Vanishing Contract Law

English contract law provides the invisible framework that underpins and enables much contracting activity in society, yet the role of the law in policing many of our contracts now approaches vanishing point. The methods by which contracts come into existence, and notionally create binding obligations, have transformed over the past forty years. Consumers now enter into contracts through remote and automated processes on standard terms over which they have little control. This book explores the substantive weakening of the institution of contract law in a society heavily dependent on contracts. It considers significant areas of contracting activity that affect many people but that escape serious and sustained legal scrutiny. An accessibly written and succinct account of contract law's past, present and future, it assesses the implications of a diminished contract law and the possibilities, if any, for its revival.

Catherine Mitchell is a reader in private law at the University of Birmingham. She has published widely on contract and has been cited by the House of Lords, the Singapore Court of Appeal and the Law Commissions of England and Scotland.

Law in Context

Series editors: Professor Kenneth Armstrong *University of Cambridge*
Professor Maksymilian Del Mar *Queen Mary, University of London*
Professor Sally Sheldon *University of Kent*

Editorial advisory board Bronwen Morgan University of New South Wales
Emeritus Professor William Twining University College London

Since 1970, the Law in Context series has been at the forefront of a movement to broaden the study of law. The series is a vehicle for the publication of innovative monographs and texts that treat law and legal phenomena critically in their cultural, social, political, technological, environmental and economic contexts. A contextual approach involves treating legal subjects broadly, using materials from other humanities and social sciences, and from any other discipline that helps to explain the operation in practice of the particular legal field or legal phenomena under investigation. It is intended that this orientation is at once more stimulating and more revealing than the bare exposition of legal rules. The series includes original research monographs, coursebooks and textbooks that foreground contextual approaches and methods. The series includes and welcomes books on the study of law in all its contexts, including domestic legal systems, European and international law, transnational and global legal processes, and comparative law.

Books in the Series

Acosta: *The National versus the Foreigner in South America: 200 Years of Migration and Citizenship Law*
Ali: *Modern Challenges to Islamic Law*
Alyagon Darr: *Plausible Crime Stories: The Legal History of Sexual Offences in Mandate Palestine*
Anderson, Schum & Twining: *Analysis of Evidence, 2nd Edition*
Ashworth: *Sentencing and Criminal Justice, 6th Edition*
Barton & Douglas: *Law and Parenthood*
Baxi, McCrudden & Paliwala: *Law's Ethical, Global and Theoretical Contexts: Essays in Honour of William Twining*
Beecher-Monas: *Evaluating Scientific Evidence: An Interdisciplinary Framework for Intellectual Due Process*
Bell: *French Legal Cultures*

Bercusson: *European Labour Law, 2nd Edition*
Birkinshaw: *European Public Law*
Birkinshaw: *Freedom of Information: The Law, the Practice and the Ideal, 4th Edition*
Blick: *Electrified Democracy: The Internet and the United Kingdom Parliament in History*
Broderick & Ferri: *International and European Disability Law and Policy: Text, Cases and Materials*
Brownsword & Goodwin: *Law and the Technologies of the Twenty-First Century: Text and Materials*
Cane & Goudkamp: *Atiyah's Accidents, Compensation and the Law, 9th Edition*
Clarke: *Principles of Property Law*
Clarke & Kohler: *Property Law: Commentary and Materials*
Collins: *The Law of Contract, 4th Edition*
Collins, Ewing & McColgan: *Labour Law, 2nd Edition*
Cowan: *Housing Law and Policy*
Cranston: *Making Commercial Law Through Practice 1830–1970*
Cranston: *Legal Foundations of the Welfare State*
Darian-Smith: *Laws and Societies in Global Contexts: Contemporary Approaches*
Dauvergne: *Making People Illegal: What Globalisation Means for Immigration and Law*
David: *Kinship, Law and Politics: An Anatomy of Belonging*
Davies: *Perspectives on Labour Law, 2nd Edition*
Dembour: *Who Believes in Human Rights?: Reflections on the European Convention*
de Sousa Santos: *Toward a New Legal Common Sense: Law, Globalization, and Emancipation*
Diduck: *Law's Families*
Dowdle: *Transnational Law: A Framework for Analysis*
Dupret: *Positive Law from the Muslim World: Jurisprudence, History, Practices*
Emon: *Jurisdictional Exceptionalisms: Islamic Law, International Law, and Parental Child Abduction*
Estella: *Legal Foundations of EU Economic Governance*
Fortin: *Children's Rights and the Developing Law, 3rd Edition*
Garnsey: *The Justice of Visual Art: Creative State-Building in Times of Political Transition*
Garton, Probert & Bean: *Moffat's Trusts Law: Text and Materials, 7th Edition*
Ghai & Woodman: *Practising Self-Government: A Comparative Study of Autonomous Regions*
Glover-Thomas: *Reconstructing Mental Health Law and Policy*
Gobert & Punch: *Rethinking Corporate Crime*
Goldman: *Globalisation and the Western Legal Tradition: Recurring Patterns of Law and Authority*
Haack: *Evidence Matters: Science, Proof, and Truth in the Law*
Harlow & Rawlings: *Law and Administration, 4th Edition*

Harris: *An Introduction to Law, 8th Edition*
Harris, Campbell & Halson: *Remedies in Contract and Tort, 2nd Edition*
Harvey: *Seeking Asylum in the UK: Problems and Prospects*
Herring: *Law and the Relational Self*
Hervey & McHale: *European Union Health Law: Themes and Implications*
Hervey & McHale: *Health Law and the European Union*
Holder & Lee: *Environmental Protection, Law and Policy: Text and Materials, 2nd Edition*
Jackson & Summers: *The Internationalisation of Criminal Evidence: Beyond the Common Law and Civil Law Traditions*
Kostakopoulou: *The Future Governance of Citizenship*
Kreiczer-Levy: *Destabilized Property: Property Law in the Sharing Economy*
Kubal: *Immigration and Refugee Law in Russia: Socio-Legal Perspectives*
Lewis: *Choice and the Legal Order: Rising above Politics*
Likosky: *Law, Infrastructure and Human Rights*
Likosky: *Transnational Legal Processes: Globalisation and Power Disparities*
Lixinski: *Legalized Identities: Cultural Heritage Law and the Shaping of Transitional Justice*
Loughnan: *Self, Others and the State: Relations of Criminal Responsibility*
Lunney: *A History of Australian Tort Law 1901–1945: England's Obedient Servant?*
Maughan & Webb: *Lawyering Skills and the Legal Process, 2nd Edition*
McGaughey: *Principles of Enterprise Law*
McGlynn: *Families and the European Union: Law, Politics and Pluralism*
Mertens: *A Philosophical Introduction to Human Rights*
Moffat: *Trusts Law: Text and Materials*
Monti: *EC Competition Law*
Morgan: *Contract Law Minimalism: A Formalist Restatement of Commercial Contract Law*
Morgan & Yeung: *An Introduction to Law and Regulation: Text and Materials*
Nash: *British Islam and English Law: A Classical Pluralist Perspective*
Ng, *Political Censorship in British Hong Kong: Freedom of Expression and the Law (1842–1997)*
Nicola & Davies: *EU Law Stories: Contextual and Critical Histories of European Jurisprudence*
Norrie: *Crime, Reason and History: A Critical Introduction to Criminal Law, 3rd Edition*
O'Dair: *Legal Ethics: Text and Materials*
Oliver: *Common Values and the Public–Private Divide*
Oliver & Drewry: *The Law and Parliament*
Palmer & Roberts: *Dispute Processes: ADR and the Primary Forms of Decision-Making, 1st Edition*

Palmer & Roberts: *Dispute Processes: ADR and the Primary Forms of Decision-Making, 3rd Edition*
Picciotto: *International Business Taxation*
Probert: *The Changing Legal Regulation of Cohabitation, 1600–2010: From Fornicators to Family, 1600–2010*
Radi: *Rules and Practices of International Investment Law and Arbitration*
Reed: *Internet Law: Text and Materials*
Richardson: *Law, Process and Custody*
Roberts & Palmer: *Dispute Processes: ADR and the Primary Forms of Decision-Making, 2nd Edition*
Rowbottom: *Democracy Distorted: Wealth, Influence and Democratic Politics*
Sauter: *Public Services in EU Law*
Scott & Black: *Cranston's Consumers and the Law*
Seneviratne: *Ombudsmen: Public Services and Administrative Justice*
Seppänen: *Ideological Conflict and the Rule of Law in Contemporary China: Useful Paradoxes*
Siems: *Comparative Law, 3rd Edition*
Stapleton: *Product Liability*
Stewart: *Gender, Law and Justice in a Global Market*
Tamanaha: *Law as a Means to an End: Threat to the Rule of Law*
Tuori: *Properties of Law: Modern Law and After*
Turpin & Tomkins: *British Government and the Constitution: Text and Materials, 7th Edition*
Twining: *General Jurisprudence: Understanding Law from a Global Perspective*
Twining: *Globalisation and Legal Theory*
Twining: *Human Rights, Southern Voices: Francis Deng, Abdullahi An-Na'im, Yash Ghai and Upendra Baxi*
Twining: *Jurist in Context: A Memoir*
Twining: *Karl Llewellyn and the Realist Movement, 2nd Edition*
Twining: *Rethinking Evidence: Exploratory Essays, 2nd Edition*
Twining & Miers: *How to Do Things with Rules, 5th Edition*
Wan: *Film and Constitutional Controversy: Visualizing Hong Kong Identity in the Age of 'One Country, Two Systems'*
Ward: *A Critical Introduction to European Law, 3rd Edition*
Ward: *Law, Text, Terror*
Ward: *Shakespeare and Legal Imagination*
Wells & Quick: *Lacey, Wells and Quick: Reconstructing Criminal Law: Text and Materials, 4th Edition*
Young: *Turpin and Tomkins' British Government and the Constitution: Text and Materials, 8th Edition*
Zander: *Cases and Materials on the English Legal System, 10th Edition*
Zander: *The Law-Making Process, 6th Edition*

International Journal of Law in Context: A Global Forum for Interdisciplinary Legal Studies

The *International Journal of Law in Context* is the companion journal to the Law in Context book series and provides a forum for interdisciplinary legal studies and offers intellectual space for ground-breaking critical research. It publishes contextual work about law and its relationship with other disciplines including but not limited to science, literature, humanities, philosophy, sociology, psychology, ethics, history and geography. More information about the journal and how to submit an article can be found at www.journals.cambridge.org/ijc

Vanishing Contract Law

Common Law in the Age of Contracts

CATHERINE MITCHELL
University of Birmingham

CAMBRIDGE
UNIVERSITY PRESS

CAMBRIDGE
UNIVERSITY PRESS

Shaftesbury Road, Cambridge CB2 8EA, United Kingdom

One Liberty Plaza, 20th Floor, New York, NY 10006, USA

477 Williamstown Road, Port Melbourne, VIC 3207, Australia

314–321, 3rd Floor, Plot 3, Splendor Forum, Jasola District Centre, New Delhi – 110025, India

103 Penang Road, #05–06/07, Visioncrest Commercial, Singapore 238467

Cambridge University Press is part of Cambridge University Press & Assessment, a department of the University of Cambridge.

We share the University's mission to contribute to society through the pursuit of education, learning and research at the highest international levels of excellence.

www.cambridge.org
Information on this title: www.cambridge.org/9781009077392

DOI: 10.1017/9781009082600

First published 2022
First paperback edition 2024

A catalogue record for this publication is available from the British Library

Library of Congress Cataloging-in-Publication data
Names: Mitchell, Catherine, 1966- author.
Title: Vanishing contract law : common law in the age of contracts / Catherine Mitchell, University of Birmingham.
Description: Cambridge, United Kingdom ; New York, NY : Cambridge University Press, 2022. | Series: Law in context | Includes bibliographical references and index.
Identifiers: LCCN 2022003232 (print) | LCCN 2022003233 (ebook) | ISBN 9781316514139 (hardback) | ISBN 9781009077392 (paperback) | ISBN 9781009082600 (epub)
Subjects: LCSH: Contracts–England. | Contracts–English-speaking countries–Philosophy.
Classification: LCC KD1554 .M585 2022 (print) | LCC KD1554 (ebook) | DDC 346.4202–dc23/eng/20220131
LC record available at https://lccn.loc.gov/2022003232
LC ebook record available at https://lccn.loc.gov/2022003233

ISBN 978-1-316-51413-9 Hardback
ISBN 978-1-009-07739-2 Paperback

Contents

Preface

Contracts are a powerful instrument in modern society. They are a mechanism through which we can be conferred with new capacities and capabilities, a way of changing status and generating rights and obligations that did not exist before. Many of our most important relationships are created, structured or constituted by voluntarily assumed, consensual and legally enforceable obligations. Contracts are the means by which we not only satisfy many of our day-to-day needs but also pursue the larger projects and plans that confer meaning on our lives. Contract norms permeate our existence, suffusing our interactions with symbolism and imagery: haggling and handshakes; small print and signatures; promising and performing; commitments and constraints. Contract trappings are so familiar to us that it is easy to overlook the significance of contract itself, particularly when much modern contracting activity is conducted through automated methods in online environments. The ambivalent attitude that most of us display towards contracts – an inevitability that must be tolerated in order to get what we want – means that the prevalence of contract norms in society, as well as the implications of their increasing dominance, mostly escapes our notice.

It seems it has also escaped the notice of the law of contract. The English law of contract provides an invisible framework that underpins and enables contractual liability. However, the role of general contract law in policing our contracts approaches vanishing point. Against the backdrop of the contractualisation of society, this book examines the role of English contract law in regulating modern contracts. It is prompted by the observation that, notwithstanding the expansion of the role of contract in all our lives, the general principles of contract law as applied and developed by the judiciary are increasingly formal and minimalistic in character, reverting to the precepts of the much-maligned classical contract model. Though contract law has been pronounced dead, or dying, many times previously, it is clear that contracting itself is very much alive and well – just not regulated (much) by traditional contract law. This work will examine the contraction of contract law, draw out the effects of it and assess the possibilities, if any, for the revival of common law. The substantive weakening of the institution of contract law in a society heavily dependent on contracts may not be regarded as a problem – there are plenty of other forms of regulation that can substitute for the law. But I believe it has implications that should be identified and addressed. I have tried to undertake this task here. I hope anyone with an interest in contract law will find something of value in it.

Acknowledgements

I have been researching and writing this book, on and off, since 2019 and have incurred various debts in the process. My first acknowledgement is to the Leverhulme Trust. I was very fortunate to be awarded a Research Fellowship by the Trust, which allowed me a year free of teaching duties at Birmingham Law School (BLS) in 2019–2020 to pursue the project. Thank you to Synda Obaji for filling in for me at BLS. Haward Soper provided excellent research assistance, which continued long past the point his formal contract had come to an end (there's a lesson there). I am also grateful to Roger Brownsword, Hugh Collins and Christian Twigg-Flesner. Sheena Robertson helped me with the award admin. The College of Arts and Law at the University of Birmingham granted research leave immediately prior to the Research Fellowship, which helped to get me started. At BLS I extend my thanks to Katharina Möser, Lorraine Talbot, Richard Young and members of the school's Regulation and Governance research group, who had the early ideas foisted upon them in a lunchtime seminar and provided some helpful feedback. Likewise the participants in a senior seminar I was invited to give at Dublin City University in February 2019, organised by Rónán Condon. Thanks also to academic partners in contract who attended the Contract, Commercial and Consumer subject section keynote address I gave at the Society of Legal Scholars Conference, University of Central Lancashire, September 2019. I am grateful to Finola O'Sullivan, Marianne Nield and the anonymous reviewers at Cambridge University Press. The errors and weaknesses in the work remain all mine.

The majority of the book was written during the height of the Covid-19 pandemic. In view of the diverse set of challenges presented during that unprecedented time, I am indebted to Tom for not ignoring my calls and for giving me one thing less to worry about. Finally, I would not have come anywhere near to completing this project without the support and encouragement of Alex, my companion in lockdown and in life. I dedicate the book to him with my love and thanks.

Table of Cases

Australia

Canada

European Union

Singapore

United States

Table of Statutes

Regulations and Directives

1

Vanishing Contract Law

1.1 Introduction

We may be living in an 'age of statutes'[1] but it is also clear that we exist in the era of contracts. Contract is one of the principal normative frameworks for social organisation. Many of our most significant relationships are created, structured or constituted by voluntarily assumed, consensual and legally enforceable obligations. One would assume, therefore, that contract law plays an important role in a contractualised economy and society.[2] In one sense this is true. Contract law notionally controls many aspects of the contracting process – how we become bound to contracts, how we might lawfully escape from the obligations they impose, what can and cannot be the subject of a contractual obligation – and thus is central to the operation of the market.[3] Yet in another important sense contract law, and the judicially created common law in particular, is disappearing. The law is increasingly disengaged from the realities of our contracting experience. Perhaps counterintuitively, the growth of contract and private ordering in society since the latter half of the twentieth century has not led to the emergence of a reinvigorated common law. Instead, the common law has largely retired from the field as general regulator of

[1] Guido Calabresi, *A Common Law for the Age of Statutes* (Harvard University Press, 1982), p. 181; quoted in Andrew Burrows, *Thinking about Statutes: Interpretation, Interaction, Improvement* (Cambridge University Press, 2017), p. 1; see also Patrick S. Atiyah, 'Freedom of Contract and the New Right' in *Essays on Contract* (Oxford University Press, 1990), pp. 355, 363ff.

[2] On contractualisation see John Wightman, *Contract: A Critical Commentary* (Pluto Press, 1996), p. 3; Hugh Collins, *The Law of Contract*, 4th ed. (Butterworths, 2003), Chapter 6; see also Margaret Jane Radin, 'The Deformation of Contract in the Information Society' (2017) 37 *Oxford Journal of Legal Studies* 505.

[3] Nathan B. Oman, *The Dignity of Commerce* (University of Chicago Press, 2016); Hanoch Dagan, Avihay Dorfman, Roy Kreitner and Daniel Markovits, 'The Law of the Market' (2020) 83 *Law and Contemporary Problems* ii; Collins, *The Law of Contract*, p. 107.

agreements, reverting to an abbreviated and formal model redolent of the classical law and perceiving its primary purpose as to enforce the express terms of the contract, provided the process of reaching agreement was free of vitiating factors.[4] On the occasions when contracts and contracting processes are subject to judicial scrutiny, they are mostly held not to offend the individualistic contract norms of the common law, notwithstanding that the formal contract structures that accompany even the simplest transactions often fail to embody the liberal contract ideals of voluntariness and consent. Freedom of contract and sanctity of contract have reasserted themselves as the basic DNA of contractual commitments. It is a model of contract designed primarily with commercial contractors in view.

From a particular perspective contract law diminishment seems unavoidable, unremarkable and not necessarily confined to contract.[5] The common law of contract has been supplemented and modified,[6] and sections of it have been abolished entirely, by legislation dealing with discrete areas of contract doctrine or with certain varieties of contractual relationship.[7] Fragmentation of contracts and the creation of specific rules and regulatory regimes to govern areas such as consumer protection and employment rights have generated doubts about the continuing relevance of general principles of contract law for some time.[8] The identification and vindication of individual legal entitlements tend to be marginalised by modern systems of regulatory enforcement aimed

[4] Jay M. Feinman, 'Un-Making Law: The Classical Revival in the Common Law' (2004) 28 *Seattle University Law Review* 1, 55. For a comprehensive defence of formalism in contract law, see Jonathan Morgan, *Contract Law Minimalism: A Formalist Restatement of Commercial Contract Law* (Cambridge University Press, 2013).

[5] On the idea of private law concepts becoming redundant see Steve Hedley, 'Tort: The Long Goodbye' (8 April 2020) https://ssrn.com/abstract=3571950

[6] The Equality Act 2010 prohibits refusal to contract with a person on the basis of a protected characteristic in relation to some goods and services. Contracting around the provisions is also prohibited (s142). The Insolvency Act 1986 (as amended by the Corporate Insolvency and Governance Act 2020) invalidates contract terms that terminate supply contracts on the grounds of a counterparty's insolvency (s 233B(3)).

[7] Consumer contract regulation is now almost entirely a matter of statute, notably the Consumer Rights Act 2015. Also see the Unfair Terms in Commercial Contracts Regulations 1999; Consumer Protection (Distance Selling) Regulations 2000; Consumer Protection from Unfair Trading Regulations 2008; Consumer Contracts (Information, Cancellation and Additional Charges) Regulations 2013; Consumer Protection (Amendment) Regulations 2014; Alternative Dispute Resolution for Consumer Disputes (Competent Authorities and Information) Regulations 2015. Intervention is not confined to consumer contracts; see, for example, Commercial Agents (Council Directive) Regulations 1993.

[8] See, for example, Ian R. Macneil, 'Whither Contracts?' (1969) 21 *Journal of Legal Education* 403, 403.

at rectifying market-wide problems. Non-legal norms, such as desire to protect reputation, still matter to most contractors and present powerful incentives to perform as agreed.[9] Contract law has also come under pressure from contemporary trends in dispute resolution. Individuals can seek dispute resolution through informal means, such as following complaints procedures mandated by a supplier or industry governing body or escalating an unresolved issue to a specialist organisation charged with facilitating settlement. Legal claims that arise can be processed through electronic platforms that promise prompt online dispute resolution.[10] There are also structural problems around the limitations of the litigation and trial process and an expensive and inaccessible court system. Notwithstanding contract law's reversion to its traditional role in overseeing commercial contracting, a multitude of alternatives to law exist for contract management in the commercial sphere. In complex forms of economic activity involving exchange between independent firms, the rules of the common law of contract are mostly defaults that apply only to the extent the parties do not stipulate for anything else.[11] Common law stagnation appears likely to be compounded further by the advent of new forms of transacting in the market, facilitated by novel technologies developed specifically to bypass the scrutiny of national legal institutions. Contrary to the views of some commentators, it is not a given that these changes will transform the common law.[12]

Contract law's reversion to a classical-style model may be presented as a natural and inevitable response to the shrinking demand for judicially created contract rules from all apart from a certain class of commercial contractor. But it is nonetheless a troubling response because it insulates much of our contracting life from effective legal scrutiny and challenge. Modern society is replete with examples of how the proliferation of contract as one of the chief structures of social organisation has been accompanied by the substantial denigration of contract law norms, with little by way of an effective response

9 For analysis of adverse publicity in a regulatory context see Peter Cartwright, 'Publicity, Punishment and Protection: The Role(s) of Adverse Publicity in Consumer Policy' (2012) 32 *Legal Studies* 179.

10 See the MoneyClaimOnline service for issuing claims for fixed sums up to £100,000; the Civil Money Claim site for claims up to £10,000; and the Claims Portal (www.claimsportal.org.uk/) for processing personal injury claims up to £25,000.

11 Wightman, *Contract: A Critical Commentary*, pp. 1–2; Morgan, *Contract Law Minimalism*, pp. 87–88; Ian Ayres and Robert Gertner, 'Filling Gaps in Incomplete Contracts: An Economic Theory of Default Rules' (1989) 99 *Yale Law Journal* 87; Ian Ayres and Robert Gertner, 'Majoritarian vs Minoritarian Defaults' (1999) 51 *Stanford Law Review* 1591.

12 Collins, *The Law of Contract*, p. 39ff.

from courts and judges. That it is possible for a customer shopping online to be taken to have agreed to the retailer's standard conditions of sale simply by making a purchase or clicking on a box labelled 'Agree' is largely the result of our law of contract. Similarly, that a driver, by the action of driving into a public car park and parking their car, has supposedly agreed to pay a fine if they stay beyond the prescribed time limit is down to the operation of contract legal rules. An employee settling a sexual harassment claim against an employer is required to sign a non-disclosure agreement as a condition of the settlement, which effectively prevents them from revealing their experience. The common law has bequeathed a dubious legacy in legitimising a bureaucratic, planning model of contract that encourages contract commitment by stealth and inertia.[13] Yet common law engagement with the deeper policy questions raised by the use of contracts in these contexts, particularly when characterised by economic inequality between the parties, has been largely non-existent. Restrictions on the operation of freedom of contract are a matter for parliament and not the courts.[14] As a result, the classical law intellectual baggage of autonomy, individualism and objectivity reigns supreme in the common law, distorting our understanding of contract and crowding out alternative normative standards based on contractual justice, collective action and responsibility.[15]

Is it a matter of concern that a significant amount of contracting activity is conducted beyond any effective legal scrutiny or control? And to what extent have judges contributed to common law diminishment through their value choices in contract decision-making? Ultimately these questions boil down to a single enquiry: what is at stake if contract assumes primary place as the main social institution for organising, constructing and understanding some of our most significant relationships without robust legal principles at its base? It seems that an enquiry into the implications of a disengaged – or vanishing – contract law in a society heavily dependent on private ordering through contracts is overdue. In the following chapters we explore how contract law has relinquished its role as general overseer of contracting activity in favour of an attenuated model of limited range and applicability. We examine what has

[13] Ian R. Macneil, 'Bureaucracy and Contracts of Adhesion' (1984) 22 *Osgoode Hall Law Journal* 5, 8.

[14] Judicial statements along these lines are numerous. See, for example, Lord Scarman in *National Westminster Bank plc* v. *Morgan* [1985] 1 AC 686, 708.

[15] See Steve Hedley on this critique of the lack of 'collective' and indeed suspicion of the idea in private law theory: 'The Rise and Fall of Private Law Theory' (2018) 134 *Law Quarterly Review* 214, 228ff.

replaced contract law. We consider the implications of common law's declining role in an era when contracting has become ubiquitous throughout society and what possibilities exist for common law revival.

In the remainder of this chapter, the broader themes of the book are presented, the initial arguments that inform the rest of the work are introduced and some preliminary issues of scope addressed. It should be noted at the outset that the work is concerned with English contract law. Its methodology is primarily doctrinal – judicial pronouncements are taken at face value as an accurate expression of the values beneath, and it naturally takes case law as the prime evidence of common law trends. It appreciates, however, the practical reality that common law is not an expression of the whole of contract regulation but is superseded in many respects by other forms of contract governance. With this pragmatic realisation in mind, the work is not overly concerned with private law theory – perhaps because of the difficulty for any unifying theory to explain and justify the fragmented realm of contract. That said, the dominance of some theories (particularly the economic analysis of law) has contributed to the problem of common law disengagement from some pressing policy issues affecting modern contracting practice. This is discussed further where relevant below. In addition, to this author it has long seemed to be the case that only a broadly relational contract theory comes close to capturing the diverse considerations and forces affecting contracts and their regulation. Aspects of this theory are referred to, therefore, when its insights appear particularly pertinent.

1.2 Diminishing Contract Law

One claim in the book is that contract law, particularly in the hands of judges, has diminished in scope and significance. This diminishment claim is explored more fully in Chapters 2 and 3, where changing trends in contract law are examined. In brief, the claim is that the recent resurgence of formalist values in contract adjudication impoverishes contract law and renders it inadequate as a general tool of contract regulation. At first blush, this claim looks unsustainable. First, there appears to be no decline in contract matters coming before courts. Appeal courts have delivered a number of judgments over recent years touching upon important areas of contract law principle: contract formation;[16]

[16] *Wells* v. *Devani* [2020] AC 129.

illegality;[17] remedies and penalties;[18] interpretation of contracts;[19] implied terms;[20] consideration;[21] and the legal validity of commonly used terms.[22] A concept of relational contracts has been developing in the lower courts, in an attempt to modify, in some contexts, the operation of the classical law model of self-interested and adversarial commercial dealing.[23] These instances could be taken as indications of the continued relevance and vibrancy of the common law of contract. However, an argument about diminishment is not rebutted by demonstrating that courts continue to rule on contract cases. What also matters is the kind of rules that result from judicial decisions, as well as the contribution they make to contract regulation. Nor is the attempt to develop a special category of relational contracts any indication that the classical law is in abeyance. At most, the jurisprudence of relational contracts is exceptional, an enclave surrounded by an increasingly formal law committed to upholding commercially oriented interests and party autonomy.[24] Appeal courts remain reticent about the development and have not given unequivocal endorsement to doctrinal advances that bear a relationalist imprint.[25]

A second initial criticism is that the work misunderstands the function of the common law rules of contract. They are designed to enable contracting between sophisticated commercial contractors operating in complex markets

[17] *Patel* v. *Mirza* [2017] AC 467.

[18] *Morris-Garner and another* v. *One Step (Support) Ltd* [2019] AC 649; *Cavendish Square Holding BV* v. *Makdessi; ParkingEye Ltd* v. *Beavis* [2016] AC 1172; *Lowick Rose Llp (in liquidation)* v. *Swynson Ltd* [2018] AC 313; *BV Nederlandse Industrie van Eiprodukten* v. *Rembrandt Enterprises Inc* [2020] QB 551.

[19] *Arnold* v. *Britton* [2015] AC 1619; *Wood* v. *Capita Insurance Services Ltd* [2017] AC 1173.

[20] *Marks and Spencer plc* v. *BNP Paribas Securities Services Trust Co Ltd* [2016] AC 742.

[21] *Simantob* v. *Shavleyan* [2019] EWCA Civ 1105; *MWB Business Exchange Centres Ltd* v. *Rock Advertising Ltd* [2017] QB 604 (CA).

[22] Notably the 'no oral modification' clause: *Rock Advertising Ltd* v. *MWB Business Exchange Centres Ltd* [2019] AC 119 (SC).

[23] *Yam Seng Pte Ltd* v. *International Trade Corporation* [2013] EWHC 111; *Sheikh Tahnoon Bin Saeed Bin Shakhboot Al Nehayan* v. *Kent* [2018] EWHC 333; *Amey Birmingham Highways Ltd* v. *Birmingham City Council* [2018] EWCA Civ 264; *Alan Bates and Others* v. *Post Office Limited (No 3)* [2019] EWHC 606.

[24] Zhong Xing Tan, 'Disrupting Doctrine: Revisiting the Doctrinal Impact of Relational Contract Theory' (2019) 39 *Legal Studies* 98, 100.

[25] *Mid Essex Hospital Services NHS Trust* v. *Compass Group UK and Ireland Ltd (t/a Medirest)* [2013] EWCA Civ 200; [2013] BLR 265; *MSC Mediterranean Shipping Company SA* v. *Cottonex Anstalt* [2016] EWCA Civ 789.

with access to legal advice.[26] Apart from some basic rules controlling the worst excesses of dishonest behaviour, contract law's function is not to regulate markets but to facilitate self-regulation. It does this by conferring on contracting parties a wide power to contract around its default rules and by enforcing that self-governance on the basis of party autonomy. Thus, the resurgence of classical values in the law is not evidence of diminishment but the natural realignment of the law with the interests of the economic group that the rules serve. The common law has returned to its primary role as enforcer of private ordering in commercial contexts, transferring responsibility for identifying and protecting the public interest in exchange activities, a task that the common law was always constitutionally and institutionally ill-equipped to perform, to statute and regulation.[27] The common law's attempt during the latter half of the twentieth century to regulate agreements characterised by inequality of bargaining power was an aberration now thankfully abandoned.

There are three immediate responses to this line of argument. First, the argument obscures how the values of freedom of contract and party autonomy that underpin a commercially oriented model of contract law reflect broader political trends and choices that are not stable and unvarying through time but are contingent and contested.[28] The argument also presents contract law development as neutral, concealing the extent to which the classical model of contract aligns itself with a particular version of contract, marginalising the impact that other contract types are permitted to have upon the law. Common law is not predisposed to follow a single path, as is amply demonstrated by examining other common law jurisdictions that have taken a different direction to English law when confronted with substantially the same dilemmas.[29]

[26] Catherine Mitchell, 'Contracts and Contract Law: Challenging the Distinction between the Real and Paper Deal' (2009) 29 *Oxford Journal of Legal Studies* 675; *Commercial Law and Commercial Practice* (Hart Publishing, 2013), p. 91ff; Dori Kimel, 'The Choice of Paradigm for Theory of Contract: Reflections on the Relational Model' (2007) 27 *Oxford Journal of Legal Studies* 232, 247.

[27] Jonathan Morgan, 'Opting for "Documentary Fundamentalism": Respecting Party Choice for Entire Agreement and Non-Reliance Clauses' in Paul S. Davies and Magda Raczynska (eds.) *Contents of Commercial Contracts: Terms Affecting Freedoms* (Hart Publishing, 2020), pp. 239–40.

[28] Feinman, 'Un-Making Law', 58.

[29] In Canada, see *Bhasin* v. *Hyrnew* [2014] SCC 71 on good faith as an organising principle in contract law and *Uber Technologies Inc* v. *Heller* [2020] SCC 16 on unconscionability; in Australia, *Andrews* v. *Australia and New Zealand Banking Group Ltd* (2012) 247 CLR 205; *Paciocco* v. *Australia and New Zealand Banking Group Limited* [2016] HCA 28 on the operation of the penalty rule.

Indeed, it is also reflected in English law by the faltering attempt to develop an alternative relational contract jurisprudence.

Second, the argument is complacent. It is true that it is unnecessary for the modern law of contract to do anything like the work required of it a century or more ago. Specialist regulatory regimes have moved into the territory where contract law and judicial action may have once exercised the main form of control.[30] But there is still plenty for general contract law to do. This includes regulating relationships that are an uneasy fit with the discrete model of contract associated with the classical law – franchising, supply chains, joint ventures, distributorships – and developing protection for small businesses that do not benefit from legislation designed with the consumer in mind. The common law may also be the primary source of the relevant rights and rules in a wide and often unpredictable variety of contracting scenarios. The decision in *Arnold* v. *Britton* is a good example of a non-commercial contract (lease for holiday chalets) to which no other set of rules except the common law applied.[31] Similarly, *Beavis* v. *ParkingEye*[32] presents a common contracting scenario that, due to the sometimes-narrow application and interpretation of controlling statutes, is also subject to the common law rules. The fallout from algorithmic contracting may present a further common law frontier.[33] Worryingly, contract terms that appear to operate in a relatively benign fashion in the ordinary business context, and whose legal meaning is settled, can easily be deployed to more insidious effect in a different contracting environment. Compare, for example, a confidentiality clause between employer and employee that protects a trade secret, with a non-disclosure agreement designed to conceal wrongdoing. The possibility that the rules developed in one context should apply unmodified in the other without serious legal consideration is absurd. But contract law's modern tendency is to eschew contract context in favour of upholding contract terms, eliding these two scenarios much more readily.

Third, and more practically, legislation and regulation rarely render common law completely redundant. The law governing a contract is often an awkward patchwork of legislative provisions, the rules of a specific

30 See, for example, the discussion in Collins, *Law of Contract*, 8, of the modern regulatory approach to the problem arising in *Carlill* v. *Carbolic Smoke Ball* [1893] 1 QB 256.

31 [2015] AC 1619. 32 [2016] AC 1172.

33 Already being considered in other jurisdictions: *Quoine Pte Ltd* v. *B2C2 Ltd* [2020] (I) SGCA 02.

regulatory regime and the common law.[34] There is no guarantee that these different sources, when considered together, will produce a consistent, comprehensive or normatively appealing legal position. This might strengthen the case for an attenuated common law (why overcomplicate an issue by layering judge-made rules on top of legislation and regulation?). But if anything the problem of regulatory overload affects legislation and regulation designed to respond to a single problem. There is no requirement that legislation be coherent and consistent, whereas the need for coherence in the common law is an important constraint.[35] Simple, widely applicable principles – the kind produced by common law – can help to unify an area of law and make underlying values operative in one situation applicable to analogous ones. Legal judgments provided by courts may be required by regulators whose power does not extend to providing authoritative determinations of legal rights or remedies under the regulatory regime. In addition, express contract terms often seek to reverse or lessen the impact of legislative provisions with an enabling or protective effect.[36] Controls on the ability of contracting parties to contract around legislation may be found within the legislation itself. If the legislation is silent, whether it should be possible to contract around legislative provisions, and the interpretation of exculpatory terms that attempt to do so, is a matter for judicial determination.[37] Common law application is not confined to commercial agreements, though it may appear so. As such, maintaining its general principles is important.

1.3 The Formalist Revival in Modern Contract Law

One of the arguments presented in this book is that the contractualisation of society has coincided with the return to a more formal style of contract law in

34 Consider, for example, privity of contract, where legislation, contract terms and common law all intersect, or control of bank and credit charges in consumer contracts, which may be subject to control under statute (Consumer Rights Act 2015; Consumer Credit Act 1974), under the common law (rules on penalties and unconscionability) and under regulation by the Financial Conduct Authority and the Competition and Markets Authority.

35 Neil MacCormick, *Legal Reasoning and Legal Theory*, revised ed. (Oxford University Press, 1994); Ronald Dworkin, *Law's Empire* (Fontana, 1986).

36 As appears to have been the case with the Contract (Rights of Third Parties) Act 1999; see also the attempt by way of 'basis of the contract' clauses to contract around the controls on excluding liability for misrepresentation under s 3 Misrepresentation Act 1967. This is discussed further in Chapter 3.

37 See early cases on the operation of the Unfair Contract Terms Act 1977, especially *Smith* v. *Eric S Bush* [1990] 1 AC 831.

the courts. The re-emergence of formalist and classical values can be observed in a number of developments in contract law over the past few years. These changes have signalled a judicial retreat from the more contextual and standards-based method of legal reasoning previously adopted by courts. The changes include the return to plain-meaning contract interpretation;[38] an emphasis on upholding express contract terms at the expense of the application of established contract doctrine;[39] a generally negative response in superior courts to attempts in lower courts to develop a relational category of contracts or to expand the role of good faith;[40] the burgeoning acceptance that contract terms can nullify the operation of legal claims and rights that a party might otherwise enjoy under general contract law;[41] and the marginalisation of equity, except in the service of insulating the express contract terms from challenge.[42] These moves reflect and reinforce contract law's increasing orientation towards upholding commercial interests and the belief that these interests are best served by a 'formal, simple, and . . . classical' law.[43]

In intellectual terms the predominance of commercial concerns and interests in contract legal reasoning has been encouraged by the economic analysis of contract law in contract scholarship. It is often noted that economic analysis has become the primary theoretical framework within which contract legal rules are explained and a strong formalist and liberal justification for them defended.[44] The focus on efficiency seeks to justify contract law instrumentally in terms of what it contributes to achieving the economic goals of commercial contractors operating in markets. Dagan and Heller assert that contract law has become synonymous with the commercial transaction, minimising the influence that other contracts (involving marriage, the consumer or the

[38] For a fuller examination of these factors, see Catherine Mitchell, *Interpretation of Contracts*, 2nd ed. (Routledge, 2018).

[39] *Rock Advertising Ltd* v. *MWB Business Exchange Centres Ltd*, above n. 22.

[40] See further Chapter 7.

[41] Margaret Jane Radin in *Boilerplate: The Fine Print, Vanishing Rights and the Rule of Law* (Princeton University Press, 2013) explores this phenomenon in depth in the US consumer context.

[42] In particular, the development of 'contractual estoppel' in relation to upholding 'basis of the contract' clauses: Gerard McMeel, 'Documentary Fundamentalism in the Senior Courts: The Myth of Contractual Estoppel' (2011) *Lloyd's Maritime and Commercial Law Quarterly* 185; Jo Braithwaite, 'The Origins and Implications of Contractual Estoppel' (2016) 132 *Law Quarterly Review* 120.

[43] Robert E. Scott, 'The Case for Formalism in Relational Contract' (2000) 94 *Northwestern University Law Review* 847 at 852.

[44] Scott, above. See also David Charny, 'The New Formalism in Contract' (1999) 66 *University of Chicago Law Review* 842.

employment relationship) have upon the general law.[45] The contribution of contract law to functioning markets – indeed the assimilation of contracting and market activity[46] – casts a long shadow in contract theory. Even the most unlikely of contract cases are sought to be located and explained in terms of their support for markets.[47] The common law has exercised some control over creeping contractualisation through the rule that parties must intend to create legal obligations through their agreement and also through public policy. The role of public policy in curbing contractualisation appears to be diminishing however, allowing the norm of party autonomy to encroach more readily into areas where its operation was previously held in check by courts. The changed status of ante-nuptial agreements is a good example. In dissenting in part from the majority Supreme Court opinion that such agreements should carry some weight in the question of financial provision on divorce (reversing the long-held position of the courts that such agreements were void as contrary to public policy) Lady Hale was alert to the problems of applying commercial contract norms of certainty in the law and party autonomy to a couple contemplating marriage.[48]

Commercial contract norms have come to dominate contracts legal reasoning in other respects, perhaps most notably in the assimilation of 'the contract' with the physical (or electronic) text containing express terms. Written contracts increasingly manifest an introspective quality. Contract terms may seek to control the immediate contracting environment and inhibit the creation of any obligations beyond those written into the text of the agreement. The 'acknowledgement of non-reliance' clause can prevent a claimant bringing an action for misrepresentation.[49] The 'entire agreement' clause can preclude collateral warranties and obligations arising outside the

45 Hanoch Dagan and Michael Heller, *The Choice Theory of Contracts* (Cambridge University Press, 2017), pp. 7–8.

46 Robert E. Scott, 'The Paradox of Contracting in Markets' (2020) 83 *Law and Contemporary Problems* 71, 71: '. . . not only are contracts in all markets, but markets are also in all contracts . . . as markets change in character, so too will the contracts that are embedded in them'.

47 See Nathan Oman's explanation of *Hamer* v. *Sidway* 27 NE 256 (NY 1891) in *The Dignity of Commerce* – enforcing the bargain may 'extend well-functioning markets', p. 103; Brian H. Bix, 'Contract Law and the Common Good' (2018) 9 *William & Mary Business Law Review* 373, 383.

48 *Granatino* v. *Radmacher* [2011] 1 AC 534 [132]; see also Lady Hale, 'Legislation or Judicial Law Reform: Where Should Judges Fear to Tread?' *Society of Legal Scholars Conference* (7 September 2016) 3.

49 *Springwell Navigation Corp* v. *JP Morgan Chase Bank* [2010] EWCA Civ 1221.

main statement of express terms and conditions.[50] The 'no oral modification' clause can prevent attempts to undermine the original contract text by reference to agreed but informal variations.[51] Courts appear content to uphold these terms, further augmenting the power of the paper statements of obligations. Desire to appease commercial interests can also be detected elsewhere. There has been some liberalisation of the operation of the penalty rule. A clause setting a level of liquidated damages, or fine, that exceeds the claimant's likely losses from breach may be enforceable if the claimant can demonstrate a legitimate interest in securing performance of the primary contractual obligation and the sum claimed is proportionate to that legitimate interest.[52] The bar for unenforceability of liquidated damages clauses is high – the amount must be disproportionate or otherwise 'extravagant, exorbitant or unconscionable'.[53] While such terms may be subject to legislative control in a consumer contract, regulation in commercial contracts is largely a common law matter. The reassertion of formalist values within the law is not without cost. It will be argued that one result of this formalist shift has been the lack of engagement between contract law and some recurring problems produced by the contractualisation of society, as well as a reluctance by courts to adopt any broad regulatory role when those problems do come before them for determination. The formalist turn in contract law is considered further in Chapter 3.

1.4 Private Ordering and Regulation

If general contract law has withdrawn from any significant role in general contract regulation, what has replaced it? One of the themes of the book is that private ordering has supplanted contract law as the main form of contract governance. At its broadest, private ordering identifies a sphere of norm/rule-making and enforcement not derived directly from state authority to create law, nor dependent on the state's monopoly on the use of force.[54] It is familiar in commercial contracting. Although private ordering, at least between commercial parties, is often a response to globalisation of trade that requires regulation stretching beyond national boundaries, it is not confined to

[50] *Inntrepreneur Pub Co Ltd* v. *East Crown* [2000] All ER (D) 1100.

[51] *Rock Advertising Ltd* v. *MWB Business Exchange Centres Ltd*, above n. 22.

[52] See *Cavendish* v. *Makdessi*, above n. 18.

[53] Per Lord Mance, *Cavendish* v. *Makdessi* [152].

[54] Annelise Riles, 'The Anti-Network: Private Global Governance, Legal Knowledge, and the Legitimacy of the State' (2008) 56 *American Journal of Comparative Law* 605–06.

transnational private regulation.[55] While private ordering may rely on *contracts* this does not necessarily entail *contract law* will be a mechanism for providing contract content, control or enforcement. Although systems may rely on legal norms for background enforcement and legitimacy, once this is assured (through entry into a contract that the law regards as valid) they operate relatively independently of the legal system. The contract itself dictates the obligations assumed, methods of sanctioning, enforcement and dispute resolution processes. Other institutions may play an important role in ensuring contract compliance: trade associations, public regulatory authorities and international organisations such as arbitral tribunals.

In many respects, this is an entirely positive development. Commercial parties, for example, can create a much more detailed and tailored set of rules for governing their relationship than anything that can be supplied by law. In other contexts, legal support for private ordering and self-regulation protects the parties from oppressive or overweening state intervention in the pursuit of their own good and prioritises autonomous decision-making. But private ordering also entails contract proliferation. Although not new in any respect,[56] the prevalence of private ordering through contracts is one result of the privatisation and marketisation of previously publicly owned or administered sectors of society and the economy.[57] Direct state provision in many areas has been augmented or supplemented by service delivery through private contracts between citizen and service provider or replaced with state procurement of essential public services through private companies[58] and the creation of internal markets within state-funded organisations.[59] Contracting regimes have been used by successive governments in the United Kingdom since the 1980s to serve diverse policy purposes, including social control of citizens and

[55] Lisa Bernstein, 'Opting Out of the Legal System: Extralegal Contractual Relations in the Diamond Industry' (1992) 21 *Journal of Legal Studies* 115.

[56] Collins, *Law of Contract*, pp. 4–5, tracing 'contractualisation' back to the classical era of the nineteenth century.

[57] For a brief description of this movement since the 1970s, see Anthony Ogus, *Regulation: Legal Form and Economic Theory* (Hart Publishing, 2004), pp. 8–12; Philip Arestis and Malcolm Sawyer, 'The Neoliberal Experience of the United Kingdom' in Alfredo Saad-Filho and Deborah Johnston (eds.) *Neoliberalism: A Critical Reader* (Pluto Press, 2005), p. 199.

[58] For example, the now-ended practice of using private sector Community Rehabilitation Companies to supply rehabilitation and probation services for low-risk offenders: HC Justice Committee, *Transforming Rehabilitation*, HC 482 (June 2018); HM Prison and Probation Service, *The Proposed Future Model for Probation: A Draft Operating Blueprint* (June 2019).

[59] The National Health Service being the most notable example: Ian Harden, *The Contracting State* (Open University Press, 1992), Chapter 3; Sally Wheeler, 'Modelling the Contracts of the Future' (2017) 26 *Griffith Law Review* 593, 595ff.

welfare reform.[60] While analysis of the privatisation agenda over the last forty years is beyond the scope of this work, its role in expanding the realm of markets, and therefore also contracts, is undeniable. Changes in the economic organisation and production methods of firms and technological advances affecting the way citizens procure goods and services have been significant social drivers behind the expansion of contracting in liberal societies, particularly contracting on standard terms. The shift to provision via market mechanisms has been accompanied not only by a rhetoric attaching pre-eminence to market values but also by the construction of a consumer ideal-type with the requisite capacities to navigate through this landscape of increased choice: self-reliant and self-interested, reasonably well-informed and with a sense of individual responsibility.[61] These values have saturated our social frameworks to the extent that contract norms are symbolically deployed to mould or encourage certain attitudes, often in quite manifestly unsuitable contexts.[62] The law has played a part in elevating contracts to the dominant position in our society that they now occupy, often by simply doing nothing in the face of pronounced change in contracting behaviour and the extension of contract norms.

Privatisation has also been accompanied by specific market regulation. Regulation is a form of centralised law-making, applying across whole markets or to particular type of contract or specific contract problems. The market-wide focus of regulation contrasts with contract law, which upholds the private rights of contracting individuals and firms.[63] Nevertheless, the advent of the regulatory state has had a marked impact on common law development. Specialist regulatory authorities now play a central role overseeing the conduct of markets (such as privatised utilities or financial services), assuming many contract law functions in the process. Regulators act as gatekeepers

[60] Peter Vincent-Jones, 'The New Public Contracting: Public versus Private Ordering?' (2007) 14 *Indiana Journal of Global Legal Studies* 259, 261; Peter Vincent-Jones, *The New Public Contracting* (Oxford University Press, 2006), p. 233, with particular reference to offender rehabilitation, where hierarchical control is supplanted by a 'contract' emphasising the values of choice, responsibility and agency of the offender in relation to their behaviour.

[61] Cf. the concept of the 'average consumer' in EU consumer law, described as 'reasonably well-informed and reasonably observant and circumspect': Recital 18, Unfair Commercial Practices Directive 2005/29/EC; Consumer Rights Act 2015 s 64(5).

[62] The use of 'behaviour' and 'homework' contracts between schools, parents and pupils are a good example. A report recommended pupils agree to such contracts upon first entry to school (which can be as young as age 4) and renewed thereafter: Social Market Foundation, *Commission on Inequality in Education* (2017), pp. 8 and 64–65.

[63] Ogus, *Regulation: Legal Form and Economic Theory*, p. 3

determining the mandatory requirements for suppliers seeking entry to particular markets, such as consumer credit or banking services. They can deploy a variety of remedial measures, including negative publicity affecting reputation, civil enforcement through the courts and ultimately criminal sanctions on non-complying businesses.[64] Regulators have wide investigatory and evidence-gathering powers and can, ultimately, undertake direct intervention in a market by determining price caps on the supply of a product or developing essential information disclosure rules. Depending on the enabling statutory regime, regulatory bodies may issue rules for the conduct of business in particular markets, which may be authoritative as any national law.[65] These responses to the systemic problems generated by contracts within markets are beyond the capacity of courts applying the contract law rules. Ultimately, regulation and legislation can focus transparently on the public interest in a way that courts cannot.

Despite contract law and the regulatory environment 'represent[ing] different paradigms',[66] they cannot operate entirely independently of each other. Legislation and regulation may not create a gap-free legal universe, and general private law rights may exist and overlap with regulation. The rules and processes promulgated by regulatory bodies may run in tandem with, or contrary to, the position on an individual's private rights under the general law as interpreted and applied by courts. In addition, regulation will rarely override the common law completely, and private law may be used by individuals or firms to challenge the actions of regulators, test the limits of regulatory power or determine the interpretation of regulations. Similarly, regulators may issue 'guidance' on legal rights and responsibilities that is not authoritative but is intended to state the regulator's interpretation of what the requisite laws require. This guidance is usually addressed to the providers of the regulated goods and services who are subject to the legislation or regulation.[67] We examine the interface between law and regulation further in Chapter 4, only noting here that the animating principles of the common law of contract often

[64] See, for example, Competition and Markets Authority, *Consumer Protection: Enforcement Guidance* CMA 58 (2016) 23.

[65] See, for example, the Financial Conduct Authority, *Handbook*, www.handbook.fca.org.uk/

[66] Roger Brownsword, Rob A. J. van Gestel and Hans-W Micklitz (eds.) *Contract and Regulation: A Handbook on New Methods of Law Making in Private Law* (Edward Elgar Publishing, 2017), p. 6.

[67] See, for example, Competition and Markets Authority, *Unfair Contract Terms Guidance* CMA 37 (31 July 2015), at para 1.8.

conflict with regulatory purposes. Though in many cases, authoritative legal interpretations of common law, legislation and regulation can come only from the courts, common law and regulation may be misaligned. The result is that no clear or consistent message is delivered on contract's underlying norms, what is appropriate behaviour in contractual relationships and what can and cannot be achieved through contractual mechanisms.

1.5 Common Law Development: A Redundant Project?

It might be argued that this project replicates the error of investing common law with more significance than it is due. Common law is a relatively minor source of contract rules when compared with legislation, market-specific regulation and actual contract practice. The private law of obligations appears immune to the social forces that produce these alternative systems of contract governance, rarely incorporating them within its own doctrines. To acknowledge these would undermine the aspiration of common law to coherence around a set of identifiable principles, such as party autonomy or sanctity of contract.[68] As such, it remains a residual and reactive law, ill-equipped for any general regulatory role. Its dependence on the vagaries of litigation also prevents common law from actively pursuing a coherent programme of reform or development. These features render common law liable to capture by a relatively narrow set of contractors. Litigation remains out of reach for many individuals, compounding the problem of contract law's lack of exposure to a diverse range of contract problems. The decline in funding for civil legal aid under the Legal Aid, Sentencing and Punishment of Offenders Act 2012 means that contract litigation is dominated by disputes between sophisticated, well-resourced and professionally represented complex commercial organisations. It is hardly surprising that the law reflects their concerns and is tailored towards protecting their interests. Such contractors may prefer a law that upholds terms that they have agreed without recourse to vague standards, policy considerations or justifications based on the public benefits that can be derived from developing general principles of law that are readily adapted across differing contract contexts.[69]

68 Steve Hedley, 'Looking Outward or Looking Inward? Obligations Scholarship in the Early 21st Century' in Andrew Robertson and Tang Hang Wu (eds.) *The Goals of Private Law* (Hart Publishing, 2009), pp. 193, 202.

69 Morgan, *Contract Law Minimalism*, p. 87.

The problem with this argument, of course, is that the common law rules are not just applicable to commercial contractors. While contract law development is undoubtedly influenced by exogenous factors concerning who can afford to litigate cases to trial and judgment, these forces have not rendered common law entirely redundant in other contexts. There are plenty of contract problems that would benefit from exposure to judicial legal reasoning, not only for the purposes of formulating a common law position on the some of the intractable problems of contractualisation but also to allow the resolution of these contract problems to influence common law development in turn. We say more about this in Chapter 5, but suffice to say here that common law has an important public-facing role that is easily suppressed when contract principles are relegated to the status of default rules designed to prompt commercial contractors to contract around them.[70] This overlooks the communicative function of the law: '[w]hat the default rule project does best is to *express a message*: our society values autonomy more than contractual fairness.'[71] The normative dimension to contract is most obviously expressed through the mandatory rules of law on vitiating factors. However, these doctrines – unconscionability, say, or public policy – are eclipsed by a contract law tailored to the demands of a commercial audience and concerned to preserve its competitive edge in the market for law. It is of course the case that the rules that reflect contract's deeper values are marginal to most ordinary (low stakes) contract disputes and are in any case difficult to litigate. The rules on misrepresentation and unconscionable bargains, for example, are complex, and claims are not easily pursued through courts by less sophisticated contractors without legal advice. Many of the legal principles in these areas of law are arcane and overlapping (for example, undue influence and economic duress; mistake and misrepresentation) and are ripe for the kind of restatement recently undertaken in the doctrine of illegality. The equitable foundation to many of contract's openly normative doctrines (unconscionable bargains; undue influence), or their location at the juncture between principles of contract and tort, or between common law and legislation, makes establishing liability difficult and prone to failure in the face of technical legal arguments advanced by the other side. The common law rules of contract can

[70] In a different context, Lord Reed asserted the important public role of courts and the public interest in dispute resolution in *R (on the application of UNISON)* v. *Lord Chancellor* [2020] AC 869 (concerning the introduction of fees for bringing a case to the Employment Tribunal) [66]–[85].

[71] David A. Hoffman and Eric Lampmann, 'Hushing Contracts' (2019) 97 *Washington University Law Review* 165, 209; *R (on the application of UNISON)* per Lord Reed [71].

easily be turned to serve, by and large, those that don't necessarily need to rely on them (well-resourced commercial contractors who can contract around the law through express terms), while largely bypassing those sections of the community that might benefit from greater legal scrutiny of their contracts.

1.6 Common Law Legitimacy

One of the effects of formalism is to recast judges in passive role as contract-enforcers, rather than authors and developers of contract law. Increased formalism in contract legal reasoning reflects some enduring fears about the legitimacy of judicial law-making. These include concerns about judicial activism and lack of transparency in the common law. These difficulties have prompted renewed calls for common law codification.[72] Critiques of the nature of the judicial role have appeared across different strands of legal scholarship. Most notably, the neo-formalist model of contract, rooted in the law and economics movement, is now well established and exerts a persistent influence over contract law theory. On this account, the role of the judge applying contract law is to uphold a strong version of party autonomy, enforce the self-regulation of the parties and not impose outcomes.[73] The most important consideration is the near certainty of enforceability and the application of stable and predictable rules, enabling the parties to contract for an alternative scheme with the reassurance that judicial interference will be limited. To instil moral justification or normative values (other than efficiency) into the rules is redundant to these purposes.[74] Reciprocal fairness is regarded as a non-contractual norm that courts enforcing contract laws have

[72] Eva Steiner, 'Challenging (Again) the Undemocratic Form of the Common Law: Codification as a Method of Making the Law Accessible to Citizens' (2020) 32 *Kings Law Journal* 27. Codification efforts in English contract law seem to have lost momentum, although see Andrew Burrows, *A Restatement of the English Law of Contract* (Oxford University Press, 2016). For an overview of the various attempts at codification of English contract law, see Neil Andrews, *Contract Law*, 2nd ed. (Cambridge University Press, 2015), pp. 609–10. See also A. Diamond, 'Codification of the Law of Contract' (1968) 31 *Modern Law Review* 361; John Eldridge, 'Contract Codification: Cautionary Lessons from Australia' (2019) 23 *Edinburgh Law Review* 204–29.

[73] See, for example, Lord Toulson in *Prime Sight Ltd* v. *Lavarello* [2014] AC 436 (PC) [47]; Paul S. Davies, 'Bad Bargains' (2019) 72 *Current Legal Problems* 253.

[74] Richard A. Posner, 'The Path Away from the Law' (1997) 110 *Harvard Law Review* 1039–41; describing O. W. Holmes approach to law in, 'The Path of the Law' (1897) 1 *Boston Law School Magazine* 1.

no business inflicting on contractors.[75] Under this sort of account, the function of contract law is to serve and preserve freedom of contract, not to mandate the circumstances when interference in freedom of contract is justified. The result, as Trakman notes, is a marked 'judicial reluctance to invoke normative values to impose responsibilities on parties'.[76] More politicised attacks on the nature of judicial reasoning have emanated from strands of the critical legal studies movement, that denied that legal reasoning was politically impartial, autonomous and determinate.[77] The possibility of finding the answer to a legal problem in the existing legal materials by application of the appropriate set of legal skills and that common law reasoning attempts to reconcile a body of inconsistent case law and construct a principled explanation of it were denounced as myths obscuring the highly discretionary and open-ended nature of legal reasoning. In an environment bordering on anti-judicial, the retreat to formalist judging and the appeal of party autonomy and freedom of contract is understandable, even justifiable.

More broadly in private law theory, Hedley has argued that narrow, internal approaches to the justification of private law imply a 'distrust of collective action or purpose'[78] and a denial that legal institutions (and private law itself) can be instrumental to the achievement of public goals or operate for the common good.[79] In his discussion of Atiyah's *The Rise and Fall of Freedom of Contract*, Hedley notes that Atiyah regarded freedom of contract as a policy choice that was liable to modification or outright displacement by other competing policies, such as welfarism or paternalism.[80] Freedom of contract has since been elevated to a supposed foundational and neutral principle of contract law and the prime justification for enforcement of contracts. It is probably no coincidence that this take on private law has resonated at a time when state intervention is viewed with suspicion, where there is a belief that

75 Robert E. Scott, 'The Death of Contract Law' (2004) 54 *University of Toronto Law Journal* 369, 390.

76 Leon E. Trakman, 'Public Responsibilities beyond Consent: Rethinking Contract Theory' (2016) 45 *Hofstra Law Review* 217–18.

77 See, for example, Duncan Kennedy, *A Critique of Adjudication* (Harvard University Press, 1998).

78 Hedley, 'Rise and Fall of Private Law Theory', 214. See also John Gardner, 'The Contractualisation of Labour Law' in Hugh Collins, Gillian Lester, and Virginia Mantouvalou (eds.) *Philosophical Foundations of Labour Law* (Oxford University Press, 2018), p. 33.

79 Hedley, 'Rise and Fall of Private Law Theory', 216.

80 Hedley, 'Rise and Fall of Private Law Theory', 216–17. See also Feinman, 'Un-Making Law', 58.

law intrudes too readily upon the liberty of the individual,[81] and judges are castigated for making political decisions.[82] Many contract theorists share the view that contract law is largely unconcerned with furthering any public purposes. The idea that there is a public interest in private contractual arrangements is substantially diluted on this kind of account. Hedley identifies 'suspicion of judicial purposes' and the illegitimacy of judges engaging with policy issues as hallmarks of this approach to private law.[83] It is scarcely surprising that the benefits of a classical and formal style of contract law have been reasserted, and with it a shift in the rationale for adjudication. Atiyah observed that the nineteenth-century judge 'was much more concerned, even in the civil law, with the influence of his decision on the behaviour of people in the future. The long-run effects of all law, the civil law as well as the criminal law, were regarded as more important than the task of doing justice in the individual case.'[84] Contrast this sentiment with the more individualistic view that '[c]ourts apply law to resolve disputes'[85] and that 'the purpose of commercial law is to provide the contract law that commercial parties want'.[86] Yet, these individual instrumental justifications for contract fail to engage with a basic question: if there is no public interest in contracts, why does the state create a machinery of enforcement?[87]

The question of the limits on judicial authority has particular resonance in contract law, where almost every judicial development draws fire for judicial law-making or for threatening party autonomy and legal certainty. Clear warnings against judicial activism in contract interpretation were issued by Lord Neuberger in *Arnold* v. *Britton*: 'it is not the function of a court when interpreting an agreement to relieve a party form the consequences of his imprudence or poor advice. Accordingly, when interpreting a contract, a judge

[81] Lord Sumption, 'Law and the Decline of Politics'; Reith Lecture, Lecture 1 (21 May 2019): 'We have expanded the range of individual rights, while at the same time drastically curtailing the scope of individual choice'.

[82] Concerns about judicial activism and overtly political judgments have surfaced recently in relation to Brexit: *R (Miller and another)* v. *The Secretary of State for Exiting the European Union* [2018] AC 61; *R (Miller)* v. *The Prime Minister* and *Cherry* v. *Advocate General for Scotland* [2020] AC 373. These kinds of argument are well established in the human rights (especially in relation to ss 3 and 4 of Human Rights Act 1998) and judicial review arena: David Campbell and James Allan, 'Procedural Innovation and the Surreptitious Creation of Judicial Supremacy in the United Kingdom' (2019) 46 *Journal of Law and Society* 347, 351.

[83] Hedley, 'Rise and Fall of Private Law Theory', 231.

[84] Patrick S. Atiyah, *The Rise and Fall of Freedom of Contract* (Oxford University Press, 1979), p. 394.

[85] Morgan, *Contract Law Minimalism*, p. 85.

[86] Morgan, *Contract Law Minimalism*, p. 87.

[87] Morris R. Cohen, 'The Basis of Contract' (1933) *Harvard Law Review* 553, 562.

should avoid re-writing it in an attempt to assist an unwise party or to penalise an astute party.'[88] This restraint would be welcomed by many contract scholars as judicial recognition of the institutional and democratic constraints on common law legal reasoning,[89] as well as the promotion of a stable law for the commercial contracting community that facilitates self-regulation and the efficient disposal of disputes.[90] Manifestations of these attitudes can be seen in the law's negative reaction to the idea that contracts involve good faith duties, its individualistic approach to the contracting process, and emphasis on procedural rather than substantive justice. This is not to say that the courts do not recognise that contracts might have unwelcome or negative social effects. However, it appears to be no part of the judicial mandate to address these. Rather, the responsibility lies with the parties to change their terms: a problem produced by the operation of a contract is to be resolved by the creation of a different contract.[91] Or else the solution lies with a government agency that can tackle the market failure that is assumed to lie at the root of the problem.

The displacement of policy assessment in legal development by individualistic modes of analysis and reasoning is evident across contract law.[92] The controls on penalties, for example, have abandoned the policy-based test of whether a stipulated payment is a genuine pre-estimate of loss and not a punishment, in favour of a fact-dependent determination of whether a contractor has a 'legitimate interest' (which is relatively easy to establish) in encouraging a counterparty to perform their primary obligations rather than breach. The existence of a legitimate interest can justify payments in excess of likely losses. Similarly, the language of proportionality has permeated contract doctrine in the area of illegality, penalties and remedies, suggesting the court's task is to assess the relative strength of the different considerations involved in an effort to identify an overriding factor.[93] This focuses judicial determination of contract rights away from 'top-down' normative justifications, in favour of a

88 *Arnold* v. *Britton*, above n. 19 [20].

89 John Gava and Janey Greene, 'Do We Need a Hybrid Law of Contract? Why Hugh Collins Is Wrong and Why It Matters' (2004) 63 *Cambridge Law Journal* 605; John Gava, 'Dixonian Strict Legalism: Wilson v. Darling Island Stevedoring and Contracting in the Real World' (2010) 30 *Oxford Journal of Legal Studies* 519; John Gava, 'How Should Judges Decide Commercial Contract Cases?' (2013) 30 *Journal of Contract Law* 133.

90 Morgan, *Contract Law Minimalism*, p. 89.

91 For example, Lord Neuberger in *Arnold* v. *Britton*, above n. 19 [64]–[65].

92 Cohen, 'The Basis of Contract', 562.

93 Zhong Xing Tan, 'The Proportionality Puzzle in Contract Law: A Challenge for Private Law Theory' (2020) 33 *Canadian Journal of Law and Jurisprudence* 215, 215–16.

'bottom-up' evaluation of the relative merits of the parties' interests, on the assumption that these can be weighted. Tan writes, 'Proportionality thus presents itself as a substantive justificatory framework for the accommodation of plural and competing values.'[94] Nevertheless, while invoking a process of balance in proportionality reasoning, some of these values enjoy presumptive status in a formal and classical contract law, rendering them difficult to depose by appealing to alternative considerations. Thus, party autonomy and the economic interests that a commercial contractor may seek to protect by contract terms carry almost overriding importance in business-to-business contracting, notwithstanding the mediation of these values through a supposedly neutral and pragmatic analysis of 'proportionality' with the other interests involved.[95] The reduction of legal reasoning to such a balancing exercise may assuage fears of judicial overreaching, but the values employed are then easily transplanted to other contexts – such as business-to-consumer contracts – marginalising the broader policy issues that might raise doubts about the appropriateness of this move.

1.7 Future Challenges and Possibilities for Revival

Changes to dispute resolution methods, and the general anti-litigation message imparted by government, courts and those with an interest in promoting alternative dispute resolution, are likely to compound the formalist turn in contract law. Contract litigation, already dominated by commercial contractors, is likely to increasingly reflect and serve the interests of business. In turn, the pressure to ensure English law remains the law of choice for the international commercial contracting community can be expected to encourage and strengthen the formalist tendency. We examine this, and the related concerns about the privatisation of justice, in Chapter 6. A further impulse towards formalism in contract may be generated by the increased automation of the contracting process. Hitherto, contract law has proved remarkably resistant to change in the light of technological advances in how we interact,

94 Tan, 'Proportionality Puzzle', 217.

95 Duncan Kennedy, 'A Transnational Genealogy of Proportionality in Private Law' in Roger Brownsword, Hans-W. Micklitz, Leone Niglia and Stephen Weatherill (eds.) *The Foundations of European Private Law* (Hart Publishing, 2011), pp. 185–86; see also Nicola Lacey, 'The Metaphor of Proportionality' (2016) 43 *Journal of Law and Society* 27, arguing that proportionality is a neo-liberal construct that contributes to the 'attenuation of the welfare and other social and political institutions designed to provide a measure of distributive justice and to counter pure market power', 43–44; Tan, 'Proportionality Puzzle', 239–40.

and consequently in how we make and perform agreements. While there have been attempts at regulation at the global and European level, common law has lagged behind in responding to specific issues, such as exactly when a contract might be created through a process of email exchanges or whether parties can be bound to terms through processes such as shrink-wrap, browse-wrap and click-wrap. Many will take this as a reassuring sign of the law's inherent adaptability. Lack of specific laws dealing with new technologies may be indicative of the general ability of commercial contractors to adjust working practices in the light of innovation without too much difficulty, and certainly without the need for a ruling on the legal implications of their actions. Nothing here necessarily disturbs the law's confidence that it still fulfils the function of background enforcer keeping everyone broadly in line, even if the rules have not developed markedly since the nineteenth century. Although this gives the appearance that new technologies have not been unduly disruptive to the common law rules of contract, it is questionable how far the model can stretch before it becomes so distorted it is transformed into something new or else is rendered entirely redundant.

Emerging information and communication technologies, such as distributed ledgers, blockchains and smart contracts, may force the domestic law of contract to confront this issue head on. Although in their infancy, these technologies have the potential to remove the requirement for state institutions to enforce certain varieties of agreement, replacing them with private and autonomous forms of control facilitated electronically through computer software and cryptography.[96] Smart transacting relies on the underlying computer code and software to execute an agreement automatically. Performance of the smart contract is therefore autonomously guaranteed by the code, presenting the possibility of a further alternative to the law. English law's current autonomy-driven stance is likely to support contracting in this way. If the parties have consented to execute their arrangement via smart methods (assuming that the parties intend the law to have any role at all in the agreement), then presumably this will be enforceable, subject to consumer protection legislation or other bespoke regulation that might be developed. Once contract law gives the green light to the possibility that contracts could be performed automatically (and potentially irreversibly) in this way, then it appears to have little further role to play, except in cases where the transaction

[96] Kevin Werbach and Nicolas Cornell, 'Contracts *Ex Machina*' (2017) 67 *Duke Law Journal* 313; Kevin Werbach, 'Trust, But Verify: Why the Blockchain Needs the Law' (2018) 33 *Berkeley Technology Law Journal* 487.

may be affected by fraud, mistake, misrepresentation, illegality, and so on. Given that algorithmic contract is likely to produce both opportunities and challenges that cannot yet be anticipated, how contract law reacts to these challenges will be an important test of how far freedom of contract extends. This is considered further in Chapter 6.

In Chapter 7 we explore the possibilities for common law revival. Chief amongst the possibilities is the potential found in the concept of relational contracting. Legal recognition of relational contracts may weaken the formalist grip on contract law. Although contract law has started to engage seriously with the idea of relational contracting, the development is tentative and vulnerable to absorption by traditional contract law doctrine, especially implied terms. This is the natural response to any development reckoned to threaten the certainty of a formal law. English law contrasts unfavourably here with other common law jurisdictions manifesting an anti-formal tendency by articulating general organising principles of contract upon which a more specific relational contract jurisprudence could be based. English law has not taken this step, fuelled perhaps by a reluctance to undermine certainty in English law, affecting the attractiveness of its legal services sector in the international market for commercial law and dispute resolution.

1.8 Conclusion

Private ordering through contracts has expanded considerably over the last forty years, following developments in privatisation and the marketisation of previously state-owned or administered sections of the economy. Technological developments have made it easier to 'contractualise' common activities not previously reliant on contract forms. The methods by which contracts come into existence, and notionally create binding obligations, have transformed. Consumers now enter into contracts through remote and automated processes on standard terms over which they have little control. Much of this contracting activity – both in the consumer and commercial sphere – escapes serious and sustained legal scrutiny. Judicial determination of contract legal rights has been replaced in many areas by privately administered dispute resolution processes. Contracting in some specific markets is subject to rules generated and enforced by a regulatory body, not the law courts. The common law response to these developments has been to exhibit a degree of self-exclusion by reasserting broadly classical values in judicial legal reasoning, most notably a strong commitment to freedom of contract and party autonomy. The shift towards comprehending most contract law rules as *defaults* – and hence dispensable according to an act of individual will – champions autonomy as the single value that contract law serves, eclipsing other normative values that should inform contract law, such as distributive justice, the promotion of social welfare, good faith and the protection of reasonable expectations. A formal and classical system of contract law rules may suit commercial contractors but the significance of the law extends beyond this group. When gaps do emerge in the pattern of contract regulation – particularly as it affects weaker parties to an exchange – the inadequacy of common law rules fashioned to appeal predominantly to commercial contractors quickly becomes apparent. One effect of this impoverishment is that many contracts appear beyond the scope of effective legal control, leaving many contract problems unresolved and the expansion of contracts largely unchecked. Instead of providing the moral foundation for economic exchange, contract law in the hands of the courts is in danger of becoming wholly optional, a minor force in a world of private dispute resolution. The return to formalist values in contract law, in a society heavily dependent on contracts, has implications that should be identified and closely examined. In what follows, this book aims to undertake this task.

We start by examining contract law trends. This serves two purposes. First, it lays the groundwork for the claim about common law diminishment. We note the previous capacity of the common law to respond to changes in the broader contracting landscape and explore how this tendency towards flexibility seems to have receded. Second, it illustrates that the law's commitment to freedom of contract, while always in the background, has been contingent. Party autonomy has not been the sole value pursued in law but has been balanced with the pursuit of other aims.

2

Contract Common Law Trends

Even a cursory examination of contract law development reveals that the commitment to freedom of contract in the common law has drifted in and out of fashion depending on changes in the broader social, economic and political landscape. Judges in the recent past recognised that freedom of contract must be modified to respond to the social welfare concerns raised by weaker parties transacting in the market and that policy goals could be pursued through law. This willingness to recognise the social effects of contracting was not an anomaly within an otherwise autonomy-centred law but a core dimension of the contract jurisdiction of the courts, developed through various doctrinal devices. This chapter briefly traces the history of contract law in order to demonstrate that the common law of contract is not immutably committed to a single value, such as facilitation of commerce, autonomy or efficiency, although it may often be presented as such. The emphasis on freedom of contract and autonomy in the modern law is not, therefore, a natural realignment with an original position that was temporarily abandoned in order to deal with the aberration presented by mass consumer contracting. Rather, it reflects a choice. Commercial concerns and interests have been permitted to capture the law of contract in opposition to an established tradition whereby contract law responded to changes in the role of contract in society. The modern tendency to invest contract law with a single purpose, or as naturally aligned with a particular interest group, is liable to distort our understandings of contract law and contracts themselves. The attenuated and diminished concept of contract law that emerges from its close association with the commercial contract seems out of keeping with contract law's complex history, particularly its early association with equity, and renders it remote from much of the reality and experience of contracting in markets.

2.1 Contract Law in the Pre-classical Period

Most legal historians and commentators agree that current contract law is 'fundamentally a creature of the nineteenth century'.[1] As to the nature of contract law prior to the classical period, opinions differ. Ibbetson, in a concise history of intellectual thought on contract, notes that the organising principle of the Aristotelian conception of contract, which retained its influence into the Middle Ages, thanks to natural law theory, was not agreement but justice in exchange.[2] This commitment gradually receded as the law adapted to meet the demands of an incipient merchant class operating in an emerging market economy.[3] The marginalisation of equitable considerations that were reflected in the earlier law is a recurring theme in many accounts of the classical era. Atiyah notes that in responding to commercial concerns during the nineteenth century, the law departed from a model of contract that encompassed equitable standards and good faith requirements.[4] Waddams also observes that equity's role in reversing manifestly unfair contracts went into decline with the passage of the nineteenth century, when the importance of certainty and predictability in the law was asserted.[5] It appears that even Lord Mansfield, often credited with cultivating the commercial characteristics of contract law by his pioneering efforts to incorporate mercantile practice into the common law,[6] was motivated as much by equity and civil law in shaping contract law as by the needs of commerce.[7] As a result, his judgments reflected both equitable

1 Morton J. Horwitz, 'The Historical Foundations of Modern Contract Law' (1974) 87 *Harvard Law Review* 917, 917.

2 David Ibbetson, 'Revolutions in Private Law?' in Sarah Worthington, Andrew Robertson and Graham Virgo (eds.) *Revolution and Evolution in Private Law* (Hart Publishing, 2018), pp. 20–23; see also A. W. B. Simpson, 'The Horwitz Thesis and the History of Contracts' (1979) 46 *University Chicago Law Review* 533, 536.

3 Simpson, 'Horwitz Thesis', 534; James Gordley, *Foundations of Private Law* (Oxford University Press, 2006), p. 288; Alan D. Morrison and William J. Wilhelm Jr, 'Trust, Reputation and Law: The Evolution of Commitment in Investment Banking' (2015) 7 *Journal of Legal Analysis* 363, noting the evolution from reliance on trust and reputation in early investment banking to contract forms during the nineteenth century: 379ff.

4 Patrick S. Atiyah, *The Rise and Fall of Freedom of Contract* (Oxford University Press, 1979), pp. 388–97. This is disputed by some, however: J. H. Baker, 'The Rise and Fall of Freedom of Contract by P.S. Atiyah' (1980) 43 *Modern Law Review* 467, 469.

5 Stephen Waddams, *Sanctity of Contracts in a Secular Age* (Cambridge University Press, 2019), pp. 27–28; see also Lord Sales, 'The Interface between Contract and Equity', *Lehane Memorial Lecture* (29 August 2019), pp. 3–4.

6 A claim made by Atiyah, *Rise and Fall*, p. 123. See also Lord Diplock, 'The Law of Contract in the Eighties' (1981) 15 *University of British Columbia Law Review* 371, 373.

7 H. G. Hanbury, 'The Field of Modern Equity' (1929) 45 *Law Quarterly Review* 196, 200.

standards and more pragmatic values.[8] While his endeavours to introduce the notion of good faith into the law and to minimise the significance attached to consideration ultimately came to nothing, the attempt illustrates that 'Mansfield cannot be taken to have been an unquestioning exponent of freedom of contract'.[9]

The development of classical contract law was also shaped by reforms to legal procedure. Swain notes that one of the most significant drivers behind the transition to modern contract law during the 1800s was the disappearance of the civil jury. Legal rules were required to replace questions of fact that were previously determined by juries, such as whether the parties had reached an agreement.[10] The decline of juries also had a substantive effect on the law, since it dispensed with 'a source of vaguely discretionary mercy'.[11] Other procedural features of the law at the time, such as the forms of action (assumpsit, covenant), effectively prevented coherent development of the common law of contract until the writ system was reformed in the period from the 1830s to the 1850s.[12] Prior to these changes, there was neither the opportunity to create a body of contract rules nor a requirement for it. Legal doctrines and grand theories had no explanatory power over the operation of the writ system. Baker therefore regards it as a mistake 'to assume that this new [classical] law replaced a previous body of law which reflected a golden age of fairness and equity'.[13] However, this is because the contract law familiar to us now did not exist before the 1800s as there was no method of creating it.[14] It was only with the decline of juries and forms of action that judges had the incentive to develop substantive principles and rules of contract law. Intellectual ballast for a rule-based account of contract law could be found in the nascent theory of legal positivism.[15] Treatise and

[8] Warren Swain, *The Law of Contract 1670–1870* (Cambridge University Press, 2015), p. 78.

[9] James Oldham, *English Common Law in the Time of Mansfield* (University of North Carolina Press, 2004), p. 79.

[10] Swain, *Law of Contract 1670–1870*, p. 29; see also Baker, 'Rise and Fall of Freedom of Contract', 469.

[11] Atiyah, *Rise and Fall*, p. 394.

[12] Swain, *Law of Contract 1670–1870*, p. 16. The forms of action were abolished by s 3 of the Common Law Procedure Act 1852; Geoffrey Samuel, *A Short Introduction to Judging and to Legal Reasoning* (Edward Elgar Publishing, 2016), pp. 24–25.

[13] Baker, 'Rise and Fall of Freedom of Contract', 469; J. H. Baker, 'From Sanctity of Contract to Reasonable Expectation?' (1979) 32 *Current Legal Problems* 17, 20.

[14] Baker, 'Rise and Fall of Freedom of Contract', 469.

[15] Atiyah, *Rise and Fall*, p. 342.

textbook writers, most notably Pothier and later Chitty, played a role in augmenting the authority of the classical law, often by imposing a coherent structure on the subject matter that it lacked in practice. This desire that the law manifest coherence perhaps reflected the lingering influence of natural law theory.[16] Two of its effects were, however, to minimise the significance of rogue elements that did not fit the model, for example equity,[17] and to champion the importance of agreement and individual will as the core of contractual liability.[18]

It is difficult to draw robust conclusions from an admittedly very superficial foray into legal history. Nonetheless, debates about the values reflected in contract before the classical law took shape focus on the extent of equity's influence on the pre-classical law, not on whether it had any influence at all. The defining norms of early contract law therefore reflect a certain mutability rather than unity. It appears beyond serious doubt that the decline of the jury, the end of Lord Mansfield's era as Lord Chief Justice in 1788 and the drive to consolidate contract doctrine effectively sidelined what was perceived as an ad hoc and uncertain equitable jurisdiction.[19] Marginalising equity may have reduced the scope for the operation of judicial discretion in contract disputes, but it also served to detach the common law from considerations of good conscience in transactions, except through the operation of some limited doctrines imported into the common law. The passing of the Supreme Court of Judicature Acts of 1873 and 1875, mandating fusion between law and equity, did not have the requisite effect of producing a unified law.[20] Thus the enduring association of equity with an expanded form of judicial discretion serves to minimise its influence over the common law of contract even to this day.

16 'Belief in natural law theory . . . leads to the idea that the legal system of a legitimate regime must consist of a coherent body of rules': Edward L. Rubin, 'From Coherence to Effectiveness: A Legal Methodology for the Modern World' in Rob van Gestel, Hans-W. Micklitz and Edward L. Rubin (eds.) *Rethinking Legal Scholarship: A Transatlantic Dialogue* (Cambridge University Press, 2017), pp. 310, 314.

17 Swain, *Law of Contract 1670–1870*, p. 201; A. W. B. Simpson, 'Contract: The Twitching Corpse' (1981) 1 *Oxford Journal of Legal Studies* 265, 269.

18 Although it is often argued that contract law reflected these themes long before, see, for example, Baker, 'Rise and Fall of Freedom of Contract', 467.

19 John Joseph Powell, *Essay upon the Law of Contract and Agreements*, vol 1 (J. Johnson, 1790), pp. ix–x; Oldham, *English Common Law in the Time of Mansfield*, pp. 103–06.

20 Andrew Burrows, 'We Do this at Common Law but that in Equity' (2002) 22 *Oxford Journal of Legal Studies* 1, 3.

2.2 The Classical Law of Contract

The decline of equity's influence on the common law in favour of a more rigid doctrine,[21] along with the rise of the contract treatise amongst scholars and the burgeoning commitment to precedent amongst the judiciary,[22] spurred classical law development. *Atiyah's Introduction to the Law of Contract* identifies the years 1770–1870 as the classical period of the law of contract.[23] The idea of agreement became central to explaining how contractual obligation arose and why legal enforcement was justified. Commitment to rules and the operation of precedent became more important, and commercial considerations came to motivate doctrinal development. Atiyah argues that privity of contract was a judicial reaction to the increasing complexity of commercial agreements.[24] Similarly, the rise of the executory contract, ensuring the enforceability of future exchange planning, was directly linked to the demands of a market economy, and commodity markets in particular.[25] The perception of contracts as instruments of future planning had the effect of emphasising contracts as abstractions, with legal significance being attached to the creation of liability at the point of agreement rather than the point of action. This transition found legal expression in the rules relating to offer and acceptance.[26]

Classical law's theoretical underpinnings included a strong commitment to party autonomy and freedom of contract (aligned with the laissez-faire political ideology of the nineteenth century). The classical model assumed the parties prioritised individual self-interest, informed by hard economic rationality, over the finer qualities, such as good faith or co-operation, necessary to maintain a continuing and long-term relationship. In more general terms, the classical law period bequeathed an enduring idea of the features a system of

[21] Horwitz, 'Historical Foundations of Modern Contract Law', 917–18, tracing the idea to Powell's *Essay upon the Law of Contracts and Agreements.*

[22] At least in the nineteenth century, Swain, *Law of Contract 1670–1870*, p. 167; Waddams, *Sanctity of Contracts in a Secular Age*, p. 27; David Ibbetson, *A Historical Introduction to the Law of Obligations* (Oxford University Press, 2001), pp. 224–25.

[23] Stephen A. Smith, *Atiyah's Introduction to the Law of Contract*, 6th ed. (Oxford University Press, 2005), pp. 9–11; see also Hugh Collins, *The Law of Contract*, 4th ed. (Butterworths, 2003), pp. 3–7; Roger Brownsword, *Contract Law: Themes for the Twenty-First Century*, 2nd ed. (Oxford University Press, 2006), Chapter 3.

[24] Atiyah, *Rise and Fall*, p. 414.

[25] Atiyah, *Rise and Fall*, pp. 420, 463. Contra to the idea of the executory contract being a novel development, see Simpson, 'Contract: The Twitching Corpse', 275–76.

[26] Atiyah, *Rise and Fall*, pp. 426–27.

contract law should possess: embodiment in determinate rules, not judicial discretion; autonomy of law from political discourse and disagreement; and grounding in a coherent and rational structure of identifiable concepts and principles, derived from precedent and applicable through formal and deductive modes of legal reasoning.[27] Contractual justice was perceived in procedural rather than substantive terms. There were limited avenues of escape from a concluded agreement and a tight rein on judicial intervention in contracts on paternalistic grounds of fairness or reasonableness.[28] A degree of rationalisation for these classical law values was found in the will theory of contractual obligation: liability was voluntarily assumed and based on consent, not legal imposition.[29] As Collins observes, 'not only was the law of contract a convenient way of understanding the social relations of a market economy, but it also represented a particular theory of the legitimacy of state power, one that limited the exercise of such power in the name of respecting the liberty of citizens under the banner of freedom of contract.'[30] Needless to say, the long-held estimation of equity as a 'roguish thing'[31] was reinforced by the classical law. The codification of commercial sales law into statute further hardened judicial sentiments against the incursion of equity into commercial matters. In the 1920s, Lord Atkin observed that the Sale of Goods Act 1893 had rendered equity redundant in sales:

> It would have been futile in a code intended for commercial men to have created an elaborate structure of rules dealing with rights at law, if at the same time it was intended to leave, subsisting with the legal rights, equitable rights inconsistent with, more extensive, and coming into existence earlier than the rights so carefully set out in the various sections of the Code.[32]

[27] Thomas C. Grey, 'The New Formalism', Stanford Public Law and Legal Theory Working Paper Series, 5 (6 September 1999), available at http://papers.ssrn.com/paper.taf?abstract-id=200732; Jay M. Feinman, 'Un-Making Law: The Classical Revival in the Common Law' (2004) 28 *Seattle University Law Review* 1, 4–5. For a classic statement of formal analogical legal reasoning method, see Edward H. Levi, 'An Introduction to Legal Reasoning' (1948) 15 *University of Chicago Law Review* 501.

[28] For a brief statement see Atiyah, *Rise and Fall*, pp. 388–89.

[29] See Smith, *Atiyah's Introduction to the Law of Contract*, p. 10; Ibbetson, *Historical Introduction to the Law of Obligations*, p. 22[illegible].

[30] Collins, *The Law of Contract*, p. 6.

[31] Attributed to seventeenth-century jurist John Selden, *The Table-Talk of John Selden* (Cambridge University Press, 2015), p. 64; see also Henry H. Brown, 'Equity' (1914) 26 *Juridical Review* 338, 338.

[32] Wait (Re) [1927] 1 Ch 606, 635–36.

The conceptual neatness of the classical law belied a more complex reality of contractual dealing that had to be moulded to fit its rules and doctrines. A particular source of tension for the will theory emanated from the law's insistence that an objective method be used to determine what were notionally matters of individual will and intention, such as whether an agreement was reached and on what terms. Far from examining their actual wills, the intention of the parties was identified using contract law rules that became entrenched through precedent. Similarly, the rules of offer and acceptance imposed a highly artificial simplicity on the process of contract creation, tending to denigrate the significance of the pre-contract negotiating period and gloss over any substantive inequalities of bargaining power between the parties. While the law deemed formalities unnecessary to contract creation, aside from the presence of consideration, the commitment to objectivity resulted in a tendency to disassociate the contract from the actual agreement of the parties in favour of the written document that recorded it. The extent of contractual liability was circumscribed by agreement, supplemented by interpretation and implied terms. Although these doctrines provided scope for judicial intervention into the agreement, this was limited due to the commitment to plain meaning in the case of interpretation and strict rules regarding when implication was justified. This lent the law certainty and predictability, which contributed to contract law's supposed efficacy as a baseline security for transactions and as a tool for contract planning, especially between independent firms. Vitiating factors (duress, mistake) were recognised but kept within tight bounds. Restraint of trade aside,[33] there was little appetite amongst the judiciary to develop a robust common law response to matters of wider public interest that were generated by the operation of contracts. The problem that contracts could be used to neutralise freedom through establishing anti-competitive practices was not addressed – freedom of contract entailed that these restrictive agreements were enforceable.[34] This reticence on the part of judges to engage with policy appears motivated by the combination of inadequate information, a lack of confidence in dealing with policy issues and concerns about institutional constraints on the judiciary.[35] Judicial

[33] Ibbetson, *Historical Introduction to the Law of Obligations*, pp. 249–51; Swain, *Law of Contract 1670–1870*, pp. 245–48. For the main cases on restraint of trade, see *Egerton* v. *Earl of Brownlow* [1853] 4 HLC 1; *Nordenfelt* v. *Maxim Nordenfelt Guns and Ammunition Co Ltd* [1894] AC 535.

[34] Atiyah, *Rise and Fall*, p. 697 ff; Betty Mensch, 'Freedom of Contract as Ideology' (1981) 33 *Stanford Law Review* 753, 759.

[35] Atiyah, *Rise and Fall*, p. 384.

disengagement from these matters more or less remained the position until the mid-twentieth century.[36]

2.3 Contract Law Transformations

In 1981 A. W. B. Simpson published a review article on three works of contract law. Under examination were Atiyah's recently published *The Rise and Fall of Freedom of Contract*, the fifth and latest edition of Treitel's *The Law of Contract* and the twenty-fifth edition of *Anson's Law of Contract*, which by that time was under the editorial stewardship of A. G. Guest. In a less than generous appraisal, Simpson described *Anson's* as an 'archaeological site'.[37] He also noted that the basic structure of Treitel had remained unaltered across several editions.[38] Simpson's review epitomises the conviction held by many in the 1980s that the classical law of contract was 'crumbling fast'.[39] Attacks on the classical model emanated from different factions of the scholarly community. Socio-legal and empirical studies of contract revealed the minor contribution of contracts and contract law to functioning business relationships and market activity. In the 1960s Ian Macneil began publishing work heralding his relational theory of contract.[40] The theory mounted a considerable challenge to many of the assumptions upon which the classical law was based, not least that contracts were discrete transactions between antagonistic strangers.[41] Trust, co-operation and reputation were shown to play significant roles in contract creation, performance and enforcement.[42] In the 1970s Grant

36 Atiyah, *Rise and Fall*, p. 742. For cases recognising the court's power to disallow abuse of a stronger bargaining position in relation to restraint of trade, see *Esso Petroleum Co Ltd v. Harper's Garage (Stourport) Ltd* [1968] AC 269; *Schroeder Music Publishing Co Ltd v. Macaulay* [1974] 1 WLR 1308; contra *Alec Lobb (Garages) Ltd* v. *Total Oil (GB) Ltd* [1985] 1 WLR 173.

37 Simpson, 'Contract: The Twitching Corpse', 266.

38 Simpson, 'Contract: The Twitching Corpse', 265.

39 Patrick S. Atiyah, *An Introduction to the Law of Contract*, 5th ed. (Oxford University Press, 1995), p. 15.

40 David Campbell, 'Ian Macneil and the Relational Theory of Contract' in David Campbell (ed.) *The Relational Theory of Contract: Selected Works of Ian Macneil* (Sweet and Maxwell, 2001), pp. 3, 5.

41 Culminating in the groundbreaking Ian R. Macneil, 'The Many Futures of Contract' (1974) 47 *Southern California Law Review* 691.

42 Seminally, Stewart Macaulay, 'Non-contractual Relations in Business: A Preliminary Study' (1963) 28 *American Sociological Review* 55; Hugh Beale and Tony Dugdale, 'Contracts between Businessmen: Planning and the Use of Contractual Remedies' (1975) 2 *British Journal of Law and Society* 45.

Gilmore criticised contract as little more than an elaborate patchwork of judicial opinions forced into existence as a distinctive field of law through academic effort. He famously predicted the death of contract from an encroaching law of tort and from the principles of unjust enrichment.[43] Cracks in the edifice of the classical model had long been appearing. Expansion of other branches of private law was deemed necessary to overcome contract law's self-imposed doctrinal constraints. Tort law coursed into areas traditionally regarded as the province of contract, facilitated by a weakened judicial commitment to upholding privity of contract and relaxation of the rules against recovery of pure economic loss.[44] This gave rise to a feeling in some quarters that tort was compensating for contract law's inflexibility.[45] Others argued that a rigid distinction between contract and tort drawn on the basis of the voluntariness of the obligation could no longer be sustained.[46] Principles of restitution were also deployed to address some recurring problems resulting from the operation of contract doctrine, such as ensuring payment for work done where a contract between the parties was anticipated but never concluded[47] or when an admitted breach of contract went wholly uncompensated because the claimant had not suffered a financial loss.[48]

The most significant peril, however, to the explanatory and justificatory power of the classical law emanated from general social changes of the twentieth century. Atiyah identified three related factors that substantially undermined the classical model: first, the emergence of the standard form contract; second, the decline of free choice and intention as foundations of contract liability, largely in response to increasing complexity in contract law and a healthy cynicism regarding the supposed equality of access to markets; and third, the rise of the consumer as a contracting force.[49] The combination of the first and the third of these factors proved particularly problematic for the common law of contract. The prevalence of non-negotiated terms in

43 Grant Gilmore, *The Death of Contract* (Ohio University Press, 1974).

44 *Hedley Byrne & Co Ltd* v. *Heller & Partners Ltd* [1964] AC 465; *Junior Books Ltd* v. *Veitchi Co Ltd* [1983] 1 AC 520; *White* v. *Jones* [1995] 2 AC 207; *Henderson* v. *Merrett Syndicates Ltd* [1995] 2 AC 145.

45 Basil S. Markesinis, 'An Expanding Tort Law – The Price of a Rigid Contract Law' (1987) 103 *Law Quarterly Review* 354.

46 Gilmore, *The Death of Contract*; Patrick S. Atiyah, 'Contracts, Promises and the Law of Obligations' in Patrick S. Atiyah (ed.) *Essays on Contract* (Oxford University Press, 1990), pp. 10, 54.

47 *British Steel Corp* v. *Cleveland Bridge and Engineering Co Ltd* [1984] 1 All ER 504.

48 *Attorney General* v. *Blake* [2001] 1 AC 268.

49 Smith, *Atiyah's Introduction to the Law of Contract*, pp. 15–19.

consumer contracts required the common law to consider openly the role of substantive fairness in contracts made on non-negotiated terms between parties of unequal bargaining power. Legal rules founded on principles of freedom of contract and individual will appeared manifestly unsuited to this task, though judges were able to adapt and develop common law to offer some protection to weaker parties. Some of the problems emerging from mass consumer contracting on standard terms were resolved by legislative intervention (key enactments were the Consumer Credit Act 1974 and the Unfair Contract Terms Act 1977). Commentators seeking to incorporate these developments within a general account of contract law, rather than exclude them as irrelevant, identified a transformation in the law away from justifications based on freedom of contract towards more market-regulatory modes that stressed the importance of preventing domination, ensuring equivalence in exchange and upholding co-operation in contractual dealings.[50] The re-establishment of values characteristic more of equity than classical contract law was pursued not through a reliance on formalistic rules but a more contextual (standards-based) style of legal reasoning in contract cases.[51] This change in legal reasoning dynamic was not indicative of an unmoored judicial discretion to tackle contract unfairness in an unprincipled fashion. The Unfair Contract Terms Act 1977 required judges to assess the reasonableness of some varieties of contract term. Judges were able to give structure to this seemingly open-ended power by developing the relevant criteria through case determination.[52]

Given the amorphous quality of the common law, it was perhaps inevitable that the values informing legislative intervention in contracts were harnessed and deployed by the judiciary to effect change elsewhere in contract law. Judges had already ameliorated some of the difficulties generated by the classical law through common law development. The courts showed some willingness to look behind contractual labels, descriptors and technical legal meanings (as with 'conditions' and 'warranties') to implement a more realist,

[50] Collins, *The Law of Contract*, Chapter 2, p. 29.

[51] Collins, *The Law of Contract*, p. 35; Hugh Collins, *Regulating Contracts* (Oxford University Press, 1999); Duncan Kennedy, 'Form and Substance in Private Law Adjudication' (1976) 89 *Harvard Law Review* 1685.

[52] *Photo Production Ltd* v. *Securicor Transport* [1980] AC 827; *George Mitchell (Chesterhall) Ltd* v. *Finney Lock Seeds Ltd* [1983] 2 AC 803; *Smith* v. *Eric S. Bush* [1990] 1 AC 831; John N. Adams and Roger Brownsword, 'The Unfair Contract Terms Act: A Decade of Discretion (1988) 104 *Law Quarterly Review* 94.

consequences-led approach to the conduct of the business relationship.[53] Some of the characteristic doctrines of the classical period were questioned. Notably, the Law Commission in 1986 decided that legislative reform of the parol evidence rule was unnecessary, as for all intents and purposes the rule no longer existed.[54] More paternalistically, the 1970s saw the inception of the doctrine of economic duress and the recognition of illegitimate pressure in bargaining.[55] Principles derived from equity, such as estoppel, permitted courts to implement a more just and fair approach to contract matters at the expense of the formal rules of the common law.[56] Undue influence, the new legislation on unfair terms, and implied terms were all utilised to achieve a more balanced and fair position between parties of unequal bargaining power.[57]

These inroads into the classical law were not accepted uncritically. Sensing the change in direction in contract law, and questioning its legitimacy, warnings emanated from the senior judiciary that major common law reform – particularly in the attempt to develop a general doctrine addressing 'inequality of bargaining power' – was a matter for the legislature rather than the judges.[58] They also warned that commercial contractors could be left to form their own bargain in the expectation of minimal legal intervention.[59] Though Atiyah had no difficulty in the 1990s in regarding contract law as a mixture of obligations imposed in the absence of consent and assumed obligations,[60] the attempt to re-interpret and remould the classical law in light of a countervailing standard of reliance-based liability drew considerable adverse comment, and some

[53] For example, *L Schuler AG* v. *Wickman Machine Tool Sales Ltd* [1974] AC 235. The innominate term was also a development in this respect: *Hong Kong Fir Shipping Co Ltd* v. *Kawasaki Kisen Kaisha Ltd* [1962] 1 All ER 474.

[54] Law Commission, *Law of Contract: The Parol Evidence Rule* No 154 (1986), paras 1.7, 2.45 and 3.8.

[55] *North Ocean Shipping Co Ltd* v. *Hyundai Construction Co Ltd* [1979] QB 705.

[56] *Central London Property Trust Ltd* v. *High Trees House Ltd* [1947] KB 130; on estoppel by conduct see *Panchaud Frères SA* v. *Etablissements General Grain Co* [1970] 1 Lloyd's Rep 53: 'what one has here is something perhaps in our law not yet wholly developed as a separate doctrine – which is more in the nature of a requirement of fair conduct – a criterion of what is fair conduct between the parties', per Lord Justice Winn, 59.

[57] *Lloyds Bank Ltd* v. *Bundy* [1975] QB 326; *Smith* v. *Eric S. Bush* [1990] 1 AC 831; *Paragon Finance plc* v. *Nash and others* [2002] 1 WLR 685.

[58] *National Westminster Bank plc* v. *Morgan* [1985] AC 686, per Lord Scarman, 708.

[59] *Photo Productions Ltd* v. *Securicor Transport Ltd* [1980] AC 827.

[60] Atiyah, *Introduction to the Law of Contract*, p. 287.

aspects of expanding tort liability were reversed.[61] There was little inclination to permit tortious liability to undermine the contractual allocation of risk in commercial network situations.[62] The requirement for courts to adopt a broad policing function over contractor behaviour and to develop concepts (such as unconscionability, inequality of bargaining power, reasonableness and good faith) to execute this task receded as statute assumed responsibility for contract control and judges withdrew from any enhanced role. Atiyah regarded *Photo Productions Ltd* v. *Securicor Transport Ltd*[63] and *National Westminster Bank plc* v. *Morgan*[64] as common law watersheds in this respect.[65] Judges in these cases fully accepted that, in the commercial sphere at least, freedom of contract was the overriding principle and that there was little need for the common law to develop doctrine to tackle contractual unfairness – consumers were protected by the enactment of the Unfair Contract Terms Act 1977, and commercial contractors had no need of general controlling principles.[66] Around the same time, the United Kingdom's membership of the European Union was becoming an important source of rules, particularly in business-to-consumer contracts. The EU pursuit of single market objectives through harmonised laws removed any stimulus to develop common law along protectionist lines, although not the need for courts to interpret and apply standards-based tests of contractual fairness.[67] Judges were required to engage with questions such as whether terms were contrary to good faith, and whether this caused a significant imbalance in the rights and obligations arising under the contract between the parties. These new rights were not always interpreted in a way that benefitted consumers. As we will see in Chapter 3, courts often imported classical law ideas into the legislative and regulatory scheme, undermining its consumer protection rationale. The mood of the time was caught by Lord Diplock. Writing extra-judicially in the early 1980s, he remarked that 'the nineteen-eighties may well see an extension of the principle that the court will

[61] Notably in *Junior Books* v. *Veitchi* above n. 44; *D & F Estates Ltd* v. *Church Commissioners for England* [1989] AC 177; *Murphy* v. *Brentwood District Council* [1991] 1 AC 398.

[62] See, for example, *New Zealand Shipping Company Ltd* v. *A M Satterthwaite & Company Limited (New Zealand) (The Eurymedon)* [1975] AC 154; see *Tai Hing Cotton Mill Ltd* v. *Liu Chong Hing Bank Ltd* [1986] 1 AC 80, per Lord Scarman at 107.

[63] [1980] AC 827. [64] [1985] AC 686.

[65] See Smith, *Atiyah's Introduction to the Law of Contract*, pp. 153, 310–11, respectively.

[66] Nelson Enonchong, 'The Modern English Doctrine of Unconscionability' (2018) 34 *Journal of Contract Law* 211, 217.

[67] Seminally, Council Directive 93/13/EEC of 5 April 1993 on unfair terms in consumer contracts. Enacted in the United Kingdom by way of Unfair Terms in Consumer Contracts Regulations 1994 and 1999, now absorbed into Consumer Rights Act 2015.

not uphold unconscionable bargains'. However, the tensions this generated within contract law and the fear that these developments might taint commercial contract law were never far from the surface. Lord Diplock went on to say, '[the court] will I hope bear in mind the realities of how modern trade and commerce are conducted, and in particular, in commercial transactions the nearly universal practice of insurance.'[68]

2.4 Relational Theory and Welfarism

Naturally, the confused state of the law drew censure and it appeared necessary to develop an alternative theoretical model to the classical law that incorporated contract's new directions rather than ignored them as aberrations.[69] Relational theory was one contender. Ian Macneil had criticised the emphasis in classical law on contract as a discrete and abstract entity, to be analysed in isolation from the complex web of social relations that surrounded it. The relational theory of contract highlighted the importance of social norms – trust, maintaining reputation and preserving productive business relationships – to contracting.[70] Macneil sought a much richer normative account of contract than could be provided by the classical law, although it was open to question how far he thought his theory could inform contract legal reasoning.[71] The indeterminate nature of relational theory, and its attention to the social context of the agreement at the expense of the legal contract, made it difficult to translate into a method judges could use to decide contract disputes. Nevertheless, relational theory had a profound influence on contract scholarship. In the 1970s Atiyah predicted that future contract law would see the courts paying greater attention to the realities of business relationships. He maintained that 'contract as an instrument for the planning of future exchanges has been replaced by contemporaneous exchanges, or short-term exchanges or long-term relationships in which exchanges can be made but on terms which are open to continuous adjustment as long as the

[68] Lord Diplock, 'Law of Contract in the Eighties', 382.

[69] See David Campbell, 'The Undeath of Contract: A Study in the Degeneration of a Research Programme' (1992) 22 *Hong Kong Law Journal* 20.

[70] Macaulay, 'Non-contractual Relations in Business: A Preliminary Study'; Ian Macneil, *The Relational Theory of Contract: Selected Works of Ian Macneil*, David Campbell (ed.) (Sweet & Maxwell, 2001).

[71] See generally Catherine Mitchell, *Contract Law and Contract Practice* (Hart Publishing, 2013), Chapter 6.

relationship lasts'.[72] In making these predictions, Atiyah was likely influenced by relational contract theory and by empirical research on business attitudes towards legal contracts.

Similarly, David Campbell and Hugh Collins used the findings of relational theory to argue that the classical law model of economic relationships was built upon a flawed foundation of discrete contracts and self-interested contracting parties at variance with reality. The result was that the discrete model required supplementation by a number of 'exceptional' counter-norms that effectively weakened the structure of the classical law, revealing its lack of internal coherence.[73] The exceptions did not lead to any sustained challenge to the classical model of contracts and contract law; they simply heralded the false dawn of 'neo-classical' law.[74] Legislative intervention in contract law did not help in building coherence. Statutes tended to operate only in certain areas of the law, and often as a supplement to the common law rather than an outright replacement or codification.[75] Others saw the rule/counter-rule structure of the law as entirely natural: 'You can only create a body of law once; having committed yourself to explicit doctrine the only way ahead is to find ways around it.'[76] Despite these scholarly critiques and predictions about contract's future directions, the law still focused on agreement as the linchpin of contractual liability, rather than the expectations generated by actions or relationships.[77] In a review article from 1996, Donal Nolan wrote: 'The challenge facing contract lawyers today is ... to identify which features of the classical law should be discarded and which retained.'[78] Despite the willingness of the modern law to undermine many of the precepts of the classical model, the fact that Nolan's question was still pertinent in

[72] Atiyah, *Rise and Fall*, pp. 716–17.

[73] David Campbell and Hugh Collins, 'Discovering the Implicit Dimensions of Contracts' in David Campbell, Hugh Collins and John Wightman (eds.), *Implicit Dimensions of Contract* (Hart Publishing, 2003), pp. 25–27.

[74] Ian R. Macneil, 'Contracts: Adjustment of Long-Term Economic Relations under Classical, Neoclassical and Relational Contract Law' (1978) 72 *Northwestern University Law Review* 854; Jay M. Feinman, 'Relational Contract Theory in Context' (2000) 94 *Northwestern University Law Review* 737, 748; 'Un-making Law: The Classical Revival in Common Law', 1, 3. See also Oliver E. Williamson, *The Economic Institutions of Capitalism* (Free Press, 1985), pp. 68–72.

[75] Notable in the Law Reform (Frustrated Contracts) Act 1943; the Misrepresentation Act 1967; the Contract (Rights of Third Parties) Act 1999.

[76] Baker, 'From Sanctity of Contract to Reasonable Expectation?', 21.

[77] Atiyah, *Rise and Fall*, p. 754.

[78] Donal Nolan, 'The Classical Legacy and Modern English Contract Law' (1996) 59 *Modern Law Review* 603, 603.

the mid-1990s was testament to the influence that the classical law, and the principle of freedom of contract, continued to exert.

For some theorists, the development of neo-classical law throughout the twentieth century could be linked to wider social and political transformations occurring at the time, particularly increased state intervention in markets. Adams and Brownsword interpreted neo-classical law as reflecting the division of contract regulation into 'market-individualist' and 'consumer-welfarist' branches.[79] Market individualism was itself split into two types: *static market individualism*, which broadly corresponded with the aspects of classical law that reflected the concerns of commercial contractors operating in discrete markets, and *dynamic market individualism*, where law placed more weight on the informal normative frameworks associated with long-term co-operative commercial relationships when resolving disputes.[80] Contract law vacillated between these two rule-sets depending on the social context of the parties' agreement. The theory of welfarism in contract, upon which the 'consumer-welfarist' idea was based, emerged from the paternalistic shift in the law in the decades from the 1940s to the 1970s, prompted by the advent of mass consumer contracting on standard terms.[81] The welfarist strand within contract law during this period chimed with the social and economic policy of post-war governments that recognised the state's important role in satisfying basic needs by providing for its citizens public goods and services that were not procured effectively through markets (such as health services, education and housing).[82] In terms of contract, the consumer-welfarist approach in legal thinking was not necessarily confined to consumer contracts. It was argued that the animating values of consumer welfarism could be detected across contract law more generally, embodied in principles such as proportionality, the reversal of unjust enrichment (or the avoidance of windfalls to one party from the vagaries of contract doctrine[83]), the protection from exploitation by a stronger party and the prevention of bad faith reliance on formal contract

[79] John N. Adams and Roger Brownsword, 'The Ideologies of Contract' (1987) 7 *Legal Studies* 205.

[80] Roger Brownsword, 'Contract Law, Co-operation, and Good Faith: The Movement from Static to Dynamic Market-Individualism' in Simon Deakin and Jonathan Michie (eds.) *Contracts, Cooperation, and Competition: Studies in Economics, Management, and Law* (Oxford University Press, 1998), pp, 255, 272–79.

[81] John Wightman, *Contract: A Critical Commentary* (Pluto Press, 1996), pp. 114–15. Problems of boilerplate in the US context are explored in Margaret Jane Radin, *Boilerplate: The Fine Print, Vanishing Rights and the Rule of Law* (Princeton University Press, 2013), pp. 7–11.

[82] David Harvey, *A Brief History of Neoliberalism* (Oxford University Press, 2007), p. 71.

[83] Law Reform (Frustrated Contracts) Act 1943.

rules to secure unbargained-for advantages.[84] By 1994 it appeared to the editors of a collection of essays entitled *Welfarism in Contract Law* that it was 'trite to say that the modern law of contract [in England] is distinguished by its protectionist concern for weaker contracting parties'.[85] The authors associated this with 'domestic politics of the twentieth century', which were 'distinguished by their interventionism, most conspicuously in the form of the modern Welfare State'.[86] However, the authors acknowledged that most of modern contract law was contained in legislative enactments.

It was not clear how far the common law at the time could be regarded as a bastion of welfarism, though certainly courts were not blind to issues of distributional justice, inequality of bargaining power and the consequences of market failure in their judgments.[87] Partly this is connected to a lack of precision over what 'welfarism' means and requires. It could denote a fairly minimalistic concept that relies on the precepts of classical law to a degree, supplemented by measures designed to provide a safety net for vulnerable individuals at risk of exploitation by stronger parties operating in the market (minors, those with disabilities affecting their ability to exercise judgment, those susceptible to pressure, duress and so on), to more expansive conceptions recognising contracting across all contexts as *fundamentally* a co-operative process where some attention must be paid to the interests of the other party for the contractual gains to be obtained.[88] A broader conception of welfarism associated it with a style of judicial reasoning that relied less on formalistic doctrine and more on flexibility in the application of the rules. This found more concrete expression in the idea that the organising principle of contract was not freedom of contract or formalism but the protection of the 'reasonable expectations of the parties'.[89]

84 Adams and Brownsword, 'The Ideologies of Contract', 210–12.

85 Roger Brownsword, Geraint Howells, Thomas Wilhelmsson, 'General Introduction' in Roger Brownsword, Geraint Howells, Thomas Wilhelmsson (eds.) *Welfarism in Contract Law* (Dartmouth, 1994), pp. 1–2.

86 Above n. 85. 87 See cases referred to at n. 36.

88 Roger Brownsword, 'The Philosophy of Welfarism and Its Emergence in the Modern English Law of Contract' in Brownsword, Howells and Wilhelmsson (eds.) *Welfarism in Contract Law*, above n. 85, at pp. 21, 29–38.

89 Baker, 'From Sanctity of Contract to Reasonable Expectation?'; Lord Steyn, 'Contract Law: Fulfilling the Reasonable Expectations of Honest Men' (1997) 113 *Law Quarterly Review* 433, 442; Roger Brownsword, 'After Investors: Interpretation, Expectation and the Implicit Dimension of the "New Contextualism"' in David Campbell, Hugh Collins and John Wightman (eds.) *Implicit Dimensions of Contract* (Hart Publishing, 2003), p. 103; Catherine Mitchell, 'Leading a Life of its Own? The Roles of Reasonable Expectation in Contract Law' (2003) 23 *Oxford Journal of Legal Studies* 639.

Reference to the reasonable expectations of contractors had already appeared in the Unfair Contract Terms Act 1977 as part of the controls on standard form exclusion clauses.[90] But the broader principle of protecting 'reasonable expectations' explained a range of contract law doctrinal advances beyond limiting the operation of unfair terms. These included the attempt to render the contract remedial regime more responsive to the different kinds of harm suffered by contractors on breach, especially consumers suffering losses that were not readily compensated by a difference-in-value method of assessment.[91] Reliance and the protection of the expectations of third parties were also explicit in the enactment of a comprehensive legislative exception to the privity rule in 1999.[92] In allied developments, there was some common law engagement with good faith in procedural terms, notably in relation to incorporating onerous terms into a contract,[93] as well as in specifying the limits on the exercise of contractual discretions.[94] Some commentators interpreted this concern with reasonableness as the modern manifestation of the older judicial equitable powers.[95] Expectations-based justifications spread into the commercial sphere, though the primacy attached to reasonable expectation was insufficient, at least in some commercial contexts, to subvert the overall assumption of self-interested dealing.[96] The doctrine of consideration was rendered less troublesome in contract modifications by judicial intervention, justified on the basis of upholding commercial expectations.[97] The 'legitimate expectation' of contractors, rather than traditional offer-acceptance analysis, was advanced to justify the imposition of contractual liability in a tendering scenario.[98] A transition from the 'plain meaning' method to contextualism in contract interpretation was openly articulated, suggesting a permanent shift

[90] Under s 3(2)(b)(ii) of Unfair Contract Terms Act 1977.

[91] *Ruxley Electronics and Construction Ltd* v. *Forsyth* [1996] AC 344; *Farley* v. *Skinner* [2001] 3 WLR 899.

[92] Contracts (Rights of Third Parties) Act 1999.

[93] *Interfoto Picture Library Ltd* v. *Stiletto Visual Programmes Ltd* [1989] QB 433.

[94] *Abu Dhabi National Tanker Co* v. *Product Star Shipping Ltd (The Product Star) (No 2)* [1993] 1 Lloyd's Rep 397; *Paragon Finance plc* v. *Nash and others* [2002] 1 WLR 685.

[95] Baker, 'From Sanctity of Contract to Reasonable Expectation?', 30.

[96] *Walford* v. *Miles* [1992] 2 AC 128.

[97] *Williams* v. *Roffey Bros & Nicholls (Contractors) Ltd* [1991] 1 QB 1.

[98] *Blackpool and Fylde Aero Club* v. *Blackpool Borough Council* [1990] 1 WLR 1195; John N. Adams and Roger Brownsword, 'More in Expectation than Hope: The Blackpool Airport Case' (1991) 54 *Modern Law Review* 281.

away from the formalism of the classical law towards an alternative expectations-based contract model.[99]

In the age of welfarism and reasonable expectation it was easy to dismiss classical contract law as a 'twitching corpse'.[100] It also presented a pleasingly tidy narrative, exploited by Atiyah in the title of the final chapter of *The Rise and Fall of Freedom of Contract*, commencing with the development of the classical law during the nineteenth century and its seeming demise during the course of the twentieth. Despite the intellectual momentum gathering behind the effort to construct a new conception of contract, whether based on welfarism, relationalism or 'reasonable expectations', with the possible exception of the principles of contract interpretation, there was no systematic or serious attempt by the judiciary to reformulate contract law's fundamental foundations along more realist lines or with co-operation as its underpinning ethic. This was notwithstanding the case law developments that seemed to reflect exactly these values. In many respects, the welfarist era represents a missed opportunity for contract law. The ease with which the recent common law appears to have shed the garb of neo-classical law vindicates the view that ultimately the welfarist philosophy did not represent a wholesale rejection of classical precepts but a compromise position, an add-on to the classical law, which has left little residual trace and few lasting effects. Similarly, while a vast literature sprang up exploring the 'Europeanisation' and harmonisation of contract law,[101] and the more ambitious possibility of unifying the different private law systems of Europe under a single civil code,[102] the 'Europeanisation' project was criticised in some quarters as failing to appreciate the distinctive characteristics of English contract law[103] or the impossibility

99 *Investors Compensation Scheme* v. *West Bromwich Building Society* [1998] 1 WLR 896; Lord Hoffmann's restatement channelled the earlier dicta of Lord Wilberforce in *Prenn* v. *Simmonds* [1971] 1 WLR 1381, 1383–84; *Reardon Smith Line Ltd* v. *Yngvar Hansen-Tangen* [1976] 1 WLR 989, 995. Lord Wilberforce traced authority for a more liberal approach to 1877 and the judgment of Lord Blackburn in *River Wear Commissioners* v. *Adamson* (1877) 2 App Cas 743.

100 Simpson, 'Contract: The Twitching Corpse'.

101 For an overview see Christian Twigg-Flesner, *The Europeanisation of Contract Law*, 2nd ed. (Routledge, 2013). Important developments here were Ole Lando and Hugh Beale (eds.) *The Principles of European Contract Law, Parts I and II* (Kluwer, 2000); Study Group on a European Civil Code/Research Group on the Existing EC Private Law (Acquis Group) (eds.) *Principles, Definitions and Model Rules on European Private Law – Draft Common Frame of Reference* (Sellier, 2009).

102 Arthur S. Hartkamp, Martijn W. Hesselink, Ewoud Hondius, C. Mak and Edgar Du Perron (eds.) *Towards a European Civil Code*, 4th ed. (Wolters Kluwer, 2010).

103 Pierre Legrand, 'Against a European Civil Code' (1997) 60 *Modern Law Review* 44.

of seamless integration of different legal systems.[104] Welfarism as associated with paternalism drew criticism for allowing the essential virtues of freedom of contract and choice to be sacrificed in the pursuit of fairness via market interventions and the recognition of the social dimension of contracting. In short, welfarist contract law was condemned as anti-contract.[105]

In light of the rise of the consumer and the programme of state intervention across society, there were perhaps two alternative paths the common law of contract could have taken. The first was to undergo what Collins referred to as 'productive disintegration', that is, assimilate the innovations triggered by consumer contracting, and other welfarist developments, into the common law more fully, dismantling the classical law in the process.[106] The new common law may have sought to build coherence around principles of contractual justice rather than freedom of contract. Such a law may have incorporated the reality of inequality of bargaining power, recognition and control of contract abuses and the protection of reasonable expectations as its central concerns. The second was to jettison the new developments as out of sync with contract law and re-focus the common law as a tool to facilitate commerce. The growth of market-specific regulation set contract law on the second path. Ultimately, the welfarist concern with the protection of vulnerable participants in the market is manifest in regulation, not in the contract reasoning of generalist courts.[107] The closed nature of the legal system was reasserted, rendering it unreceptive in response to the wider social concerns that were generated by the prevalence of contracting in modern society.[108] The rise of regulation was predicted in some respects by Atiyah, although he understandably failed to forecast its extent. Atiyah associated the waning of contract in the twentieth century with increasing government interference in markets, culminating in the creation of the welfare state, a programme of nationalisation of industry and the consequent growth of bureaucratic institutions charged with allocating resources and administering this expanded

[104] Gunther Teubner, 'Legal Irritants: Good Faith in British Law or How Unifying Law Ends up in New Divergences' (1998) 61 *Modern Law Review* 11.

[105] David Campbell, 'Relational Contract and the Nature of Private Ordering: A Comment on Vincent-Jones' (2007) 14 *Indiana Journal of Global Legal Studies* 279, 281–82. See also David Campbell, 'Reflexivity and Welfarism in the Modern Law of Contract' (2000) 20 *Oxford Journal of Legal Studies* 477.

[106] Collins, *Regulating Contracts*, p. 53.

[107] See, for example, Financial Conduct Authority, *Guidance for Firms on the Fair Treatment of Vulnerable Customers* (FG21/1, February 2021).

[108] Collins, *Regulating Contracts*, p. 32.

machinery of the state.[109] He identified the social changes – democratisation, the rise of monopolies and lack of competition, and the growth of trade unions[110] – that contributed to the decline of contract in favour of administrative hierarchies and centralised governance processes. He noted that commitment to freedom of contract still remained relatively strong in the courts in this period,[111] although it seemed to him that administrative law was assuming greater responsibility for areas traditionally regarded as the preserve of contract.[112]

Atiyah's prediction about the future importance of administrative law was prescient.[113] Public law concepts such as 'Wednesbury-reasonableness' have found their way into reasoning about the constraints on the exercise of contractual discretionary powers,[114] and proportionality and legitimate/reasonable expectations have found a foothold in contract law. However, what Atiyah failed to appreciate was the effect of the huge growth in private dispute resolution, a general legal acquiescence in the face of parties self-legislating over contract governance via express contract terms in the commercial sphere (private ordering) and the importance of regulation in the consumer sphere. The role of contract law as a public provider of applicable rules to govern the contract diminished accordingly, reducing the field for the operation of general contract law and falsifying Atiyah's forecast that some residual judicial power was still necessary 'to deal with unconscionable contracts in cases not caught by [Unfair Contract Terms Act 1977] or the EC [unfair terms] Directive or any other statutory provisions'.[115]

Notwithstanding the increased significance of contracting in all our lives, the expectation that the common law would develop rules to address problems arising in consumer contracts, or other instances of bargaining inequality, has not been realised. The expansion in contracting has instead spawned a variety of regulatory agencies governing market activity that have effectively assumed responsibility for enforcing contracts and providing systems of redress. Legislation and regulation by the state address instances of market failure that

109 Atiyah, *Rise and Fall*, pp. 717–18.

110 Atiyah, *Rise and Fall*, pp. 596ff. 716ff. See also Campbell, 'Relational Contract and the Nature of Private Ordering: A Comment on Vincent-Jones', 282ff.

111 Atiyah, *Rise and Fall*, p. 599.

112 Atiyah, *Rise and Fall*, p. 718ff.

113 Atiyah, *Rise and Fall*, p. 726. See also Jack Beatson, 'Public Law Influences in Contract Law' in Jack Beatson and Daniel Friedmann (eds.) *Good Faith and Fault in Contract Law* (Oxford University Press, 1995).

114 *Braganza* v. *BP Shipping Ltd* [2015] 1 WLR 1661.

115 Atiyah, *Introduction to the Law of Contract*, p. 302.

often become apparent through the use and abuse of contracts.[116] We return to the relationship between contract law and regulation in Chapter 4. In the next section of this chapter, we explore how the growth of regulation provided the fuel for a judicial revival and reassertion of formal classical law values within traditional contract law.

2.5 The Common Law of Contract in the Twenty-First Century: The Regeneration of a Research Programme

Despite the apparent weakening commitment to the classical law in the welfarist era, contract law has not died and we have not witnessed the 'degeneration of [the classical law] research programme'.[117] Brownsword's observation in 2006 that 'the suggestion that freedom of contract is in decline invites further analysis and needs to be approached with some caution' was pertinent.[118] The common law of contract appears to have returned to what is perceived by many, particularly from within the law and economics branch of contract scholarship, to be its core mission of facilitating commercial dealing, with a renewed commitment to freedom of contract and autonomy. The formalist shift in contract legal reasoning can be interpreted as the natural, perhaps even inevitable, result of the liberation of the common law from responsibility for policing business-to-consumer transactions. The rise of neo-formalism was also rooted in the critique of standards-based contract legal reasoning and the incorporation of business practices into law.[119]

116 Whittaker notes that in the United Kingdom the regulation of contracts between firms is regarded broadly as a matter of competition law, rather than contract law, contrasting this with French law under the French Civil Code (2016), which created a judicial power to review contract terms between firms for unfairness under Arts 1110 and 1171: Simon Whittaker, 'Unfair Terms in Commercial Contracts and the Two Laws of Competition: French Law and English Law Contrasted' in (2019) 39 *Oxford Journal of Legal Studies* 404.

117 Campbell, 'The Undeath of Contract: A Study in the Degeneration of a Research Programme', 20.

118 Brownsword, *Contract Law: Themes for the Twenty-First Century*, p. 65; Roger Brownsword, 'The Law of Contract: Doctrinal Impulses, External Pressures, Future Directions' (2014) 31 *Journal of Contract Law* 73, 75.

119 Robert E. Scott, 'The Case for Formalism in Relational Contract' (2000) 94 *Northwestern University Law Review* 847; David A. Charny, 'The New Formalism in Contract' (1999) 66 *University of Chicago Law Review* 842; Omri Ben-Shahar, 'The Tentative Case against Flexibility in Commercial Law' (1999) 66 *University of Chicago Law Review* 781; Richard A. Epstein, 'Confusion about Custom: Disentangling Informal Customs from Standard Contractual Provisions' (1999) 66 *University of Chicago Law Review* 821; William J. Woodward, 'Neoformalism in a Real World of Forms' (2001) *Wisconsin Law Review* 971;

While superficially attractive, it is too simple to suggest that this resurgent formalism in the common law is the reassertion of a historical status quo that was temporarily suspended in order to deal with problems generated by the advent of contracting on standard terms in the consumer society. Dagan et al. observe that '[a]ppreciating the significance of law as the infrastructure of markets reveals that no particular market structure is inevitable. Instead, every market order is the result of a complex set of legal and political choices.'[120] Contract law not only reflects the 'underlying economic structures of society' but also, inevitably, the political ideologies that support those economic structures.[121]

In his 1988 essay, *Freedom of Contract and the New Right*, Atiyah rejected the idea that the political changes that fomented the revival of freedom of contract in the final decades of the twentieth century echoed the conditions that led to freedom of contract's rise in the 1800s. The assertion of freedom of contract during the latter period was connected to a left-wing commitment to democracy, the right of individual self-determination and rejection of the paternalism associated with the political system of the time.[122] The rise of neo-formalism in the twentieth century, on the other hand, was rooted in societal changes following the privatising and marketisation agenda pursued by governments in the United Kingdom since the late 1970s. Atiyah attributed marketisation to the decline of trust in inefficient public bureaucracies and a renewed faith in the capacity of the market to deliver savings and choice. This faith in markets was apparent even amongst governments occupying the left-of-centre political ground. Contract served as both the enabling tool and symbolic representation of the reliance on market mechanisms. The direct provision of public goods by the state was divested and replaced by agencies

John E. Murray, 'Contract Theories and the Rise of Neoformalism' (2002) 71 *Fordham Law Review* 869; William C. Whitford, 'Relational Contracts and the New Formalism' (2004) *Wisconsin Law Review* 631. In the UK, see Jonathan Morgan, *Contract Law Minimalism: A Formalist Restatement of Commercial Contract Law* (Cambridge University Press, 2013). For a slightly different formalist perspective, stressing the institutional and constitutional constraints on the common law, see John Gava, 'False Lessons from the Real Deal: Campbell, Collins and Wightman on Implicit Dimensions of Contract – Discrete, Relational, and Network Contracts?' (2005) 21 *Journal of Contract Law* 182.

[120] Hanoch Dagan, Avihay Dorfman, Roy Kreitner and Daniel Markovits, 'The Law of the Market' (2020) 83 *Law and Contemporary Problems* i, i.

[121] Nolan, 'The Classical Legacy and Modern English Contract Law', 619.

[122] Patrick S. Atiyah, 'Freedom of Contract and the New Right' in *Essays on Contract* (Oxford University Press, 1990), pp. 355, 357.

and other providers through outsourcing of services, giving rise to the 'contracting state'.[123] The reassertion of market-oriented values of individual autonomy and self-reliance also attached to the consumer, who by this time was deemed sufficiently educated (or at least literate) to be able to take care of themselves and exhibit less dependence on the state.[124] Other diverse factors, such as the burgeoning rights movement, also contributed to the ideological elevation of the freedom of contract principle.[125] Atiyah concluded that while freedom of contract generated negative externalities, 'contracts should still be left to the market'.[126]

In terms of legal scholarship, the decline of trust in public institutions identified by Atiyah also incorporated a mistrust of the judiciary. Modes of legal reasoning that drew little adverse comment in an earlier period were subject to censure by the latter part of the twentieth century. The once-accepted inevitability of judicial discretion alluded to by H. L. A. Hart in *The Concept of Law*[127] was challenged by theories castigating judges for using policy arguments in legal reasoning.[128] Contract's classical revival gained support from various critiques of relational contract theory emanating from within economic analysis of law. The latter theoretical strand has focused attention on contract law as default rules in the service of an underlying market ideology. This line of scholarship (styled 'neo-formalism' or 'anti-anti-formalism' in the literature) maintains that the findings of empirical studies and relational theory vindicate the formalism of the classical law. Contextual, relational or standards-based legal regimes are criticised for their increased cost, uncertainty and unpredictability. In American legal scholarship the contextual shift in legal reasoning, especially the call for contract law to incorporate the norms of the business relationship (such as co-operation, good faith, industry-generated

[123] Ian Harden, *The Contracting State* (Open University Press, 1992); Mark R. Freeland, 'Government by Contract and Public Law' (1994) *Public Law* 86; Jody Freeman, 'The Contracting State' (2000) 28 *Florida State University Law Review* 155; Peter Vincent-Jones, *The New Public Contracting* (Oxford University Press, 2006).

[124] This attitude could be traced back much earlier, thus the Crowther Report *Consumer Credit* Cmnd 4596 (HMSO, 1971), which led to the Consumer Credit Act 1974, was of the view that 'people themselves must be the judge of what contributes to their material welfare', para 3.9.1; Atiyah, 'Freedom of Contract and the New Right', p. 358.

[125] Atiyah, 'Freedom of Contract and the New Right', p. 356.

[126] Atiyah, 'Freedom of Contract and the New Right', p. 360.

[127] H. L. A. Hart, *The Concept of Law*, 1st ed. (Oxford University Press, 1961).

[128] Ronald Dworkin, *Law's Empire* (Fontana, 1986); Duncan Kennedy, 'A Transnational Genealogy of Proportionality in Private Law' in Roger Brownsword, Hans-W. Micklitz, Leone Niglia and Stephen Weatherill (eds.) *The Foundations of European Private Law* (Hart Publishing, 2011), pp. 185, 216–17.

understandings and expectations), has been criticised as precipitating not the death of contract but the 'death of contract law', that is, the flight of contracting parties from the operation of national contract law[129] in favour of private and formal dispute resolution processes, over which parties exercise greater control and that offer reduced risk of unpredictable outcomes.[130]

It is not suggested here that these wider trends have exerted direct influence on legal reasoning methods in contract. Rather, the present judicial tendency towards formalism in contract decision-making is consistent with these developments. There is an important difference in the new formalism, however. We are not seeing a movement from contextual standards, or reasonable expectations-based justifications, back to bright-line rules in contract law but from standards to contract terms. Whereas the classical law found expression in formal contract rules and doctrines, current contract law places contract texts and express terms at the centre of its analysis. In the commercial sphere this has been matched by the expansion of private ordering to facilitate contract governance. The result of these diverse forces is that general common law rules of contract occupy ever more niche territory. The formalist and introspective shift in contract law is also in keeping with the direction of travel of private law and obligations scholarship more generally. In the United Kingdom, the intellectual trend is towards internally focused accounts of the values of private law. Tort theory, for example, has undergone a similar turn towards 'traditional' rights-based, corrective justice or interpretivist theories that eschew any instrumental or public-facing justification for private law.[131] Implicit in these accounts is the idea that 'common law safeguards important values of personal responsibility and limited government which legislation necessarily … disregards'.[132] Classical contract law may court substantive

129 Robert E. Scott, 'The Death of Contract Law' (2004) 54 *University of Toronto Law Journal* 369–70.

130 Lisa Bernstein, 'Merchant Law in a Merchant Court: Rethinking the Code's Search for Immanent Business Norms' (1996) 144 *University of Pennsylvania Law Review* 1765; 'The Questionable Empirical Basis of Article 2's Incorporation Strategy: A Preliminary Study' (1999) 66 *University of Chicago Law Review* 710; 'Private Commercial Law in the Cotton Industry: Creating Co-operation through Rules, Norms and Institutions' (2001) 99 *Michigan Law Review* 1724.

131 Steve Hedley, 'Looking Outward or Looking Inward? Obligations Scholarship in the Early 21st Century' in Andrew Robertson and Tang Hang Wu (eds.) *The Goals of Private Law* (Hart Publishing, 2009), pp. 193, 196–97.

132 Hedley, 'Looking Outward or Looking Inward?', pp. 202. This trend is perhaps more apparent in tort scholarship than in contract – see, for example, Ernest Weinrib, *The Idea of Private Law* (Harvard University Press, 1995); Allan Beever, *Rediscovering the Law of Negligence* (Hart Publishing, 2007); Robert Stevens, *Torts and Rights* (Oxford University Press, 2007) – and in

redundancy, but it can demonstrate a degree of doctrinal coherence without fear of contamination by legislation, regulation or the need to resolve systematically the contract problems that occur outside the commercial sphere.[133] The risk of contract law stagnation in light of these trends is also likely to be exacerbated by the withdrawal of the United Kingdom from the European Union. The question of whether English contract law should develop a good faith doctrine, which appeared central to the legal harmonisation project of the European Union, has receded. Similarly, the general European influence over English contract law – both in letter and spirit – has diminished in the light of Brexit. Neither have changes in contracting practice brought about changes in law. Contract law has not adapted to new frameworks for organising productive activity, such as collaborative networks. Nor has contract law responded systematically to the increased automation of contracting, despite the patent potential of artificial intelligence to assume control over aspects of contract creation, performance and enforcement.[134]

In claiming that contract law has returned to a more classical style of legal reasoning, we may be regarded as going against the grain. Some private law and contract scholars have argued that contract law has travelled in the reverse direction. Varuhas claims that private law is moving away from protecting the interests of right holders to upholding policy goals. Although Varuhas's observation is more pertinent in the law of tort, it is also manifest in contract by 'greater judicial willingness to make deep inroads into party autonomy, and to superimpose on parties' agreed rights substantive obligations based in public interest concerns and social expectations'.[135] This claim about contract is mostly substantiated by attention to problematic remedies cases where the courts have not provided the claimant with the cost of curing a breach of contract on the grounds that facilitating the cure is economically wasteful of societal resources or where courts have refused specific performance because it would compel a business to trade at a loss.[136] On this basis, the courts'

unjust enrichment, Peter Birks, *An Introduction to the Law of Restitution*, revised ed. (Oxford University Press, 1989).

133 Cf. Hedley, 'Looking Outward or Looking Inward?', 202.

134 Brownsword, 'The Law of Contract: Doctrinal Impulses, External Pressures, Future Directions', 81ff.

135 Jason N. E. Varuhas, 'The Socialisation of Private Law: Balancing Private Right and Public Good' (2021) 137 *Law Quarterly Review* 141, 141–42. See also Magda Raczynska and Paul S. Davies, 'Freedom of Contract and Terms Affecting Freedoms' in Paul S. Davies and Magda Raczynska (eds.) *Contents of Commercial Contracts: Terms Affecting Freedoms* (Hart Publishing, 2020), pp. 1, 4–5.

136 *Co-operative Insurance Society Ltd* v. *Argyll Stores (Holdings) Ltd* [1998] AC 1.

engagement with policy concerns is connected with economic efficiency and community goals of increasing social welfare. The increased willingness of courts to imply terms and control contract discretions according to criteria derived from administrative law are also regarded as a manifestation of this trend towards societal welfare in contract.[137] However, the cases relied upon (from employment law and consumer law) are exactly where one might argue social values should have a role. There are few references in Varuhas's work to arm's length commercial deals, in relation to which much traditional contract law has been forcefully reasserted.

2.6 Conclusion

The foregoing analysis has tried to show that the classical model of contract is not a natural or essential feature of contract law driven by coherent theory or intellectual imperatives but has been moulded by certain pragmatic influences that have exerted themselves in different ways at different times. Contract law has never wholly embraced a single model without qualification, whether committed to a more formal or more contextual law. The need to develop common law solutions to the problems generated by consumer contracting necessitated some relaxation of the strict classical law rules. This move was not easily confined just to consumer contracts, and there was plenty of scope for cross-fertilisation. Under the Unfair Contract Terms Act 1977, courts were required to assess the reasonableness of contract terms and consider the reasonable expectations of the parties not expressed in the contract's paper text. It was perhaps inevitable that these values would impinge on judicial reasoning in some commercial contract disputes. The consumer protection imperative that drove neo-classical law was reflected in commercial contract law by the softening of classical law in favour of the protection of reliance through doctrines such as promissory estoppel and the willingness to ease contract doctrine, notably consideration, to meet business realities. An expansive contract interpretation method was transparently advanced by a progressive judiciary. When coupled with empirical evidence of the lack of importance of contracts and law to business practice, the classical law model appeared to be under considerable pressure from realist and contextualist rivals that stressed the life of a contract outside its formal express terms.

137 Varuhas, citing *Braganza* v. *BP Shipping Ltd* (above n. 114); *Societe Generale, London Branch* v. *Geys* [2013] 1 AC 523.

The reasonable expectation principle, pursued through a broadly contextualist reasoning method, was identified as a key theme of contract law well into the second decade of the twenty-first century.[138] However, despite the apparent weakening hold of the classical law, the factors that pushed contract law in a welfarist and paternalist direction in the latter half of the twentieth century exerted much less of an influence by the turn of the twenty-first. The earlier confidence that the classical model would give way to an alternative account of contract – whether relational or welfarist-based – and that this was *necessary* for contract law coherence has all but disappeared. The contract law that has emerged from these overlapping shifts in the political landscape, in contract legal reasoning and in scholarly movements, has a decidedly neoliberal character. It is hallmarked by a decline in the exposition and development of common law doctrine and general principles (remedies for breach is perhaps the most notable exception), in favour of increased focus on express contract terms and the rules of contract law surrounding these terms (interpreting express terms, implied terms, limitations on terms). Contract law's increasing focus on commercial contractors has seen Lord Atkin's anti-equity mindset in sales law extend beyond statutory law to incorporate the common law of contract: express contract terms have become a form of commercial code, and the values of certainty and predictability have eclipsed those of justice or fairness traditionally associated with equity.[139] The regulatory capacity of contract law has declined as a result. We explore this further in the next chapter.

[138] See Brownsword, 'The Law of Contract: Doctrinal Impulses, External Pressures, Future Directions', 74.

[139] Waddams, *Sanctity of Contracts in a Secular Age*, pp. 9 and 158.

3

Contractualisation and the Common Law Retreat

Having explored a little of contract's history in the previous chapter, this chapter subjects the revival of formal and classical law values in contract law to critical examination. The emergence of a commercially oriented contract law is evident across a number of contract developments over recent years: the reassertion of party autonomy and the emphasis on contract law as default rules; the return to a more formalist style of contract interpretation; the marginalisation of equity and considerations of public policy in contract; the tendency of judges to uphold contract terms whose validity was previously regarded as questionable ('no oral modification' and 'no reliance' clauses); and the dilution of common law controls on contract terms (in relation to penalties, for example). While formalism may be entirely appropriate in many commercial contract contexts, it threatens the distinctive contribution common law makes to the regulation of contracts – its generality and its expressive role in communicating the normative values that contract supports. Law also loses its capacity to create new mandatory rules, or adapt old ones, in response to novel contract problems. In these respects, contract law is diminished.

Contract law's self-exclusion from any broader regulatory role over contracts, and its re-embrace of freedom of contract, is particularly unfortunate at a time when the role of contract in society has expanded following the privatisation and marketisation efforts of successive governments over the last forty years. The common law rules have generally not engaged with, nor reflected, the consequences of this enlargement of the contract realm. Much modern contracting activity escapes serious legal scrutiny, controlled instead via an array of privately administered processes and distinct regulation. As a result, common law principle has little to contribute towards modern contract regulation or the attempt to control dubious contract practices. These include the imposition of contractual obligations by stealth, the weakening of consent and the use of contracts for questionable purposes, such as the suppression of information that ought to be disclosed in the public interest. Current contract law tends to place the interpretation of express terms and party autonomy at the centre of the analysis, with little consideration of how changes in modern contracting practice undermine many of the assumptions upon which classical contract law rests or how a case engages wider public policy or social concerns. The first part of the chapter examines recent contract law developments that suggest the re-emergence of formalism in law. The second part explores the common law's retreat from a role as general regulator of contracting activity in the context of an increasingly contractualised society.

3.1 The Emergence of Liberal Contract Law

The revival of freedom of contract was already apparent in contract law during its welfarist period. English judges took the opportunity presented by protective legislation to reverse some of the more paternalistic developments of mid-twentieth century common law. The now defunct doctrine of fundamental breach is one illustration. Although bedevilled by doctrinal anomalies,[1] fundamental breach was perhaps the furthest the common law advanced to mounting a substantive attack on exempting terms. The 'rule of law' of fundamental breach maintained that there were some contractual obligations that were so central to performance that liability for breach of them could not be excluded. The claimant's right to damages for the breach would be left intact, irrespective of what the contract terms might otherwise dictate.[2] This principle was elevated by the Court of Appeal under Lord Denning to a matter of the inner morality of contract law.[3] The House of Lords, however, denied the existence of any such rule of law.[4] It was all a matter of contract construction.[5] In *Photo Production* v. *Securicor* it was noted that the fundamental breach doctrine had served a useful purpose that was no longer necessary with the enactment of the Unfair Contract Terms Act (UCTA) 1977 and the

[1] David Yates, *Exclusion Clauses in Contracts*, 2nd ed. (Sweet & Maxwell, 1982), Chapter 6; Brian Coote, 'The Second Rise and Fall of Fundamental Breach' (1981) 55 *Australian Law Journal* 788.

[2] Yates, *Exclusion Clauses in Contracts*, pp. 216–17.

[3] *Karsales (Harrow) Ltd* v. *Wallis* [1956] 1 WLR 936, per Lord Denning at 940; also *Charterhouse Credit Co Ltd* v. *Tolly* [1963] 2 WLR 1168; Yates, *Exclusion Clauses in Contracts*, p. 226; Stephen Waddams, *Sanctity of Contracts in a Secular Age* (Cambridge University Press, 2019), pp. 62–69.

[4] *Suisse Atlantique Société d'Armement Maritime SA* v. *NV Rotterdamsche Kolen Centrale* [1967] 1 AC 361; *Photo Production Ltd* v. *Securicor Transport Ltd* [1980] AC 827.

[5] *Suisse Atlantique*, per Viscount Dilhorne, 392.

availability of insurance.[6] Related common law innovations around inequality of bargaining power were similarly criticised.[7] A line of cases considering the application of the 'reasonable' test under the statute culminated with the freedom of contract–supporting decision of the Court of Appeal in *Watford Electronics Ltd* v. *Sanderson CFL Ltd*.[8] The reasonableness of a limitation of liability clause in contract between a family business and a software supplier was upheld. The decision sent a strong message of anti-paternalism in business dealings, which has reverberated down to this day: exclusion of almost any kind of liability is possible (with the exception of fraud) provided it is clearly expressed in the contract terms.[9] Other innovative principles challenging classical law orthodoxy have been regarded as emanating from rogue judicial decisions and have been abandoned.[10] The traditional tests for whether a liquidated damages clause is an invalid penalty have been relaxed.[11] There has been the broad rehabilitation of plain meaning interpretation methods[12] as well as the reassertion of traditional tests for implied terms.[13] We explore some of these developments here.

3.1.1 Contract Interpretation

The view that there has been a classical revival in the common law of contract is not universally shared. Some commentators have argued that recent contract law manifests a tendency towards judicial intervention at odds with the principle of freedom of contract. Raczynska and Davies, for example, argue that 'freedom of contract is becoming more limited'.[14] They point to four

6 *Photo Production*, per Lord Wilberforce, 843; Lord Diplock, 848.

7 *National Westminster Bank plc* v. *Morgan* [1985] AC 686, per Lord Scarman, 708.

8 [2001] EWCA Civ 317.

9 *Triple Point Technology Inc* v. *PTT Public Company Ltd* [2021] UKSC 29 [107]–[108]; *Mott MacDonald Ltd* v. *Trant Engineering Ltd* [2021] EWHC 754 [64]. See also *Goodlife Foods Ltd* v. *Hall Fire Protection Ltd* [2018] EWCA Civ 1371; *Persimmon Homes Ltd* v. *Ove Arup & Partners Ltd* [2017] EWCA Civ 373; *Transocean Drilling UK Ltd* v. *Providence Resources plc* [2016] 2 Lloyd's Rep 51, [2016] EWCA Civ 372.

10 Mistake in equity is an example: *Great Peace Shipping Ltd* v. *Tsavliris Salvage (International) Ltd* [2003] QB 679 (CA) [155]–[157].

11 *Cavendish Square Holding BV* v. *Makdessi; ParkingEye Ltd* v. *Beavis* [2016] AC 1172.

12 *Arnold* v. *Britton* [2015] AC 1619. See further Catherine Mitchell, *Interpretation of Contracts*, 2nd ed. (Routledge, 2018), pp. 62–71.

13 *Marks and Spencer plc* v. *BNP Paribas Securities Services Trust Co Ltd* [2016] AC 742.

14 Magda Raczynska and Paul S. Davies, 'Freedom of Contract and Terms Affecting Freedoms' in Paul S. Davies and Magda Raczynska (eds.) *Contents of Commercial Contracts: Terms Affecting Freedoms* (Hart Publishing, 2020), pp. 1, 4.

broad trends as evidence of this: (1) contextual contract interpretation methods; (2) the case law surrounding relational contracts and the implied term of good faith; (3) judicial control of contractual discretions and (4) the developing concept and use of smart contracts.[15] From another point of view, these are not examples of interference with freedom of contract but instances where courts are performing the essential task of contract regulation. We leave consideration of smart contracts and relational contracting to Chapter 6 and Chapter 7 respectively. In relation to the constraints on discretionary powers, it is clear that these are justified to control attempts by the stronger party to render their contractual promises functionally empty or to substantially undermine contract expectations. Contract involves an exchange. If the element of exchange is made illusory through the operation of express terms, then there is no contract. Freedom of contract is not absolute and, like the concept of a 'free market', is a construct whose existence depends on the operation of legal rules.[16] It is precisely the role of the law – and the judge as a custodian – to set limits on the exercise of party autonomy and regulate contract behaviour, not act as freedom of contract's uncritical defender.

Similarly, contract interpretation continues to generate controversy about judicial intervention in contracts, but the debate around contextual methods also demonstrates how contract interpretation (what the words of the contract text mean) has become a much more important source of contract disputes and judicial decision-making than almost any other part of contract law. This much has been admitted by senior members of the judiciary.[17] A rudimentary examination of judgments in the Court of Appeal indicates that references to *Investors Compensation Scheme* outnumber those considering *Williams* v. *Roffey*, *Hadley* v. *Baxendale* and *The Achilleas* combined.[18] Even decisions from the Supreme Court that appear to engage with mandatory rules of

[15] Raczynska and Davies, 'Freedom of Contract and Terms Affecting Freedoms', pp. 4–5.

[16] Hanoch Dagan, Avihay Dorfman, Roy Kreitner and Daniel Markovits, 'The Law of the Market' (2020) 83 *Law and Contemporary Problems* i, ii; Hugh Collins, *The Law of Contract*, 4th ed. (Butterworths, 2003), p. 107.

[17] Lord Hodge, 'Judicial Development of the Law of Contract in the United Kingdom' (2017) 85 *George Washington Law Review* 1587, 1588.

[18] Lexis search conducted on 28 August 2019 of Court of Appeal Civil Division decisions for all available dates. Cases referring to *Williams* v. *Roffey Bros & Nicholls (Contractors) Ltd* [1991] 1 QB 1 (on consideration) returned 17 results; *Hadley* v. *Baxendale* (1854) 9 ExCh 341 (on remoteness of damage) returned 149 results; *Transfield Shipping Inc* v. *Mercator Shipping Inc (The Achilleas)* [2009] 1 AC 61, returned 21 results; *Investors Compensation Scheme* v. *West Bromwich Building Society* [1998] 1 WLR 896 (on the contextual method of contract interpretation) returned 402 results.

contract law, such as *Braganza* v. *BP Shipping Ltd*[19] (controls on discretionary powers in contract) or *Cavendish* v. *Makdessi*[20] (penalty clause jurisdiction) also turn on matters of contract interpretation. The decline of contract doctrinal development in favour of determining the meaning of the terms used by the parties is one of the hallmarks of liberal contract law. The methods used to interpret contracts have undergone a subtle transformation. Lord Hoffmann's more extensive form of contextual interpretation, which could proceed by reference to any admissible and relevant background, has been condensed into a text-based formulation that focuses on contract language.[21] The parol evidence rule and the canons of construction, long thought buried under the influence of contextualist modes of reasoning, have been partially disinterred.[22] In *Shogun Finance Ltd* v. *Hudson*, a case concerning mistaken identity, the issue of who owned a car appropriated through hire purchase fraud and then sold to an innocent third-party purchaser was resolved by Lord Hobhouse with reference to the legal documents (an invalid hire purchase agreement taken out by the fraudster using stolen identification) and the operation of the parol evidence rule.[23]

One result of the ascendancy of contract texts in contract law is a degree of judicial disengagement from doctrinal development in favour of interpreting express terms. There are exceptions to this, of course. The illegality doctrine and remedies for breach have been the site of some important innovations.[24] Nevertheless, judges seem less inclined to resort to doctrinal analysis in decision-making. In *Rock Advertising Ltd* v. *MWB Business Exchange Centres Ltd*,[25] the Supreme Court was content to dispose of a dispute concerning an alleged contract variation on the basis of an express 'no oral modification' clause in the contract. The court chose not to provide any detailed assessment of the contract law doctrines of consideration and the part-payment rule that also impinged on the case, arguments over which have occupied academics for approaching three decades. This unwillingness to reconsider doctrine is unfortunate considering how few contract cases reach the Supreme Court.[26] The primacy of contract interpretation in contract legal

19 [2015] 1 WLR 1661.

20 *Cavendish Square Holding BV* v. *Makdessi*; *ParkingEye Ltd* v. *Beavis* above n. 11.

21 *Arnold* v. *Britton* [2015] AC 1619; *Wood* v. *Capita Insurance Services Ltd* [2017] AC 1173.

22 *Cusack* v. *Harrow LBC* [2013] 1 WLR 2022 [57].

23 [2004] 1 AC 919.

24 *Patel* v. *Mirza* [2017] AC 467; *Morris-Garner* v. *One Step (Support) Ltd* [2019] AC 649.

25 [2019] AC 119.

26 Linda Mulcahy and Wendy Teeder, 'Are Litigants, Trials and Precedents Vanishing After All?' *Modern Law Review* (forthcoming) https://ssrn.com/abstract=3880274 at 43, 46.

reasoning disengages courts from the development of common law principle in favour of resolving the individualised problems emanating from specific contract texts.

3.1.2 Contracts and Public Policy

Together with the rules on vitiating factors, public policy remains one area for the mandatory operation of contract law rules. A public policy argument is one that draws on the consequences of the decision for general society welfare, or the public interest, as part of its justification. The application of public policy concerns in contract law is very narrow. Courts wield the power to declare contracts void as against public policy only in cases where the operation of policy is already well established (contracts in restraint of trade, contracts tainted by illegality, contracts undermining the operation of the legal system or contracts involving moral impropriety[27]). It is doubtful that courts can create new heads of public policy.[28] The judicial reluctance to engage with policy considerations in contract is not new but has become more pronounced. Swain notes that the doctrine of public policy was unpopular from its inception in the nineteenth century because of judicial fears of encroaching on legislative territory.[29] Chitty observes that the doctrine is criticised for its flexibility and 'open texture' and its conflict with the competing policy of upholding freedom of contract.[30] Broader engagement with policy factors can be found in the common law, but the operation of policy in contract remains controversial. The decision in *Patel* v. *Mirza* concerning the operation of the illegality defence illustrates this particular tension. The Supreme Court was split in their reasoning between a rule-based approach to the operation of illegality and a more flexible, fact-dependent and openly policy-centred assessment of when the illegality was sufficiently damaging to the legal system that the resulting claim should be barred.[31] In justifying a multi-factor method of assessment, Lord Toulson observed that 'respect for the integrity of the justice system is not enhanced if it appears to produce arbitrary, unjust or

[27] Hugh Beale (ed.), *Chitty on Contracts*, 33rd ed. (Sweet & Maxwell, 2020), 16-008.

[28] Beale, *Chitty on Contracts*, 16-007; *Johnstone* v. *Bloomsbury Health Authority* [1992] 1 QB 333, 346.

[29] Warren Swain, *The Law of Contract 1670–1870* (Cambridge University Press, 2015), pp. 245–46. See, for example, *Multiservice Bookbinding* v. *Marden* [1979] 1 Ch 84 at 104.

[30] Beale, *Chitty on Contracts*, 16-005. On freedom of contract as a matter of public policy, see Sir George Jessel MR in *Printing and Numerical Registering Co* v. *Sampson* (1875) 19 Eq 462, 465.

[31] *Patel* v. *Mirza* [2017] AC 467.

disproportionate results'.[32] The attempt amongst a minority of their Lordships to force the disparate policy threads raised by illegality claims into a rule-framework is indicative of the distaste in some judicial quarters for the operation of policy-based, or what is perceived as discretionary, reasoning.[33]

Recent case law indicates avoidance of policy arguments by courts in favour of individualistic modes of reasoning that consider the legitimate interests of contracting parties in seeking enforcement of the terms of the agreement. The decision in *Cavendish* v. *Makdessi* liberalises the rules on penalties by abandoning the requirement that the payment be a genuine pre-estimate of loss in favour of an assessment of whether the claimant has a legitimate interest in encouraging performance rather than breach. This departs from the previous common law tests that sought to ensure the amounts claimed were consistent with the (policy) objective of damages, which is to compensate and not punish.[34] Though subject to overarching controls based on unconscionability,[35] the contract-stipulated payments can now exceed anticipated losses from breach if the party claiming the payment can demonstrate a legitimate interest in encouraging performance of the primary obligations in the contract. This naturally involves an individualistic assessment of the purposes of the provision and a party's particular motive in stipulating for the payment. Before the penalty rules are engaged there is an earlier interpretative hurdle to surmount concerning whether the payment clause creates a primary or secondary obligation. Even if interpreted as a secondary obligation triggered by a breach of contract, a legitimate interest in encouraging performance rather than breach is relatively easy to demonstrate, and the bar for establishing unconscionability in the amount (morally reprehensible[36]) is high. We return to the penalty rule in Section 3.1.5 when we consider how consumers have fared in senior courts.

A similar reluctance to consider the broader social welfare effects of contracting is evident elsewhere, particularly where courts are called upon to consider the limitations on self-interested behaviour in markets. Courts are unwilling to censure contract conduct that is not unlawful but ethically questionable. The case law on economic duress accepts that a lawful act can amount to illegitimate pressure if the threat is used in bad faith to support a demand that the stronger party is not entitled to make.[37] Exploitation of a

[32] *Patel* v. *Mirza* per Lord Toulson at [108].
[33] *Patel* v. *Mirza* per Lord Mance, Lord Clarke and Lord Sumption.
[34] *Dunlop Pneumatic Tyre Co Ltd* v. *New Garage and Motor Co Ltd* [1915] AC 79.
[35] Waddams, *Sanctity of Contracts in a Secular Age*, pp. 17–18.
[36] *Multiservice Bookbinding* v. *Marden* [1979] 1 Ch 84, 110.
[37] *CTN Cash and Carry Ltd* v. *Gallaher Ltd* [1994] 4 All ER 714.

monopoly position, however, or the normal 'rough and tumble'[38] of commercial bargaining will not usually constitute duress.[39] In a freedom of contract environment, judges are unlikely to make assessments that a commercial contractor is acting in bad faith where there is no breach of contract terms, even where the behaviour is particularly bullying or hostile or the stronger party is taking advantage of significant power disparities in the relationship. The Court of Appeal in *Times Travel (UK) Ltd* v. *Pakistan International Airlines Corporation* determined that an inquiry into what is morally or socially unacceptable in a commercial context could only be made on very narrow terms.[40] The notion that 'illegitimate pressure' could include conduct that was not unlawful but contrary to acceptable standards of behaviour was an unwelcome one, and in danger of allowing intrusion of equitable principles of unconscionability into commercial law.[41] Judicial disengagement from issues of this kind is unfortunate. Where questions of public policy are raised they invite consideration of the interests that can and cannot legitimately be made the subject of a contractual obligation and the legal limits on freedom of contract. The operation of policy and judicial controls on the excesses of self-interested behaviour helps to keep the over-extension of market norms in check.[42] The reluctance of the courts to intervene is a manifestation of a more general reticence towards allowing equitable principles to influence commercial law. We consider this in the following sections.

3.1.3 Marginalisation of Equity ...

Though historically important, equity's position in modern contract law is ambivalent. On one hand, concepts derived from equity still feature prominently in contract doctrine (rectification; undue influence; rules against penalties and forfeitures; estoppel in various forms). On the other, recent judicial

[38] *Carillion Construction Ltd* v. *Felix (UK) Ltd* [2000] All ER (D) 1696; *Adam Opel GmbH* v. *Mitras Automotive* [2007] EWHC 3252 [26].

[39] *CTN Cash and Carry Ltd* v. *Gallaher Ltd*, per Lord Steyn, 717.

[40] [2019] 3 WLR 445 [73].

[41] *Times Travel* [101]–[102].

[42] The English and Scottish Law Commissions use autonomy and libertarian arguments to justify legalising commercial surrogacy: *Building Families through Surrogacy: A New Law*, Joint Consultation Paper 244/167, (June 2019) at para 2.65. See also *XX* v. *Whittington Hospital NHS Trust* [2021] AC 275: 'it is no longer contrary to public policy to award damages for the costs of a foreign commercial surrogacy' per Lady Hale at [53]; Cressida Auckland and Imogen Goold, 'Claiming in Contract for Wrongful Conception' (2020) 136 *Law Quarterly Review* 45, 48.

encounters with these doctrines have tended to curtail their application[43] or have sought to impose rule-bound structure on their operation. Waddams notes a reluctance to develop the equitable jurisdiction of the courts since fusion in 1875, which he attributes to declining awareness of equity amongst practitioners and an unwillingness amongst judges to resort to equitable principles in their reasoning.[44] Lack of chancery experience amongst Supreme Court justices has also been blamed for the waning of equity's influence over the law.[45] The introduction of equitable concepts into commercial dealing has been discouraged for fear of imposing trustee, or fiduciary-type, duties on commercial contractors acting at arm's length.[46] These sentiments undermine the potential of equity to balance out the more commercially oriented tenets of contract law.

Concern is often expressed that equitable interventions will 'distort the parties' contractual bargain'[47] or render the law uncertain.[48] Alternatively, it is feared that the enforcement of contractual rights will be made subject to judicial value judgments about unconscionability.[49] Equitable concepts are also castigated for their antiquity. The equity-derived penalty rule has come under fire for permitting contractual allocations of risk ex ante to be reallocated ex post under the auspices of a now-vanished jurisdiction associated with penal bonds that morphed unchecked into the modern doctrine.[50] Equity's emphasis on good conscience as a standard increasingly sits uneasily with the self-interested economic rationality that is often thought to

[43] Nelson Enonchong, 'The Modern English Doctrine of Unconscionability' (2018) 34 *Journal of Contract Law* 211, 217.

[44] Waddams, *Sanctity of Contracts in a Secular Age*, pp. 34, 158–59.

[45] Man Yip and James Lee, 'The Commercialisation of Equity' [2017] 37 *Legal Studies* 647, 650.

[46] William Goodhart and Gareth Jones, 'The Infiltration of Equitable Doctrine into English Commercial Law' (1980) 43 *Modern Law Review* 489; Sir J. Mummery, 'Commercial Notions and Equitable Potions' in Sarah Worthington (ed.) *Commercial Law and Commercial Practice* (Hart Publishing, 2003), pp. 29, 42–43; *UBS AG (London Branch)* v. *Kommunale Wasserwerke Leipzig GmbH* [2017] 2 Lloyd's Rep 621, per Lady Justice Gloster at [347]; *Yeoman's Row Management Ltd* v. *Cobbe* [2008] WLR 1752, per Lord Walker at [85] and [91].

[47] *Fujitsu Services Ltd* v. *IBM United Kingdom Ltd* [2014] EWHC 752 at [126]. See also *Scandinavian Trading Tanker Co AB* v. *Flota Petrolera Ecuatoriana (The Scaptrade)* [1983] 1 QB 529 (CA), affirmed by HL [1983] 2 AC 694; *Union Eagle Ltd* v. *Golden Achievement Ltd* [1997] AC 514.

[48] *Yeoman's Row Management Ltd* per Lord Walker at [81].

[49] Irit Samet, *Equity: Conscience Goes to Market* (Oxford University Press, 2018), pp. 14–15.

[50] Jody P. Kraus and Robert E. Scott, 'The Case against Equity in American Contract Law' (2020) 93 *Southern California Law Review* 1323, 1327, 1332.

characterise the model of the contractor underlying classical contract law.[51] Lord Sumption expressed this well in observing that 'fairness has nothing to do with commercial contracts. The parties enter into them in a spirit of competitive co-operation, with a view to serving their own interest. Commercial parties can be most unfair and entirely unreasonable, if they can get away with it.'[52] This separation between the commercial model of the contractor and the fiduciary model may explain the judicial reticence to develop systematic principles in the identification and treatment of relational contracts, an issue to which we return in Chapter 7.

3.1.4 ... Except in the Service of Formalism

To the extent that equity may have a role in modern contract law, it is clearly not the equity of Lord Mansfield's time. Yip and Lee assert that the relationship between common law and equity is not so much one of fusion but the appropriation of equitable means in the service of commercial ends, altering the character of equity in the process.[53] It is hard to disagree with this assessment. Judges have not been slow to harness concepts derived from equity when they can do useful work in justifying text-based interpretations of the agreement or the application of formalistic contract law rules. The development of contractual estoppel provides an example. Contractual estoppel reinforces the effectiveness of what have become known as 'basis of the contract' clauses. The precise drafting of these clauses varies, but the most common is the 'no reliance' clause. The function of this term is to prevent liability in misrepresentation arising by removing a constituent of the claim through a formal contract acknowledgement that no representations have been made or have not been relied upon.[54] More broadly, the legal recognition of basis clauses permits parties to make a serious contractual commitment founded on a set of assumed understandings, or agreed 'facts', that they know

[51] T. T. Arvind, 'Contract Transactions and Equity' in Larry A. DiMatteo, Qi Zhou, Séverine Saintier and Keith Rowley (eds.) *Commercial Contract Law: Transatlantic Perspectives* (Cambridge University Press, 2013), pp. 146, 166; Sir Terence Etherton, 'Equity and Conscience', Eldon Professor's Lecture, Northumbria University (24 October 2017) [53]–[57]. Lord Justice Millett, 'Equity's Place in the Law of Commerce' (1998) 114 *Law Quarterly Review* 214, 216.

[52] Lord Sumption, 'A Question of Taste: The Supreme Court and the Interpretation of Contracts' (2017) 17 *Oxford University Commonwealth Law Journal* 301, 310. See also *Daventry District Council* v. *Daventry & District Housing Ltd* [2011] EWCA Civ 1153 [139].

[53] Yip and Lee, 'The Commercialisation of Equity', 648–49.

[54] *Carney* v. *N M Rothschild & Sons Ltd* [2018] EWHC 958 [73].

may be false.[55] Basis clauses have been fortified against challenge by the proposition that a party who has indicated their assent to a basis clause, through signature for example, is estopped from asserting a different state of affairs exists. Given the well-known critiques of standard form contracts it is disingenuous to manipulate the doctrine of estoppel – and develop novel forms of evidential and contractual estoppel – in the service of a form of contract imperialism that binds a contractor absolutely to a set of unnegotiated written terms proffered by the economically stronger party.[56]

When interpreted as setting out the assumed facts upon which the transaction rests, basis clauses may operate with relative immunity from the controls imposed on exempting terms by UCTA 1977.[57] This understanding of basis clauses substantially departs from a previous line of authority that denied that contract terms could define legal rights out of existence in a way that escaped the reach of the legislative protections. An early debate on the operation of UCTA 1977 centred on whether exempting terms should be understood as defensive mechanisms designed to absolve defendants from the consequences of breach of a legal duty or as legitimate devices for defining and modifying those duties.[58] The common law had already reached the position that there must be a minimum of non-excludable content in agreements. This prevented a contract being reduced to a 'mere declaration of intent'[59] through the operation of the terms. This principle was reflected in various sections of the 1977 Act.[60] In line with the welfarist thinking of the period, courts were of the view that it was not possible for parties to contract out of common law duties

55 Accepted by the Privy Council as an estoppel by convention: *Prime Sight Ltd* v. *Lavarello* [2014] AC 436 [46]–[47]. See also Jonathan Morgan, 'Opting for "Documentary Fundamentalism": Respecting Party Choice for Entire Agreement and Non-reliance Clauses' in Paul S. Davies and Magda Raczynska (eds.) *Contents of Commercial Contracts: Terms Affecting Freedoms* (Hart Publishing, 2020), pp. 239, 246–47.

56 Gerard McMeel, 'Documentary Fundamentalism in the Senior Courts: The Myth of Contractual Estoppel' [2011] *Lloyd's Maritime and Commercial Law Quarterly* 185.

57 *Watford Electronics Ltd* v. *Sanderson CFL Ltd* [2001] EWCA Civ 317, [2001] All ER (Comm) 696 at [39]–[41]. See Kwan Ho Lau and Ben Mathias Tan, 'Basis Clauses and the Unfair Contract Terms Act 1977' (2014) 130 *Law Quarterly Review* 377; Jo Braithwaite, '*Springwell*-watch: New Insights into the Nature of Contractual Estoppel', LSE Law Society and Economy Working Paper No 12/2017, p. 13.

58 Brian Coote, 'The Function of Exception Clauses' in Rick Bigwood (ed.) *Contract as Assumption: Essays on a Theme* (Hart Publishing, 2010), pp. 81, 86.

59 Lord Wilberforce, *Suisse Atlantique* v. *Rotterdamsche* [1967] AC 361, 432.

60 See for example, ss 3(2)(b), 11(3) and 13(1).

in order to evade the statutory controls.[61] This approach was applied to consumer and commercial contracts alike,[62] and it was extended subsequently to other protective legislative provisions.[63] Similarly, early authority on the scope of 'no-reliance' clauses regarded them as subject to the operation of UCTA 1977 and the Misrepresentation Act 1967.[64]

Courts since have chipped away at this line of authority, notably in *Springwell Navigation Corp* v. *J P Morgan Chase Bank*.[65] Basis clauses have proved particularly useful in shielding banks from mis-selling claims brought by investors in emerging financial markets and purchasers of interest rate hedging products (or swaps) who suffered losses following the global financial crisis.[66] Many of the claimants were small or family businesses. The contractual statements that the claimants were required to sign, acknowledging that they were given information and not 'advised' and that they relied on their own judgment, or were a 'sophisticated investor', were highly significant. These phrases serve to negate the assumption of responsibility required for common law liability to arise and, in many cases, proved conclusive in the light of the contractual estoppel argument.[67] The contractual statement that a relationship is 'not advisory' also reduces the level of protection available to the investor under Financial Conduct Authority regulation. In the words of

[61] John N. Adams and Roger Brownsword, 'The Unfair Contract Terms Act: A Decade of Discretion' (1988) 104 *Law Quarterly Review* 94. For an early critique of the approach of UCTA 1977, see Yates, *Exclusion Clauses in Contracts*, pp. 269–70.

[62] See respectively *Smith* v. *Eric S. Bush* [1990] 1 AC 831; *Phillips Products Ltd* v. *Hyland and Hamstead Plant Hire Co Ltd* [1987] 1 WLR 659.

[63] *Director General of Fair Trading* v. *First National Bank* [2002] 1 AC 481, 499 in relation to the 'core term' exception in the Unfair Terms in Consumer Contract Regulations 1994/1999.

[64] *Cremdean Properties* v. *Nash* [1977] 2 Estates Gazette LR 80, per Lord Justice Bridge at 82 and Lord Justice Scarman at 82–83; *Brikom Investments Ltd* v. *Carr* [1979] 2 All ER 753; *Thomas Witter* v. *TBP Industries* [1996] 2 All ER 573; *Goff* v. *Gaultier* (1991) 62 P & C R 388 (ChD).

[65] For other sympathetic cases see *E A Grimstead & Son Ltd* v. *McGarrigan* [1999] EWCA Civ 3029; *Axa Sun Life Services plc* v. *Campbell Martin Ltd* [2011] 2 Lloyd's Rep 1 at [34] and [64]–[65]; *Peekay Intermark Ltd* v. *Australia and New Zealand Banking Group Ltd* [2006] 2 Lloyd's Rep 511.

[66] See generally Jo Braithwaite, 'Law after Lehmans', LSE Law, Society and Economy Working Papers 11/2014.

[67] *Thornbridge Ltd* v. *Barclays Bank plc* [2015] EWHC 3430 [109]; *Carney* v. *Rothschild*, above n. 54 at [346]; *Property Alliance Group Ltd* v. *Royal Bank of Scotland plc* [2018] EWCA Civ 355; [2018] 1 WLR 3529 [98]; *Crestsign Ltd* v. *National Westminster Bank plc* [2014] EWHC 3043 [94], [114]; contra *Thomas* v. *Triodos Bank NV* [2017] EWHC 314 [68], [80]; Braithwaite, '*Springwell*-watch', pp. 10–12.

one judge, the clauses 'remove what might have been a grey area of liability' concerning the extent of the duties owed.[68]

The estoppel route to upholding such clauses conveniently sidesteps the protective statutes, replacing the balanced assessment of interests required under the reasonable test with express term *fiat.* In determining that 'basis clauses' can define the primary relationship of the parties and exclude the operation of legal claims that might otherwise arise, courts have sought to rehabilitate a line of argument that lay dormant and apparently discredited for a number of years. Not all judges have endorsed this move. In *First Tower Trustees Ltd* v. *CDS (Superstores International) Ltd* the idea that parties could contract around statutory provisions based on a sound policy through a 'duty-defining' term was treated with scepticism. Lord Justice Leggatt noted that liability under section 2(1) of the Misrepresentation Act 1967 did not depend on the operation of contract terms: 'The liability arises by operation of law independently of what the parties have agreed.'[69] The statute could not be circumvented by 'felicity in drafting the contract term'.[70]

Contractual estoppel has developed out of a judicial determination to avoid the doctrinal restrictions imposed by other types of estoppel, particularly evidential estoppel. The broad principle behind estoppel is that a party cannot deny the truth of something they have earlier asserted, and upon which another relied, if it would be unconscionable to allow them to do so. For the operation of contractual estoppel, detrimental reliance on the statement is not required, nor is it necessary to show that the representor acted unconscionably in reneging.[71] The evidential difficulty presented by the representee's knowledge that the representation (of non-reliance) is not true disappears. The motivation for the development of contractual estoppel is to promote certainty in commercial dealings. It is a formal mechanism to gird the express contract terms against challenge. Contractual estoppel supplements the common law message that the words mean what they say,[72] and a signature on a document is an objective indication of assent to the terms contained therein. McMeel notes that the estoppel argument supports several classical contract law doctrines concerning the signature rule, the objective test of agreement, the parol evidence rule and freedom of contract.[73] By using estoppel to support the

[68] *Carney* v. *Rothschild,* above n. 54 at [80]. [69] [2019] 1 WLR 637 [98].
[70] *First Tower Trustees* [99].
[71] Jo Braithwaite, 'The Origins and Implications of Contractual Estoppel' (2016) *Law Quarterly Review* 119–21 (a broadly supportive view of contractual estoppel).
[72] Braithwaite, '*Springwell*-watch', p. 11.
[73] McMeel, 'Documentary Fundamentalism', 189–91.

objective test of agreement or the signature rule, the courts manifest their own lack of faith in these rules as reliable indicators of party intent.

The substantial dilution of estoppel requirements in contractual estoppel undermines its equitable basis, deploying it for a purpose (bolstering commitment to the express terms) for which it was not originally intended. It must be doubted whether it is permissible that principles derived from equity should be brought to bear to protect powerful institutions from the consequences of laws designed to control the excesses of freedom of contract. That it is necessary to rely on equity to prop up an invidious common law stance on the conclusiveness of contract documents illustrates the weakness of the common law's own doctrinal position. More broadly, basis clauses, along with the 'no oral modification' clause and the 'entire agreement clause', are an indication of the increasing introspection found in written contracts of all varieties. Collectively these terms have a unified purpose: to ensure the agreement is bounded on all sides by whatever documents constitute the contract text and to minimise recourse to context in establishing additional obligations or legal duties. The growth of basis clauses is in keeping with the re-emergence of a classical style of contract law and the evaporating influence of welfarist concerns in the common law. The clauses are an attempt to impose 'discreteness' on the deal and to prompt a formal approach to interpretation.[74] There are circumstances in which context-limiting clauses may be justified, to control agents and employees, for example, or to delineate precisely in a negotiated agreement the obligations undertaken to the counterparty. But they also disable a court from subjecting the agreement to general rules of contract law (misrepresentation; implied terms; variation and waiver). In addition, they allow the stronger party to dictate and control the contracting environment through contract mechanisms. This includes constructing a version of the counterparty as 'well-informed' or 'sophisticated' and fully understanding all the implications of the agreement.[75]

The attempt to impose an interpretative cordon around contract texts and insulate terms from challenge gives rise to more general dangers. It bestows exceptional power on the contract paperwork, a power readily exploited by economically stronger parties. This might be justified in a situation involving a negotiated contract between genuinely evenly matched commercial

[74] Uri Benoliel, 'The Interpretation of Commercial Contracts: An Empirical Study' (2017) 69 *Alabama Law Journal* 469.

[75] See Mr Justice Christopher Clarke in *Raiffeisen Zentralbank Osterreich* v. *Royal Bank of Scotland plc* [2011] 1 Lloyds Rep 123 [304].

contractors. But what is acceptable in relation to one kind of contract term in the common law is relatively easily extended to other situations by analogy, creating a permissive environment in which other kinds of liability-denying or fact-altering clauses can flourish.[76] We discuss this further in Chapter 5, noting the difficulties surrounding non-disclosure agreements.

3.1.5 Consumer Contracts in the Senior Courts

One of the features of the classical law of contract was its lack of differentiation between different types of contracting party. Notwithstanding that protective legislation distinguished consumers from business contractors, courts displayed the occasional tendency to assimilate all contracting parties to the commercial model. This often thwarted the consumer protection rationale of legislation and regulation. In *Director General of Fair Trading* v. *First National Bank*,[77] the House of Lords first considered the operation of the EU Directive on Unfair Terms in Consumer Contracts and its enacting regulations in the United Kingdom. The case was brought by the Office of Fair Trading (OFT), the regulator responsible at the time for consumer protection. The OFT sought to challenge the bank practice of adding post-judgment interest to debts. The House of Lords took the view that a bank customer that had defaulted on a loan agreement, and who had been subject to County Court enforcement proceedings, would expect to pay interest on the debt as long as it remained outstanding. It would not constitute an 'unfair surprise' for the debtor, having paid off all the court-ordered instalments, to receive an additional bill for interest from the lender, since the contract terms provided for it. In reaching this decision, Lord Millett remarked, 'The [continuing interest] term is not only a standard term in non-negotiable loans to consumers, but in commercial loans freely negotiated between parties on equal terms and acting with professional advice ... no lawyer advising a commercial borrower would dream of objecting to the inclusion of such a term which merely reinforces and carries into effect what the parties themselves would regard as the essence of the transaction.'[78] This assimilation of consumer expectations with commercial realities had the effect of obscuring that one source of the problem of additional indebtedness for a distressed consumer was the omission by courts to

[76] Braithwaite, 'The Origins and Implications of Contractual Estoppel', 121, referring to the problem of 'contagion', that is, decisions made in the rarefied context of the global financial crisis of 2008 taking on disproportionate significance as general principles of contract law.

[77] [2002] 1 AC 481.

[78] *Director General of Fair Trading* v. *First National Bank* [56].

exercise their power to reduce interest on judgment debts to zero in the initial enforcement proceedings. The judgment of lack of unfairness in the case proceeded on the basis of an acontextual exercise of contract interpretation that ignores the background of enforcement and the consumer's reasonable expectation that a county court judgment incorporating a mandated repayment plan is likely to mark the end of the matter. The unsatisfactory nature of the judicial approach prompted an amendment to legislation to ensure that the consumer had notice of their right to seek a court order to reduce interest on judgment debts.[79]

A more conciliatory and balanced approach to relations between lenders and customers was taken by the Court of Appeal in the same case,[80] as well as in *Paragon Finance plc* v. *Nash*,[81] decided in the same year. However, the House of Lords' decision in *Director General of Fair Trading* was a harbinger of what was to follow regarding the treatment of consumer contracts by courts. Judges have been reluctant to utilise common law rules in the furtherance of consumer protection or the regulation of consumer contracts. The common law tools courts have at their disposal, such as the rule against penalties, are not generally used in a way that supports consumers seeking to challenge the effects of standard contract terms. The changes to the penalty rule made by *ParkingEye* v. *Beavis* demonstrate the inadequacy of common law as an instrument of consumer protection. The public policy justification for the penalty rule – the liquidated damages specified must be a genuine pre-estimate of loss or broadly *compensatory* – has been replaced by an ex ante perspective, that is to say, the central question is whether the impugned provision is a secondary obligation 'which imposes a detriment on the contract-breaker out of all proportion to any legitimate interest of the innocent party in the enforcement of the primary obligation'.[82] In *ParkingEye* it was conceded by ParkingEye that the £85 parking charge was not a pre-estimate of loss from overstaying in a car park, nor was it compensatory.[83] The court regarded the

79 Section 130A Consumer Credit Act 1974, as amended.

80 *Director General of Fair Trading* v. *First National Bank* [2000] EWCA Civ 27; [2000] 2 WLR 1353.

81 [2002] 1 WLR 685.

82 *Cavendish* v. *Makdessi; ParkingEye* v. *Beavis*, above n. 11 at [32]. Lord Atkinson alluded to similar considerations in *Dunlop* v. *New Garage*, above n. 34, at 92: '[Dunlop] had an obvious interest to prevent this undercutting . . . it would appear to me impossible to say that that interest was incommensurate with the sum agreed to be paid'. See also *Clydebank Engineering & Shipbuilding Co Ltd* v. *Don Jose Ramos Yzquierdo y Castaneda* [1905] AC 6, 19–20.

83 *Cavendish* v. *Makdessi; ParkingEye* v. *Beavis*, above n. 11, at [97].

charge as nevertheless justified by the legitimate interest of ParkingEye in discouraging overstaying to maximise turnover of shoppers using the facility. The £85 charge was considered proportionate to achieving that aim. If the claimant can produce *some plausible reason* why performance matters, the contractual payment is likely to be enforceable unless so clearly oppressive or manifestly unreasonable that it is unconscionable. This is likely to capture only the most obviously outrageous cases. In one post-*ParkingEye* case a lender had raised its default interest rate to 4 per cent from a market norm of 1–3 per cent and the court upheld this on the basis of the legitimate interest test.[84] Contract interpretation has also become more significant in the application of the penalty rule, as it is possible to contract around the controls by framing stipulated contractual payments (or deductions) as primary obligations. Primary obligations are not reviewable under the penalty jurisdiction.

Evident in *Cavendish* and *ParkingEye* is the ambition within the senior courts to strengthen commitment to party autonomy as *the core* contract value and a reluctance to create uncertainty for commercial contractors. Lord Neuberger and Lord Sumption suggested that the parties should expect certainty from the law and that the penalty rule is 'an interference with freedom of contract'.[85] These pronouncements are very different in tone to the previous leading authority on penalties. In Lord Dunedin's speech in *Dunlop Pneumatic Tyre Co Ltd* v. *New Garage and Motor Co Ltd*,[86] there may have been doubt about the scope of the penalty doctrine and the correct principles that govern the exercise of the penalty jurisdiction, but there was no question that the jurisdiction existed. Freedom of contract is mentioned fleetingly in Lord Parmoor's judgment. The changes wrought by *Cavendish* v. *Makdessi* extend an anti-interventionist commercial rationale into the penalty rule, which is likely to impinge on the consumer context. This became clear in *ParkingEye*. The analysis of the penalty jurisdiction adopted by the Supreme Court affected the application of the Unfair Terms in Consumer Contract Regulations

84 *ICICI Bank UK plc* v. *Assam Oil Co Ltd* [2019] EWHC 750 (Comm). See also *ZCCM Investment Holdings plc* v. *Konkola Copper Mines plc* [2017] EWHC 3288 (Comm) in which Lionel Percy QC, stated that he had seen no evidence to suggest that the agreed rate of LIBOR plus 10 per cent was 'evidently extravagant' at [38]. A rate of LIBOR plus 12 per cent was held not to be a penalty by Mr Justice Bryan in *Cargill International Trading Pte Ltd* v. *Uttam Galva Steels Ltd* [2019] EWHC 476 (Comm) on the basis of the 'legitimate interest in performance' test.

85 Supreme Court in *Cavendish* v. *Makdessi* at [33]. The Court of Appeal in *Cavendish* v. *Makdessi* [2013] EWCA Civ 1539 regarded the penalty rule as a 'blatant interference with freedom of contract' per Lord Justice Christopher Clarke at [44].

86 [1915] AC 79.

1999.[87] The parking charge was not unfair under the regulations since it did not exclude any right a consumer enjoyed under the general law, and a reasonable motorist in Mr Beavis's position would have agreed to the charge.[88] Lord Toulson disagreed: the charge caused significant imbalance between the parties precisely because 'it far exceeded any amount which was otherwise likely to be recoverable as damages for breach of contract or trespass'.[89] For the majority, contract terms rendered the common law default position – central to Lord Toulson's approach – immaterial. Lord Toulson's reasoning is more in keeping with the independent controls on unfair terms found within the regulations and their justification in consumer protection. The majority did not permit the consumer protection policy of the unfair terms regulations to undermine the effect of common law contract doctrine.[90]

The anti-consumer outcome in *ParkingEye* was not a surprise. It was foreshadowed by the bank charges litigation from 2010. In *Office of Fair Trading* v. *Abbey National plc*, the Supreme Court held that charges imposed by banks on customers with unarranged overdrafts could not be assessed for fairness under the Unfair Terms in Consumer Contract Regulations.[91] An earlier stage in proceedings had determined that the charges could not be reviewed under the penalty jurisdiction either since the payments, which were usually well in excess of the bank's actual losses from unarranged overdrafts, were not triggered by a breach of contract. It was not against any term in the contract between bank and customer for the customer to go into overdraft.[92] This finding about the limits on the penalty jurisdiction was not challenged on appeal.[93] The Unfair Terms in Consumer Contract Regulations were held inapplicable because the charges were part of an account pricing structure

87 *Cavendish* v. *Makdessi*, above n. 11 [106]: relying on *Aziz* v. *Caixa d'Estalvis de Catalunya, Tarragona i Manresa (Catalunyacaixa)* Case C-415/11, [2013] 3 CMLR 5.

88 *Cavendish* v. *Makdessi* per Lord Sumption and Lord Neuberger [107]–[108].

89 *Cavendish* v. *Makdessi* per Lord Toulson [307], [309].

90 The position may be different where there is no interface between common law and regulation. See, for example, *Lipton and another* v. *BA City Flyer Ltd* [2021] 1 WLR 2545, on Regulation (EC) 261/2004 of the European Parliament and of the Council (Denied Boarding Regulation) where the Court of Appeal noted the consumer protection rationale of the regulation throughout their judgment.

91 *Office of Fair Trading* v. *Abbey National plc* [2010] 1 AC 696.

92 *Office of Fair Trading* v. *Abbey National plc* decision of Mr Justice Andrew Smith [2008] EWHC 875; [2008] 2 All ER (Comm) 625.

93 Cf. the Australian decisions in *Andrews* v. *Australia and New Zealand Banking Group Ltd* (2012) 247 CLR 205; [2012] HCA 30; *Paciocco* v. *Australia and New Zealand Banking Group Ltd* [2016] HCA 28 deciding that the penalty rule can be applied to a broad variety of clauses, not just those secondary obligations triggered by a breach of contract.

whereby free banking could be offered to customers remaining in credit, paid for by charges for unauthorised borrowing.[94] Since freedom of contract reigns in relation to the price of the bank's services, the charges were not reviewable for fairness under the regulations, being concerned with 'the definition of the main subject matter of the contract or … the adequacy of the price or remuneration, as against the goods or services supplied in exchange'.[95] As with the level of parking charges, how banks make profits is not a matter for regulation by courts.[96] The court regarded transparency as the most important consideration (even terms falling outside the operation of the fairness test must be in plain, intelligible language). The trial judge dismissed the argument that the regulations had displaced the common law, which was no longer applicable. The judge noted that the regulations laid down the minimum level of protection available for consumers, and the latter should also be entitled to common law protection, especially when more robust.[97] A restrictive approach to the operation of common law protection is not likely to assist consumers however.

The above developments indicate a non-interventionist common law in retreat from any significant role in policing or controlling contract content. Judges have, over recent years, used case determination to turn contract law principles to the task of supporting commercial contracting. In light of the continued fragmentation of contract governance into private law and public regulatory modes,[98] it is perhaps natural that the traditional principles of contract law become focused on commercial agreements. In the commercial context, at least insofar as the parties are evenly matched economically, the common law principles can be applied unencumbered by policy-based reasoning. Business contractors are unlikely to find much use for general principles of contract law dealing with consumer protection or standards of behaviour in contract and will prefer a contract law that simply upholds their agreements. However, as Waddams has shown, the common law contains tools that may have fallen out of favour in the modern law but that could

94 *Office of Fair Trading* v. *Abbey National plc*, above n. 91, per Lord Walker [47]; Lord Phillips [62].

95 Reg 6(2) Unfair Terms in Consumer Contract Regulations 1999, sometimes referred to as the 'core terms' exemption.

96 *OFT* v. *Abbey National*, above n. 91, Lady Hale [93].

97 *OFT* v. *Abbey National* above n. 91, [331].

98 See Steve Hedley, 'Two Laws of Contract, or One?' in T. T. Arvind and Jenny Steele (eds.) *Contract Law and the Legislature* (Hart Publishing, 2020), p. 147.

usefully be revived to address the problem of unreasonable contracts.[99] If judges are reduced solely to contract interpreters, they are unlikely to have the opportunity to engage in the kind of doctrinal renewal that is necessary to develop such a power. This is unfortunate, since given the piecemeal nature of regulation, the common law is the important repository of contract law's general normative and justificatory architecture. Importantly, whether for good or ill, law both shapes and is an expression of a society's contract culture. Judicial reasoning around the kind of agreements that are enforced, how they are enforced and why they are enforced conveys an important message to society about the core values of contract law. The possibility of judicial oversight and enforcement of contracts, and the consequent communicative and educative effect of judgments, is vital in an increasingly contractualised society.

3.2 Contractualisation of Society

Contractualisation is used here to describe the grounding of social and economic relations on legally enforceable agreements, or through the symbols and trappings of legally enforceable agreements, rather than some other foundation, such as gift, trust, status or hierarchy. That we live in a contractualised society is not a novel observation. Henri Maine noted in 1861 that progressive societies had moved 'from status to contract'.[100] Collins locates the idea of a contractualised society in the work of Max Weber and Emile Durkheim.[101] The features of contractualisation have been identified in different ways.[102] Collins isolates four characteristics of contractualisation: 'the valuation in delimited (contract) terms, the measurement by a precise currency of exchange, the externalization of social effects, and the unilateral rule-making power ... emphasizing the values of preference satisfaction and a monetary currency of exchange between the parties'.[103] For Gardner,

[99] Waddams, *Sanctity of Contracts in a Secular Age*, pp. 3–4.

[100] Henry Sumner Maine, *Ancient Law* (John Murray, 1861; Cambridge University Press, 2012), p. 170.

[101] Hugh Collins, *Regulating Contracts* (Oxford University Press,1999), p. 17.

[102] See John Wightman, *Contract: A Critical Commentary* (Pluto Press, 1996), pp. 2–3; Collins, *The Law of Contract*, Chapter 6; Margaret Jane Radin, 'The Deformation of Contract in the Information Society' (2017) 37 *Oxford Journal of Legal Studies* 505; John Gardner, 'The Contractualisation of Labour Law' in Hugh Collins, Gillian Lester and Virginia Mantouvalou (eds.) *Philosophical Foundations of Labour Law* (Oxford University Press, 2018), p. 33; Peter Vincent-Jones, *The New Public Contracting* (Oxford University Press, 2006), p. xxviii.

[103] Collins, *The Law of Contract*, pp. 110–11; see also *Regulating Contracts*, pp. 17–20, Chapter 13.

contractualisation represents the prioritisation of contract norms above others. Contractualisation is

> the process by which contractual norms come, not only to be socially supported, but to enjoy a unique pre-eminence among those that enjoy social support. What kind of pre-eminence? This kind: whenever the norms of certain roles and relationships can be understood as having their source in a contract, they are so understood. They are reinterpreted as contractual norms, existing for content-independent reasons.[104]

The effect of contractualisation is the dominance of contract norms and the bestowal of independent worth on contractual forms as the source of obligations and rights.[105] Law, including judicial decision-making, supports and promotes a certain conception of contract that facilitates the process of contractualisation. Presently, this conception valorises ideological constructs associated with the market: freedom of contract; individualism; formalisation of relationships and expectations according to express contract terms; and a rational, utility-maximising model of the contractor. At the extreme, this model of contract, including its justification in abstract economic criteria and the notion of party autonomy, can be deployed to legitimise all kinds of behaviour that would provoke moral outrage when evaluated under any other normative framework.[106] In elevating the contract norm to principal position, all other aspects of social, and occasionally historical, context are obliterated. The contract norm cloaks our encounters with a veneer of normative acceptability through contract's association with ideals of assent, voluntariness and freedom. These features may or may not be genuinely present in contractual relationships. The alignment of contract law with the commercial contract accentuates and fortifies this process by encouraging discreteness in contracting – the effectuation of consent and implementation of planning – to the exclusion of other values and criteria.[107] Contract is reduced to a transaction between two disembodied economic units (firms), who are assumed, through the exercise of freedom of contract and consent, to have reached agreement on all matters material to the exchange at the moment when

[104] Gardner, 'Contractualisation of Labour Law', p. 36.

[105] Gardner, 'Contractualisation of Labour Law', pp. 36–37. See also Vincent-Jones, *The New Public Contracting*, p. 4 (footnote omitted).

[106] J. Mark Ramseyer, 'Indentured Prostitution in Imperial Japan: Credible Commitments in the Commercial Sex Industry' (1991) 7 *Journal of Law, Economics and Organization* 89; 'Contracting for Sex in the Pacific War' (2021) 65 International Review of Law and Economics (art. 105971).

[107] Ian Macneil, *The Relational Theory of Contract: Selected Works of Ian Macneil*, David Campbell (ed.) (Sweet and Maxwell, 2001), p. 21.

offer and acceptance coincide.[108] Other normative structures that support the relationship are crowded out by this bureaucratic vision of contract,[109] and alternative functions of contract law – to achieve policy aims, to ascribe moral responsibility or to control contractual injustice – are marginalised in favour of the enforcement of contract terms.[110]

That contract, and a particular model of contract, has assumed a central place in society appears beyond doubt. The accelerated pace of modern contractualisation is closely connected to – perhaps indistinguishable from – the privatisation and marketisation agenda pursued by governments of all stripes since the latter part of the twentieth century.[111] Competitive markets have been established in areas once dominated by nationalised industries – telecommunications, utilities and transport are the most obvious examples. Direct state provision in many areas has been replaced with decentralised delivery through private contracts between citizen and service provider or state procurement of goods and services through private companies.[112] Notionally independent agencies (sometimes adopting a corporate structure) are established to carry out government functions, and internal markets created within publicly funded institutions delivering essential services.[113] Contractualisation and formalisation have permeated the relationship between the state and individual, transforming the latter from citizen to consumer of public services.[114] The public interest is no longer to be found in directly improving social welfare but in ensuring competitive markets where it is assumed that increases in social welfare will follow.[115]

[108] Ian R. Macneil, 'Relational Contract Theory: Challenges and Queries' (2000) 94 *Northwestern University Law Review* 877, 878; David Campbell, 'Ian Macneil and the Relational Theory of Contract' in *The Relational Theory of Contract: Selected Works of Ian Macneil*, pp. 5–6.

[109] Gardner, 'Contractualisation of Labour Law', p. 37.

[110] Collins, *The Law of Contract*, pp. 4–5.

[111] For brief descriptions of this movement since the 1970s, see Anthony Ogus, *Regulation: Legal Form and Economic Theory* (Hart Publishing, 2004), pp. 8–12; Philip Arestis and Malcolm Sawyer, 'The Neoliberal Experience of the United Kingdom' in Alfredo Saad-Filho and Deborah Johnston (eds.) *Neoliberalism: A Critical Reader* (Pluto Press, 2005), p. 199; David Harvey, *A Brief History of Neo-liberalism* (Oxford University Press, 2007), pp. 55–63, Chapter 3; Trevor C. W. Farrow, *Civil Justice, Privatization and Democracy* (University of Toronto Press, 2014), pp. 51–57.

[112] Peter Vincent-Jones, 'Contractual Governance: Institutional and Organizational Analysis' (2000) 20 *Oxford Journal of Legal Studies* 317.

[113] Ian Harden, *The Contracting State* (Open University Press, 1992), Chapter 3; Sally Wheeler, 'Modelling the Contracts of the Future' (2017) 26 *Griffith Law Review* 593, 595ff.

[114] See Wightman, *Contract A Critical Commentary*, pp. 115–19.

[115] Arestis and Sawyer, 'The Neoliberal Experience of the UK', p. 203.

The transition to private modes of delivery has been accompanied by an ideological shift that emphasises the individual advantage derived from the provision of public goods and services over the community benefit. Contract is, of course, the chief mechanism through which this individualism is pursued and made manifest. Changes to higher education funding, for example, promote the idea of education as an individual exchange rather than a social good. The state-gift funding model of university tuition has been replaced with a contract in the form of the 'student loan agreement'. Students now bear individual responsibility for the payment of their tuition fees, though the liability is deferred until a certain income threshold is reached and repayments are administered through the taxation system. While very far from being a genuine market, the higher education system in England bears enough market trappings – the symbolic shift to a user-pays structure; the aspiration to increase competition between universities for students; the emphasis on customer satisfaction – that the relationship between student and university is converted into one of consumer and service-provider with a contract at its core, although not one likely to be scrutinised or enforced by general contract law. Oversight of the sector is undertaken by the Office for Students, whose regulatory goals include ensuring that students receive value for money from their higher education experience and in line with their rights as consumers.[116] The focus on individual benefit is manifest by the production of regular statistics on graduate outcomes and the degree subjects (and universities) that provide the student with the best chance of enhanced future earnings from their degree.[117]

This macro instance of contractualisation of a relationship can be augmented by numerous micro examples of contract encroachment into areas where it traditionally played little practical role. The simple purchase of goods for cash at a high street retailer generates multiple layers of contract complexity when transferred away from physical premises and into an online environment. Of course, the small print has been an enduring feature of contracting for centuries,[118] but it is rarely evident, and certainly not necessary, in a face-to-face sale of tangible products in a bricks-and-mortar shop.[119] Conducted

[116] Dissatisfied students have recourse to the Office of the Independent Adjudicator. See the Competition and Markets Authority, *Higher Education – Undergraduate Students: Your Rights Under Consumer Law* CMA 33(a) (12 March 2015).

[117] https://assets.publishing.service.gov.uk/government/uploads/system/uploads/attachment_data/file/874410/2020_03_HE_LEO_main_text.pdf

[118] See Swain, *The Law of Contract 1670–1870*, p. 88.

[119] Mark A. Lemley, 'Terms of Use' (2006) 91 *Minnesota Law Review* 459, 466.

over the Internet, however, the same sale will be subject to a dense array of retailer standard terms and conditions that purport to govern most aspects of the transaction, even for low-value goods.[120] Consent to these contracts is often procured through processes that are less than transparent, reinforcing the control that the superior economic actor has over the transaction and facilitating commitment by stealth on the part of the stronger party and acquiescence on the part of the weaker.[121] Contract law has done little to arrest or reverse this state of affairs, and indeed aspects of the law positively promote it.

3.3 Contract Law Contribution to Contractualisation

Contractualisation is foremost a social transformation, but law nevertheless plays an important role. Gardner has observed that '[contractualisation] is a process of social change that the law helps to propel, in spite of itself . . . the law connives in contractualisation, and the law itself can offer only feeble and futile defences against it'.[122] In promulgating a particular discrete version of the contract and contracting process, the law encourages and reinforces the process of contractualisation and the formalism that accompanies it. Some features of contract contribute more to this process than others.

3.3.1 Objectivity

Objectivity in the determination of whether contractual liability has been assumed and on what terms has exercised profound influence on how contracts are created and how the obligations under them are identified. Contract law is notionally concerned with upholding the intentions of the parties but this intention is gleaned from outward signs and symbols and what has been communicated to the other party, rather than any investigation of the inner

120 Yannis Bakos, Florencia Marotta-Wurgler and David R. Trossen, 'Does Anyone Read the Fine Print? Consumer Attention to Standard-Form Contracts' (2014) 43 *Journal of Legal Studies* 1; Margaret Jane Radin, *Boilerplate: The Fine Print, Vanishing Rights and the Rule of Law* (Princeton University Press, 2013), p. 12; Lisa Bernstein and Hagay Volvovsky, 'Not What You Wanted to Know: The Real Deal and the Paper Deal in Consumer Contracts: Comment on the Work of Florencia Marotta-Wurgler' (2015) 12 *Jerusalem Review of Legal Studies* 128, 130–32.

121 Lemley, 'Terms of Use', 466; Florencia Marotta-Wurgler, 'What's in a Standard Form Contract – An Empirical Analysis of Software License Agreements' (2007) 4 *Journal of Empirical Legal Studies* 677.

122 Gardner, 'Contractualisation of Labour Law', p. 35.

will or beliefs on the part of the contractors. As a result, a contract becomes disembodied, separated from the experiences and actions giving rise to it.[123] The idea of the contract having independent significance plays a large part in contract legal reasoning. It formed the basis upon which Lord Sumption accorded validity to the no oral modification clause in an agreement.[124] The law's concern with objectivity is similarly displayed when contract legal reasoning displaces and substitutes the actual contracting parties with their reasonable counterparts, thus rendering the expectations and beliefs of contractors irrelevant. Reliance on the 'reasonable person' construct allows the courts to make certain assumptions about contracting parties. The reasonable person is possessed of certain attributes, such as knowledge of the law or at least access to reliable advice on it, which they are assumed to take, and a propensity to act prudently and rationally in relation to their economic interests, seeking the best deal possible.[125] Needless to say, these attributes, whether contracting parties are actually invested with them or not, can have a significant influence on interpretative outcomes.[126]

The legal commitment to objectivity is easily manipulated to create a form of contractual obligation in circumstances far removed from the contract paradigm of genuine voluntariness and consent. It is relatively simple to impose contractual liability on another and to have one's responsibilities and liabilities constructed entirely by contract terms. Contracting scenarios that have a propensity to generate unjust contracts and imbalanced agreements are perpetrated via general contract norms, symbols and techniques that have been given a legal imprimatur by contract law rules. Accordingly, these signs and symbols are invested with independent importance as signifying contractual commitment. The chief vehicle and manifestation of this has been the standard form contract. As one of the most potent symbols of contractualisation, the existence of the 'terms and conditions' has become so ubiquitous that it has become the stuff of parody and cliché. Standard form contracts have reduced contracting, and the assumption of contractual obligation, to a matter

[123] Patrick S. Atiyah, *The Rise and Fall of Freedom of Contract* (Oxford University Press, 1979), p. 58.

[124] 'Party autonomy operates up to the point when the contract is made, but thereafter only to the extent that the contract allows': per Lord Sumption in *Rock Advertising* v. *MWB Business Advice Centres*, above n. 25 [11].

[125] See *BNY Mellon Corporate Trustee Services Ltd* v. *LBG Capital No 1 plc* [2017] 1 All ER 497 [33].

[126] See, for example, the construct of the reasonable person used in *Cavendish* v. *Makdessi; ParkingEye* v. *Beavis*, above n. 11, per Lord Neuberger and Lord Sumption at [108].

of routine administration and minor inconvenience, not requiring any thought or reflection. In many cases, this may be entirely appropriate. But it has the effect of rendering contracting, while full of meaning as a concept, largely meaningless as a social practice and an experience. Contracting under a standard form is at once both highly significant and utterly mundane.

3.3.2 Support for Standard Form Contracting

Aspects of standard form contracting are so removed from the liberal contract ideal that some commentators have questioned whether standard forms can really be called contracts at all.[127] This essentially bureaucratic tool rose to such prominence in our experience of contracting thanks in part to legal rules concerning objective consent and the incorporation of terms whereby reasonable notice, rather than positive assent, is sufficient to ensure express terms are included in the agreement. Other factors also played a role. Professions and industries face various institutional and client pressures to keep their costs down, which militates against individualised contracting on negotiated terms.[128] The rise of the consumer society exerted considerable influence in the development of standard form contracting.[129] Macneil has observed that standard form contracting is connected to the complexity of modern bureaucracies and the 'consumer mission', that is, providing consumers with access to goods and services at relatively low cost. In his view, the phenomenon of standard form contracting cannot be challenged without dismantling the underlying commitment to the consumer mission. The hidden cost of the consumer mission is the reduced quality of consent. This mission requires that our informed 'consent' is attenuated and inferred – it is not consent now to everything that happens in the future but 'consent to relations approved by society'.[130]

[127] For the doubts, see Arthur A. Leff, 'Contract as Thing' (1970) 19 *American University Law Review* 131; W. David Slawson, 'Standard Form Contracts and Democratic Control of Lawmaking Power' (1971) 84 *Harvard Law Review* 529, 544, 566; Radin, 'The Deformation of Contract', 506–08, 530; *Boilerplate*, pp. 14 and 56ff, 80–88, 242; Robin Bradley Kar and Margaret J. Radin, 'Pseudo-contract and Shared Meaning Analysis' (2019) 132 *Harvard Law Review* 1135.

[128] Mitu Gulati and Robert E. Scott, *The 3½ Minute Transaction* (University of Chicago Press, 2013), pp. 138, 146.

[129] Atiyah, *Rise and Fall*, p. 572 ff.

[130] Ian R. Macneil, 'Bureaucracy and Contracts of Adhesion' (1984) 22 *Osgoode Hall Law Journal* 5, 20–21.

Technology has augmented the rapid expansion of standard forms by simultaneously simplifying the process of contract creation but complicating the contracting environment. Delivery of products and services online via digital platforms involves layers of forms concerning matters such as site rules, licensing of software, terms and conditions on which any goods or services are supplied, privacy and data protection policies. Lawyers too have played a significant part, since boilerplate is a variety of automated text that lawyers have invested huge resources in developing.[131] Various defences of the standard form and boilerplate provisions do nothing to address the degradation of contract norms that such forms embody and replicate.[132] Consumer protection legislation in the United Kingdom precludes some of the more worrying applications of boilerplate identified in recent US contracts literature.[133] Nevertheless, the classical law of contract, with its focus on objectivity and freedom of contract, enables and informs a mostly administrative model of what it means to contract. The standardisation of many types of relationship through contract structures, such as the standard form, together with the legal willingness to enforce these forms, taps into, and accords pre-emptive status to, a set of justificatory arguments and norms that are so entrenched in our model of contract that they are difficult to displace by counter-arguments.[134] The exercise of autonomy, for example, can be established through proxies for genuine agreement – such as clicking a box indicating one has agreed to a non-negotiated (and usually unread) set of standard terms, the legality of which may be largely untested. The common law of contract has engaged only slightly with the implications of modern methods of creating contracts, although it is clear that these contractual structures rely heavily for their legitimacy on the objective theory of agreement, its expression in the rule about the binding quality of signature[135] and the expansion of the signature rule in order to incorporate analogous signifiers of assent.

131 Gulati and Scott, *3 ½ Minute Transaction*, pp. 91–92.

132 Radin, *Boilerplate*, p. 154ff.

133 Radin attacks the compulsory arbitration agreement in *Boilerplate*, p. 130ff, but in the United Kingdom mandatory arbitration clauses are unenforceable for small claims under s 91(1) Arbitration Act 1996 and would be subject to the Consumer Rights Act 2015 s 62 unfairness test for more significant claims. Shmeul I. Becher and Uri Benoliel note the proliferation of unilateral variation clauses in US boilerplate: 'Sneak in Contracts: An Empirical and Legal Analysis of Unilateral Modification Clauses in Consumer Contracts' (2020) 55 *Georgia Law Review* 657, 664. A similar provision in the United Kingdom is likely to be subject to review under s 62 of the Consumer Rights Act 2015.

134 Radin 'The Deformation of Contract', 510.

135 *L'Estrange* v. *Graucob* [1934] 2 KB 394.

Though the law may provide the badge of validity to standard terms, their legality may be beside the point. Standard form contracts exploit term deference from both consumers and courts. If the consumer *believes* the terms are legally sound, and create commitments, then the terms have largely achieved their aim.[136] The influence exerted on the recipient of contract terms, their psychological power to persuade a contractor to take their obligations seriously, independent of the content of the terms or their legal validity, has been shown in numerous studies.[137] Wilkinson-Ryan has attributed this willingness to submit to 'regulation via unread terms'[138] to individuals' belief in the morality of promise-keeping and their antipathy towards breach.[139] These beliefs held notwithstanding the considerable artificiality of conceiving the standard form contract as a variety of promise.[140] She also attributes this response to contract terms to consumers' general tendency to rationalise their powerlessness by believing that 'overall the system functions'[141] and the desire to 'make peace with the status quo'.[142] This deference to standard form contracts can be so extreme that consumers often blame themselves for failing to read terms carefully and understand what they were agreeing to.[143] It is arguable that these findings strengthen the case for legal intervention via ex post contract review and regulation, rather than ex ante information and disclosure rules. The research also raises a more foundational point concerning how the

136 Colin P. Marks, 'Online Terms as *In Terrorem* Devices' (2019) 78 *Maryland Law Review* 247, 285–86. See also Yates, *Exclusion Clauses in Contracts*, pp. 19, 30. See also Tess Wilkinson-Ryan, 'Do Liquidated Damages Encourage Breach? A Psychological Experiment' (2010) 108 *Michigan Law Review* 633.

137 Yates, *Exclusion Clauses in Contracts*, pp. 19, 30; Tess Wilkinson-Ryan, 'Justifying Bad Deals' (2020) 169 *University of Pennsylvania Law Review* 193. See also Meirav Furth-Matzkin and Roseanna Sommers, 'Consumer Psychology and the Problem of Fine Print Fraud' (2020) 72 *Stanford Law Review* 503.

138 Wilkinson-Ryan, 'Justifying Bad Deals', 196.

139 Tess Wilkinson-Ryan, 'Legal Promise and Psychological Contract' (2012) 47 *Wake Forest Law Review* 843, 845–46; Tess Wilkinson-Ryan and Jonathan Baron, 'Moral Judgment and Moral Heuristics in Breach of Contract' (2009) 6 *Journal of Empirical Legal Studies* 405; Zev J. Eigen, 'When and Why Individuals Obey Contracts: Experimental Evidence of Consent, Compliance, Promise and Performance' (2012) 41 *Journal of Legal Studies* 67.

140 Randy E. Barnett, 'Consenting to Form Contracts' (2002) 71 *Fordham Law Review* 627: 'enforcement of private agreements is not about promising, but about manifesting consent to be legally bound', 634.

141 Wilkinson-Ryan, 'Justifying Bad Deals', 197.

142 Wilkinson-Ryan, 'Justifying Bad Deals', 240.

143 Furth-Matzkin and Sommers, 'Consumer Psychology and the Problem of Fine Print Fraud', 525. The authors conclude that 'laypeople are contract formalists', 520.

proliferation of standard terms has tapped into contract's normative framework and undermined it.[144]

3.3.3 Ease of Assuming Contractual Liability

Standard form contracting may be controlled by robust consumer protection measures for dealing with unfair terms. English law has such rules, chiefly in the Consumer Rights Act 2015, although the practical difficulties faced by consumers in bringing an individual claim before the courts mean their effectiveness in policing contract fairness is questionable. Enforcement by regulators may not yield a positive outcome in terms of changing general contract behaviour or culture. The problem of unaddressed unfairness in terms is compounded when we consider that English law takes a relatively relaxed attitude towards innovation in contract creation. The legal enquiry usually turns on how new methods of forming contracts can be rendered legally effective within the established legal rules so that the economic aims of the superior party using the technology are achieved (law refrains from putting 'spanners in the works' or 'grit in the oil'[145]). Common law permissiveness in the face of innovation in contracting has evident drawbacks. The generalising tendency of the law minimises the differences between new ways of making agreements and elides the idiosyncratic problems that each innovation may generate in order to bring them within the scope of pre-existing rules.[146] The result is that common law principles become excessively abstract and increasingly unsuited to specific application, while the detailed regulation that responds to the specific problem becomes progressively more fragmented, complex and impenetrable. Rules around electronic contracting, for example, are found in different places depending on the context (consumer credit agreements; distance selling; land transfers and registration). This leads to problems of accessibility and understandability of the rules, particularly for consumers.[147] In addition, the combination of an atrophied common law with technological innovations reinforces the contractualisation project by making it relatively easy to bind other parties to contracts on standard terms by stealth

[144] Furth-Matzkin and Sommers, 'Consumer Psychology and the Problem of Fine Print Fraud', 543.

[145] Sir Robert Goff, 'Commercial Contracts and the Commercial Court' [1984] *Lloyd's Maritime and Commercial Law Quarterly* 382, 391.

[146] A point recognised by judges, see Lord Wilberforce in *The Eurymedon* [1975] AC 154, 167.

[147] Law Commission, *Electronic Execution of Documents*, Law Com 386 (2019), para 1.3.

methods where the contractual basis of the obligation created and its implications are not wholly transparent.

Nowhere is this more apparent than contracting over the Internet. This form of contracting would benefit from sustained legal scrutiny, but as Mik states starkly, '*From a contract law perspective the Internet does not exist.*'[148] The application of the objective test of agreement and the commitment to freedom of contract ensures that there are few barriers to online contracting. Click-wrap and browse-wrap are methods by which visitors to websites are taken to assent to the standard terms that govern either their use of the site or any contract to supply goods and services, including digital content. Click-wrap acceptance requires some positive act of assent on the part of the customer, usually clicking an 'I agree' button, having had an opportunity, which need not be taken, to familiarise themselves with the content of the terms. The click fulfils the multiple functions of signalling the assent of the customer, the intention to create a contract (although the precise point of contract formation is likely to be set out in the supplier's terms and conditions) and the incorporation of its terms in a single seemingly insignificant act. Browse-wrap on the other hand does not require any positive indication of assent to the terms, although to create a valid contract there must be reasonable notice of the existence of terms and that the customer is contracting on the basis of those terms. There is no requirement that the terms are accessed, read or understood in order for them to be included in the contract.[149] These methods are not thought to raise any novel issue of contract law principle.[150]

The application of the familiar rules tends to obscure the manifest differences in the online contracting environment that the signature or notice rules exclude from consideration. On the surface, contracting over the Internet has a

148 Eliza Mik, 'The Unimportance of Being Electronic or – Popular Misconceptions about Internet Contracting' (2011) 19 *International Journal of Law and Information Technology* 324, 325, emphasis in original.

149 In English law, the classic authority is the nineteenth-century case of *Parker* v. *South Eastern Railway Co* [1877] 2 CPD 416. Elizabeth Macdonald, 'When Is a Contract Formed by the Browse-wrap Process?' (2011) 19 *International Journal of Law and Information Technology* 285.

150 Robert A. Hillman and Jeffrey J. Rachlinski, 'Standard-Form Contracting in the Electronic Age' (2002) 77 *New York University Law* Review 429; contra, see Nancy S. Kim, *Wrap Contracts* (Oxford University Press, 2013), pp. 175–76. The recent Law Commission report *Electronic Execution of Documents* suggests that an e-signature also incorporates clicking an 'I agree' button on a website, para 2.21. In *Bassano* v. *Toft* [2014] EWHC 377 it was held that clicking on 'I accept' satisfied the requirement for the debtor's signature in s 61 Consumer Credit Act 1974. See also the Law Commission, *Electronic Commerce – Formal Requirements in Commercial Transactions: Advice from the Law Commission* (December 2001), para 3.36ff.

seductive simplicity that is not present in other processes, precisely conducive to incorporating standard terms into the agreement without too much interruption to the overall online experience. One does not have to leave one's home, which contributes to a misplaced sense of security, privacy, anonymity and effortlessness in contracting.[151] The idea that one is contracting and creating legal relationship is remote, and indeed websites do their utmost to encourage this attitude of unquestioning compliance towards the terms. What is readily obvious in a paper contract – pages of small print – is much less visible in the online environment. It usually takes some effort to find the terms if the user is required to navigate through several hyperlinks. The length and complexity of the terms may be obscured by the way the text is presented on screen. Quickly scrolling down a screen in order to access the 'Agree' button can easily hide the length and complexity of the terms. Prolixity is much more obvious with traditional paper documents.[152] We might note at this point that the rules of most relevance here – objective agreement and incorporation by notice – were formulated at a time when the law had not yet faced the scale of mass contracting on standard terms. Courts may have had little sustained engagement with contracts created through online methods such as browse-wrap and click-wrap, but when confronted with difficult cases they have shown how the current rules, notably on interpretation, incorporation and the protective legislation, can be deployed to address the problems. However, these cases rarely get beyond first instance for a more authoritative and general statement of the legal principles governing online contracting.[153]

The protections offered by the statute and common law are not always effective to combat other systematised forms of contracting. The combined features of term deference, objectivity in agreement, relative ease in assuming contractual liability and validity of standard terms means contractual norms are a readily harnessed and potent force for creating liabilities. Car parking provides a prosaic illustration. The application of traditional contract law rules

151 Mik, 'The Unimportance of Being Electronic', 336, 340. For some commentators, the ability to contract from home offers positive advantages to the consumer, rendering the e-contracting scenario more balanced than in-person contracting at the seller's premises: Hillmann and Rachlinski, 'Standard-Form Contracting in the Electronic Age', 477, 485.

152 Kim, *Wrap Contracts*, p. 162; *Green* v. *Petfre (Gibraltar) Limited t/a Betfred* [2021] EWHC 842 (QB) [167], [172].

153 In *Green* v. *Petfre (Gibraltar) Limited t/a Betfred* it was assumed by the judge that terms governing use of the platform were incorporated through click-wrap [125]–[126] and [171]–[172]. The terms were held invalid under common law and the Consumer Rights Act 2015 s 64 (3) at [176]. See also *Spreadex Ltd* v. *Cochrane* [2012] EWHC 1290 at [14].

here has been problematic ever since Lord Denning grappled with the concepts of offer and acceptance in a multi-storey car park in *Thornton* v. *Shoe Lane Parking Ltd.*[154] A contractual agreement concerning use of the car parking facilities – incorporating matters such as fees, procedure for paying, use of the spaces, parking in designated areas, length of stay, maximum stay, extent of land owner's liability for loss or injury during use of the premises, consent to use of cameras and automatic number plate recognition technology, consent to driver identification and tracing through the relevant licencing authorities, liabilities for additional parking charges, methods of enforcement, identity of enforcers and enforcement fees – is created simply by an act of driving into the car park and parking one's car.[155] Transgression results in the imposition of financial penalties. Since the company administering the facility usually has no authority to levy fines, these are described as parking 'charges', imposed and enforced through the creation of a contractual relationship established through acceptance and consent.[156] Common law procedural controls will be concerned with whether reasonable notice of the terms has been given to the other party and whether terms are 'onerous' such that the company is required to take additional steps to ensure incorporation.[157] Protective legislation against unfair terms notionally also applies, under section 62 of the Consumer Rights Act 2015. The decision in *ParkingEye* demonstrates that the controls in the statute may have limited effect.

Notwithstanding the potential for legal control of the contract content, there are some troubling aspects in deploying the contract normative framework to facilitate and justify enforcement of the obligations of the car park user. The payments extracted from parking transgressors, including enforcement costs, produce income for private companies administering car parks. The administrators are therefore incentivised to develop various revenue-

[154] [1971] 2 QB 163.

[155] See David Campbell and Roger Halson, 'By Their Fruits Shall Ye Know Them' (2020) 79 *Cambridge Law Journal* 405, relating the unreported case of *One Parking Solution Ltd* v. *W* (5 February 2020) Lewes County Court, where it was held on the facts that the defendant had not 'parked' and therefore could not incur parking charges.

[156] Department for Transport, *Guidance on Section 56 and Schedule 4 of the Protection of Freedoms Act 2012: Recovery of Unpaid Parking Charges* (September 2012) s 7.1; *ParkingEye* v. *Beavis*, above n. 11, at [108].

[157] *J Spurling Ltd* v. *Bradshaw* [1956] 1 WLR 461; *Interfoto Picture Library Ltd* v. *Stiletto Visual Programmes Ltd* [1989] QB 433. For a recent failure of incorporation on this ground see *Green* v. *Petfre (Gibralter) Ltd t/a Betfred* [167].

generating schemes that are legitimised through contract and autonomy norms. This mechanism of contracting can enlarge the customer's contractual obligations considerably and to an indeterminate and unidentifiable group of counterparties to whom various aspects of the enterprise have been outsourced. Even if the parking company contracts directly with the customer, the private company outsources payment collection to an enforcing company, the enforcing company may outsource legal work in debt recovery to law firms, and so on, increasing the customer's liabilities at every stage.

Contract practices such as these have been questioned in other contexts. In an investigation of abuses in the leasehold housing market, the Competition and Markets Authority (CMA) noted that the leaseholder does not get anything in return for their obligation to pay ground rent, the entire purpose of which is to generate an income stream for the investment companies to whom freeholds are transferred by developers. The freeholder's rights are administered through managing agents who readily escalate ground rents, permission fees, lease extension and enfranchisement fees, relying on contract terms that permit this.[158] It was found that the supposed justifications for ground rent worked only to the benefit of the freeholder (for example, to permit further land purchases and developments) There was little benefit, only detriment, to the leaseholder. The argument that ground rent allows the initial purchase price of the house to be lower was not found to be substantiated by the CMA.[159] The point here is not to enter into a debate about the unconscionability or otherwise of these charges but to identify how contract mechanisms are used to create liabilities often in contravention of some relatively basic contract norms. The simplicity of the transaction and exchange belies the complexity that is generated by the use of the contract framework. More broadly, the message conveyed by the law is that parties can privatise the remedies for breach of contract in various ways, or extract other payments, all implemented through the operation of contract terms.[160] As we have seen in relation to penalties, there will be scant consideration of the contract policy that remedies should be compensatory, nor the broader and more worrying social welfare issues raised by the encroachment of contract norms into most aspects of social and economic existence.

158 Competition and Markets Authority, *Leasehold Housing: Update Report* CMA 115 (February 2020), para 76.

159 CMA, *Leasehold Housing: Update Report*, para 77(c).

160 Seana V. Shiffrin, 'Remedial Clauses: The Overprivatization of Private Law' (2016) 67 *Hastings Law Journal* 407, 410 and 420–21.

3.4 Conclusion

The removal of consumer contracts (or aspects of them) from common law control, together with some strong critiques of a more flexible, dynamic and contextual contract law, has seen the reassertion by judges of a formal, classical and commercially oriented law. The result is a common law of contract that perceives itself primarily as the enforcer of systems of self-regulation. We examine this further in the next chapter. Excessive attention to commercial concerns (and the one-dimensional view of contract law that results) does not just cause a problem for contract theory (much has to be excluded from the contract realm in order to make the theories work) but also for case determination. This is displayed in the tendency to take considerations resonating with commercial contractors and conflate them into a set of contract law imperatives or foundational ideas that are allowed to inform common law reasoning in almost all circumstances. This has a particularly deleterious effect on common law's capacity to address problems in consumer contracting.

The commercial and formalist turn in contract is poor timing, given the importance of contract to the current organisation of society and economy. Despite bestowing validity on elements of the bureaucratic contract model upon which modern contracting rests, much of our contracting activity escapes serious legal scrutiny. We see very little common law engagement with some pressing issues surrounding modern contracting (such as the imposition of contractual obligations by stealth, the weakening of consent, the use of contracts for questionable purposes). In addition, when such issues do come before a court, a formal and commercially oriented style of contract law tends to place the interpretation of express terms and party autonomy at the centre of the analysis, with minimal consideration of wider contextual issues, such as how a contractualised society undermines many of the assumptions upon which classical contract law rests or how public policy factors impinge on a contract problem. Of course, a contractualised society need not depend on contract law for contracts regulation. In the next chapter we consider this in the context of processes that have supplemented, and in some cases replaced, common law rules. These alternatives to traditional law have contributed to contract law's diminishing scope and raise considerable doubts about any future role for common law as a general regulator of contracts.

4

Private Ordering, Regulation and Contract Law

The finding that traditional common law rules of contract operate on a shrinking canvas is hardly revelatory. Legislative intervention and the advent of specific regulatory regimes across multiple fields, together with the establishment of specialist tribunals to hear disputes, have reduced the range of application for the traditional principles of contract law, as well as the opportunities for generalist judges to consider those principles during adjudication. Many contract claims will be classified and resolved according to whether they raise an issue of employment rights, residential property, competition law and so on. It would take a long and slow process of appeal for decisions on these matters to reach the senior courts where the general implications (if any) of the case for contract law could be drawn out and considered. Even across the more natural territory for the operation of general law – commercial and consumer contracts – the common law is of dwindling significance. Traditional contract law rules have been substituted with various private arrangements in the case of commercial contractors and specific market regulation for consumer contracting. We explore these developments in this chapter.

It has long been recognised that contracting is supported by a wide variety of social norms and institutions that supplement, and occasionally replace, the rules of contract law. In the commercial sphere, the alternatives to state-provided contract law rules and legal enforcement are well known and diverse. These range from general rule systems that seek to compete with national contract law rules by offering formal or informal transnational alternatives suitable for cross-border contracting (for example, the UN Convention on the International Sale of Goods 1980, a modern incarnation of the lex mercatoria) to more tailored rule sets and dispute resolution procedures promulgated by global trade associations operating in specific markets.[1] Transnational rule

[1] See, for example, Wioletta Konradi, 'The Role of Lex Mercatoria in Supporting Globalized Transactions: An Empirical Insight into the Governance Structure of the Timber Industry' in

systems are law-like in constitution and are often the result of international co-operation efforts between states. As such, they are not the main focus of concern in this chapter, notwithstanding that they may be intended to substitute for the operation of domestic legal rules.[2] The activities of trade associations, industry governing bodies and professional organisations in producing group norms to function as a form of institutionalised trust between participants is of much more interest here.[3] Such groups may wield quasi-legal authority within a market or sector by imposing norms via 'private legislation'[4] promulgated through standardised contract documentation, model forms and rule-books, codes of conduct, statements of professional standards and the like.[5] These methods represent a form of private contract regulation. The shift from public rules to private ordering is further exacerbated by the prevalent use of arbitration to resolve disputes in commercial contracts.[6] Arbitration conducted through various institutions drawing on the 'merchant court' ideal has been a feature of commercial contracting for centuries. The privatisation of rule creation allows the state to shed the direct (and expensive) administration of rule-making, monitoring and enforcement.

Volkmar Gessner (ed.) *Contractual Certainty in International Trade* (Hart Publishing, 2009), p. 49; Lisa Bernstein, 'Opting Out of the Legal System: Extralegal Contractual Relations in the Diamond Industry' (1992) 21 *Journal of Legal Studies* 115; Lisa Bernstein, 'Private Commercial Law in the Cotton Industry: Creating Co-operation through Rules, Norms and Institutions' (2001) 99 *Michigan Law Review* 1724; Thomas Dietz, *Global Order beyond Law* (Hart Publishing, 2014), pp. 167–72.

2 For helpful summaries and taxonomies of the different types, see John Linarelli, 'Global Legal Pluralism and Commercial Law' in Paul Schiff Berman (ed.) *Oxford Handbook on Global Legal Pluralism* (Oxford University Press, 2020), p. 689; Ingeborg Schwenzer, 'Global Unification of Contract Law' (2016) 21 *Uniform Law Review* 60; Ross Cranston, 'Theorizing Transnational Commercial Law' (2007) 42 *Texas International Law Journal* 597. See also Roger Cotterell, 'Transnational Communities and the Concept of Law' (2008) 21 *Ratio Juris* 1, 3.

3 Hugh Collins, 'Regulatory Competition in International Trade: Transnational Regulation through Standard Form Contracts' in Horst Eidenmüller (ed.) *Regulatory Competition in Contract Law and Dispute Resolution* (Verlag C H Beck, Hart Publishing, Nomos, 2013), pp. 121, 123; Joanne P. Braithwaite, 'Standard Form Contracts as Transnational Law: Evidence from the Derivatives Markets' (2012) 75 *Modern Law Review* 779.

4 Michael Bridge, 'Exceptions Clauses and Contractual Frustration Clauses' (2020) 136 *Law Quarterly Review* 1, 3.

5 Roger Brownsword, Rob A. J. van Gestel and Hans-W Micklitz (eds.), *Contract and Regulation: A Handbook on New Methods of Law Making in Private Law* (Edward Elgar Publishing, 2017), p. 10. See also Ronald J. Gilson, Charles F. Sabel and Robert E. Scott, 'Contract and Innovation: The Limited Role of Generalist Courts in the Evolution of Novel Contract Forms' (2013) 88 *New York University Law Review* 170, 176–77.

6 This ousting of common law courts and jurisdiction has been sanctioned at least since *Scott* v. *Avery* (1856) 5 HLC 810 where an arbitration clause was held effective.

This move also serves to reinforce the view that private ordering is the superior method for structuring economic exchange, with contract law as a last resort gap filler, or at best a limited corrective to any failures in private ordering.[7] The increasing institutionalised nature of private ordering through industry-specific standard contract terms, codes, compliance and monitoring procedures prompts questions concerning the impact of private ordering on contract law development.[8]

If private ordering has assumed law-like functions in the commercial sphere, market-specific regulation has performed a similar role, albeit through very different methods, in the consumer sphere. Many areas traditionally governed by the application of contract law rules, such as the control of unfair terms in contract, fall now within the remit of regulators such as the Financial Conduct Authority (FCA) and the Competition and Markets Authority (CMA). Regulation may interact with law in various ways. Regulators may take disputes before a court, usually when there is a legal question concerning the scope of their regulatory powers or their interpretation of the law as it affects a regulated business. They may also resort to court action to remedy breaches of law and regulation by firms. In general, regulators do not act on behalf of individuals, nor seek to uphold individual legal rights. Instead, they may force regulated businesses to institute mass customer redress regimes in the case of market-wide failures,[9] or they may take various other enforcement measures against firms. Regulators will use their delegated powers of norm creation to promulgate a form of soft law (guidance, principles, codes) that rarely requires judicial interpretation or substantive legal oversight and that may not give rise to substantive legal rights for individuals.

Direct regulation is supplemented by the actions of independent organisations, including charities and other private entities, that provide assistance with enforcement of consumer contracts (for example, the Consumers'

[7] Avery W. Katz, 'Taking Private Ordering Seriously' (1996) 144 *University of Pennsylvania Law Review* 1745, 1747.

[8] See generally, Katz, 'Taking Private Ordering Seriously', 1745. On the effectiveness of group norms, see Robert D. Cooter, 'Decentralized Law for a Complex Economy' (1994) 23 *Southwestern University Law Review* 443; 'Decentralized Law for a Complex Economy: The Structural Approach to Adjudicating the New Law Merchant' (1996) 144 *University of Pennsylvania Law Review* 1643; contra, Eric A. Posner, 'Law, Economics and Inefficient Norms' (1996) 144 *University of Pennsylvania Law Review* 1697.

[9] For example, the payment protection insurance (PPI) scandal in the United Kingdom, which generated some ten million complaints against banks and other providers: Ned Beale, 'Access to Financial Justice: Three Financial Services Conduct Scandals, and a Proposal for Reform' (2018) 33 *Journal of International Banking Law and Regulation* 153.

Association) or that offer dispute resolution services.[10] Individual complaints may be processed and resolved through various private fora that do not necessarily rely on legal principles in decision-making. Nor do these for a generate authoritative rulings that would bind other decision-makers. The various ombudsmen services are an example.[11] Ombudsman schemes deal chiefly with individual complaints arising in selected areas of the economy and society. There are ombudsmen operating in relation to privatised industries and utilities, higher education, financial and legal services, and various public services covering housing, health, local government and the police.

Private ordering and regulation evince very different forms of contract governance. Nevertheless, in terms of their relationship to contract law, some similar themes emerge. In what follows we draw out the effect of private ordering and regulation on contract law development and explore their troublesome relationship with contract doctrine. This relationship is paradoxical and ambivalent. Both regulation and private ordering rely on general contract law to a significant degree, while also resisting many of its rules and norms. Similarly, judges often ignore the regulatory context in which a contract operates, unless the regulatory framework is specifically relevant to the case. Even where relevant, the different rationales behind the common law rules of contract on the one hand and regulatory regimes on the other create 'overlapping jurisdictions' in the same field.[12] Divergences between the regulatory approach to contract enforcement and the applicable contract law rules generate confusion over the deeper normative message to be communicated about acceptable behaviour for those simultaneously subject to the general law and the specific regulation. Legal reasoning around the operation of regulations can also undermine general regulatory objectives. We return to this point later in the chapter, when we contrast the FCA review concerning the mis-sale of interest rate hedging products to 'unsophisticated' customers with case law on misrepresentation covering the corresponding scenario under the common law. Ultimately, the diversity and richness of the myriad structures that

10 Department for Business, Energy and Industrial Strategy, *Resolving Consumer Disputes – Alternative Dispute Resolution and the Court System: Final Report* (April 2018). The report noted that there were approximately ninety-five consumer ADR schemes operating in the United Kingdom in 2015, at p. 10.

11 www.ombudsmanassociation.org/about-where-ombudsmen-work.php

12 Cotterell, 'Transnational Communities', 7; Sally Engle Merry, 'Legal Pluralism' (1988) 22 *Law and Society Review* 869, 870; Bronwen Morgan and Karen Yeung, *An Introduction to Law and Regulation* (Cambridge University Press, 2007), p. 4.

facilitate productive exchange do not make contract law richer, more diverse, more nuanced and responsive but only more insular, inflexible and reactive.

4.1 Private Ordering and Contract Law

Private ordering, broadly defined, describes a process of rule-making and enforcement not derived directly from state authority to create law, nor dependent on the state's monopoly on the use of force. It encompasses a variety of bottom-up, market-based regimes that avoid the application of state-imposed rules in favour of the norms and practices generated from within the relevant community.[13] Legitimacy of the system usually derives from consensus to submit to the norms amongst those affected by them, supported by reputational sanctioning or other forms of informal remedy in case of default.[14] This form of enforcement is of course not confined to private ordering in a commercial setting. Consumers can engage in a degree of reputational sanctioning by sharing their experiences of dealing with firms through various online platforms. More seriously, negative publicity is often the first sanction deployed by a regulatory body against non-compliant businesses, particularly those with a high public profile,[15] or where non-compliance involves a breach of criminal law.[16]

More formal regimes of private ordering are often implemented through contracts. Private ordering may be facilitated by contracting, but this does not necessarily entail a strong commitment to *contract law* for regulation, enforcement or dispute resolution in the resulting relationships. The precise aim of private ordering is often to dispense with the machinery of courts and positive law.[17] Once background authority is assured through entry into a contract that the law recognises as enforceable, the private regime may operate more or less

[13] Barak D. Richman, 'Firms, Courts, and Reputation Mechanisms: Towards a Positive Theory of Private Ordering' (2004) 104 *Columbia Law Review* 2328, 2336–37; Katz, 'Taking Private Ordering Seriously', 1745; Gregory C. Shaffer, 'How Business Shapes Law: A Socio-Legal Framework' (2009) 42 *Connecticut Law Review* 147, 162.

[14] Steven L. Schwarcz, 'Private Ordering' 97 (2002) *Northwestern University Law Review* 319, 327. Famous studies of such systems include Robert C. Ellickson, *Order Without Law* (Harvard University Press 1994); Bernstein, 'Opting Out of the Legal System: Extralegal Contractual Relations in the Diamond Industry', 115; Dietz, *Global Order Beyond Law*, pp. 167–72.

[15] Such as supermarkets, see Antony Seely, *Supermarkets: The Groceries Code Adjudicator*, HC Briefing Paper 6124 (12 November 2015), p. 9.

[16] Peter Cartwright, 'Publicity, Punishment and Protection: The Role(s) of Adverse Publicity in Consumer Policy' (2012) 32 *Legal Studies* 179, 183–85.

[17] Richman, 'Firms, Courts, and Reputation Mechanisms', 2329.

independently of the legal system, thus presenting a functional alternative to it.[18] Trade associations and industry representative bodies are particularly significant in generating normative frameworks for contracting through standard contract forms and other contract documentation. These institutions, and the contract forms they produce, constitute a type of private law regime,[19] which includes authoritative processes for resolving conflict.[20] Trade associations, or individual firms, may also assume the role of a private regulator, responsible for policing the conduct of participants in the trade, occasionally at the direction of government or other public regulatory body that oversees the relevant market.[21]

The advantages to businesses engaging in effective self-regulation through contracts are manifest, especially in the area of dispute resolution.[22] Rules and procedures created and enforced by market or industry experts should be easier and quicker to administer, and yield more predictable outcomes, than the corresponding legal principles.[23] These private rules are substitutes for the law insofar as they perform functions of facilitation of the exchange (standard forms), regulation (internally generated norms, circulated through standard forms, rule-books and so on) and enforcement (specialist industry dispute resolution). Nevertheless, there are drawbacks to this form of market-generated authority. Lack of competition for the rule set (for example, UCP600 on documentary credits or the International Swaps and Derivatives Association [ISDA] Master Agreement) is a factor in according these regimes the kind of authoritative status normally reserved for legal rules.[24] While not having the legal power to compel compliance with the promulgated norms, effective coercion is still possible by the sizable impediments to contracting on an alternative basis. Standard forms generated within a market constitute a form of private legislation that is not easily resisted by any individual

[18] Schwarcz, 'Private Ordering', 324–29.

[19] Annelise Riles, 'The Anti-Network: Private Global Governance, Legal Knowledge, and the Legitimacy of the State' (2008) 56 *American Journal of Comparative Law* 605, 606.

[20] Collins, 'Regulatory Competition in International Trade', p. 122.

[21] Rory Van Loo, 'The New Gatekeepers: Private Firms as Public Enforcers' (2020) 106 *Virginia Law Review* 467. An example is the 'customer due diligence' requirements placed on banks and other financial institutions under the Money Laundering, Terrorist Financing and Transfer of Funds (Information on the Payer) Regulations 2017.

[22] Richman, 'Firms, Courts, and Reputation Mechanisms', 2341ff.

[23] Richman, 'Firms, Courts, and Reputation Mechanisms', 2342. See also Bernstein, 'Private Commercial Law in the Cotton Industry: Creating Co-operation through Rules, Norms and Institutions', 1724.

[24] David V. Snyder, 'Private Law Making' (2003) 64 *Ohio State Law Journal* 371, 377, 389 and 411.

contractor,[25] rendering the use of the form essentially non-optional.[26] Lock-in effects may be created for existing members, with possibilities of collusion, anti-competitive behaviour and discrimination.[27] Though the validity of the standard form may depend ultimately on the operation of national laws (such forms may opt into English contract law as the governing law[28]), the intention nevertheless is that such contracts operate with relative autonomy from the legal processes of the state, effectively ousting the operation of national law.[29] Engagement with the legal system is therefore likely to be limited, arising only where there is some unanticipated global crisis[30] or where aspects of the form require legal interpretation to provide certainty in a particular market.

The project to disengage substantially from the legal system is assisted by courts manifesting considerable reluctance to intervene in the operation of standard forms backed by powerful trade associations, particularly those used in global markets. The judicial policy of non-interference can be justified on the basis that freedom of contract entails that courts do not exercise a policing role over the contract form using the independent standards of the law. The courts' role is an interpretative one: working out what the terms mean, if asked, and determining whether a course of action taken by one party is in accordance with the 'rules' as set out in the standard form.[31] The importance placed on commercial certainty means that courts are not likely to interfere with meanings attributed to the contract provisions amongst the parties that use them. This attitude of standard contract deference is problematic. Conducting the entirety of productive activity largely outside the confines of the legal system of a nation state raises issues about legitimacy, accountability and the rule of law. There are three particular considerations.

[25] Michael Bridge, 'Good Faith, the Common law and the CISG' (2017) 22 *Uniform Law Review* 98, 104; Mitu Gulati and Robert E. Scott, *The 3½ Minute Transaction* (University of Chicago Press, 2013), p. 33ff; Jeffrey B. Golden, 'Setting Standards in the Evolution of Swap Documentation' (1994) 13 *International Financial Law Review* 18.

[26] Richman, 'Firms, Courts, and Reputation Mechanisms', 2339.

[27] Richman, 'Firms, Courts, and Reputation Mechanisms', 2347; See also Posner, 'Law, Economics and Inefficient Norms'.

[28] See, for example, Bridge, 'Good Faith, the Common Law and the CISG', 103 on GAFTA standard terms.

[29] Collins, 'Regulatory Competition in International Trade', p. 125.

[30] Braithwaite, 'Standard Form Contracts as Transnational Law', 790, describing the increase in litigation on the effectiveness of the ISDA Master Agreement remedies regime following the global financial crisis.

[31] *Lehman Brothers Finance AG (in liquidation)* v. *Klaus Tschira Stiftung GMBH & Anor* [2019] EWHC 379 [162]ff, [166] and [174].

First, the fact that a rule has evolved from trade usage or is mandated by a standard form developed by industry insiders may be a reliable indicator that the rule is familiar but not that the rule is normatively defensible. The norms of any social or economic group are likely to reflect the interests of its dominant members rather than a fair compromise between all the participants in the collective.[32] A standard contract promulgated by a trade association may allow the imposition onto the weaker actor of the processes and obligations mandated by the stronger party. Second, an association promulgating its own industry-wide dispute resolution procedure may render that procedure essentially compulsory, putting trade rules and practices beyond the scope of legal oversight and the conduct of the association outside effective legal control. This preference for privacy and insulation from the external control of the legal system will usually be deliberate. Third, to the extent that a powerful international trade association does engage with the law, it is likely to lobby hard with law-makers to protect its contract norms from legal intervention, irrespective of the effect on third parties, the public interest or social welfare. The result is that if an industry standard form is reviewed during litigation, courts may be very reluctant to interfere in its operation or disturb industry understandings concerning the effects of terms.[33] Standard forms may therefore depart from contract law in material respects without serious challenge from the national legal system. The law's capitulation to private ordering may not necessarily be motivated by freedom of contract (even if this is how it is presented on the surface) but by exogenous factors such as the desire to be seen as a receptive and friendly legal home for the operation of a market.[34] Notwithstanding that private ordering is 'always conditioned by enabling and limiting legal rules and is thus embedded in a specific legal framework',[35] the relationship between national law and private ordering may not be one of legal pre-eminence but a kind of mutually beneficial equilibrium.[36]

[32] Posner, 'Law, Economics and Inefficient Norms', 1718; Maria Larrain and Jens Prufer, 'Trade Associations, Lobbying, and Endogenous Institutions' (2015) 7 *Journal of Legal Analysis* 467, 471ff.

[33] See Bridge, 'Exception Clauses and Contractual Frustration Clauses', 3.

[34] John Biggins and Colin Scott, 'Public-Private Relations in a Transnational Private Regulatory Regime: ISDA, the State and OTC Derivatives Market Reform' (2012) 13 *European Business Organization Law Review* 309, 336.

[35] Horst Eidenmüller, 'Regulatory Competition in Contract Law and Dispute Resolution' in Horst Eidenmüller (ed.) *Regulatory Competition in Contract Law and Dispute Resolution* (Verlag C H Beck, Hart Publishing, Nomos, 2013), pp. 1, 5–6.

[36] Shaffer, 'How Business Shapes Law', 169.

4.2 An Illustration: The ISDA Master Agreement

We can illustrate some of these arguments about private ordering by examining ISDA. ISDA has been credited with preventing the return to older, more restrictive common law regulatory approaches to derivatives trading in the wake of the global financial crisis.[37] This arises out of ISDA's development and custodianship of a standard form contract – the ISDA Master Agreement – which governs around 90 per cent of trading in over-the-counter (OTC) financial derivatives. It has been asserted that the ISDA contract standardisation project has been 'highly successful in assuring public actors that the OTC derivatives industry was ... capable of largely self-regulating'.[38] On the face of it, drafting and promulgating a popular standard form appears fairly benign, but ISDA now wields significant power over the regulation of the OTC derivatives market. While founded primarily to develop a standard form contract to facilitate derivatives trading, the organisation has now morphed into an effective lobby group that actively seeks to ensure national law does not supplant the terms of the ISDA Master Agreement or interfere in the operation of the market.[39]

There is some evidence coming out of the English courts pointing to ISDA's success in this regard.[40] ISDA often acts as 'amicus curiae' or 'advocate to the court', advising on technical matters during litigation concerning the Master Agreement.[41] It acted in the capacity of third-party intervener both at first instance and in the Court of Appeal in *Lomas & Ors* v. *JFB Firth Rixson Inc.*[42] In this case the Court of Appeal was required to rule on the operation of certain provisions of the Master Agreement. After some inconsistent approaches in the lower courts, the case has, according to one commentator, 'restored, more or less intact, to its status quo ante the common understanding of market practitioners as to how the ISDA Master Agreement works following an Event of Default'.[43] The importance of maintaining participant expectations around the operation of the Master Agreement has recently been confirmed by the Court of Appeal in *CFH Clearing Ltd* v. *Merrill Lynch*

[37] Biggins and Scott, 'Public-Private Relations', 322.
[38] Biggins and Scott, 'Public-Private Relations', 323.
[39] Biggins and Scott, 'Public-Private Relations', 328–29; Riles, 'The Anti-network', 614–15.
[40] See generally Braithwaite, 'Standard Form Contracts as Transnational Law', 785ff and 788.
[41] See Supreme Court Rules 2009, r 35 (2009 No. 1603 (L. 17)).
[42] *Lomas & Ors* v. *JFB Firth Rixson Inc* [2012] EWCA Civ 419.
[43] Edward Murray, 'Lomas v Firth Rixson: "As you were!"' (2013) 8 *Capital Markets Law Journal* 395, 395; Braithwaite, 'Standard Form Contracts as Transnational Law', 800ff.

International.[44] In this case, contracting on the terms of the Master Agreement precluded the parties from relying on any more general market practice that may have impinged on their transaction.[45] The Court of Appeal endorsed[46] the statement of Mr Justice Briggs at first instance in *Lomas*:

> The ISDA Master Agreement is one of the most widely used forms of agreement in the world. It is probably the most important standard market agreement used in the financial world ... It is axiomatic that it should as far as possible, be interpreted in a way that serves the objectives of clarity, certainty and predictability, so that the very large number of parties using it should know where they stand.[47]

Resistance to legal interference in the operation of the standard form may extend so far as to make the form practically impervious to a negative assessment of legality by courts.[48] Individual terms in the ISDA Master Agreement, such as the basis clauses we examined in the last chapter, are difficult to challenge.[49] Maintaining the relative stability of the form as a tool of co-ordination and facilitation may be more important to courts than an authoritative determination of legal validity, given that the function of the form is to speed up the transacting process almost to the point of automation.[50]

Nevertheless, there are arguments against prioritising too highly the interests of the trade association. Firstly, it has been shown that ISDA's governance structure is over-represented with banks and intermediaries at the expense of a much more diffuse collection of end-users and investors.[51] This allows the association to further the self-interest of its prominent members over other market participants and essentially create a monopoly over the rules on which OTC derivatives are traded.[52] Less economically powerful participants in the

44 [2020] EWCA Civ 1064. 45 Above n. 44, at [41] and [48].

46 The Court of Appeal in *CFH* v. *Merrill Lynch* repeats Mr Justice Briggs's quote at [38] and endorses it at [41].

47 [2010] EWHC 3372 (Ch) at [53].

48 Gulati and Scott, *The 3½ Minute Transaction*; Omri Ben-Shahar and John A. E. Pottow, 'On the Stickiness of Default Rules' (2006) 33 *Florida State University Law Review* 651.

49 *Marz Ltd* v. *Bank of Scotland plc* [2017] EWHC 3618 (Ch).

50 Gulati and Scott, *The 3½ Minute Transaction*, pp. 10–11.

51 Braithwaite, 'Standard Form Contracts as Transnational Law', 798.

52 Frank Partnoy and David A. Skeel Jr, 'The Promise and Perils of Credit Derivatives' (2007) 75 *University of Cincinnati Law Review* 1019, 1037ff; Maciej Borowicz, 'Private Power and International Law: The International Swaps and Derivatives Association' (2015) 8 *European Journal of Legal Studies* 46, 60ff, particularly on the operation of ISDA's Credit Determination Committees.

market are under-represented in ISDA and in the litigation over the meaning of the forms.[53] Given this, the standard form may not necessarily represent the interests of all stakeholders.

Secondly, while freedom of contract suggests that disputes involving the standard contract terms should be resolved in accordance with party autonomy (insofar as not offending any mandatory rules), important policy issues may arise that are obscured by the culture of judicial deference to the form. Consider, for example, one of the legal issues arising in the wake of the collapse of Lehman Brothers: the tension between national insolvency laws (which will often vary in their provisions) and the 'flip clauses' contained in the synthetic collateralized debt obligations made on the terms of the ISDA Master Agreement. These clauses altered the legal rules concerning priority of payments to creditors on insolvency. Did this contractual amendment to the common law offend the anti-deprivation rule of insolvency in English law? The validity of the flip clause was considered in *Belmont Park Investments PTY Ltd* v. *BNY Corporate Trustee Services Ltd.*[54] Lord Collins remarked that

> party autonomy is at the heart of English commercial law ... it is desirable that, so far as possible, the courts give effect to contractual terms which parties have agreed. And there is a particularly strong case for autonomy in cases of complex financial instruments such as those involved in this appeal ... [E]xcept in the case of a blatant attempt to deprive a party of property in the event of liquidation ... the modern tendency has been to uphold commercially justifiable contractual provisions which have been said to offend the anti-deprivation rule.[55]

The economic logic of the term as a risk allocation mechanism, as opposed to a bad faith and deliberate evasion of the common law rules on insolvency, persuaded the judges that the term was valid.[56] This does not consider the

[53] Stephen J. Choi and G. Mitu Gulati, 'Contract as Statute' (2006) 104 *Michigan Law Review* 1129, 1132.

[54] *Belmont Park Investments PTY Ltd* v. *BNY Corporate Trustee Services Ltd and Lehman Brothers Special Financing Inc* [2011] 3 WLR 521. For a brief explanation of the common law rules at issue, see Roy Goode, 'Perpetual Trustee and Flip Clauses in Swap Transactions' (2011) 127 *Law Quarterly Review* 1, 3–4.

[55] *Belmont Park* n. 54 [104]–[105].

[56] See Hugh Collins, 'Flipping Wreck: Lex Mercatoria on the Shoals of Ius Cogens' in Stefan Grundmann, Florian Möslein and Karl Riesenhuber (eds.) *Contract Governance: Dimensions in Law and Interdisciplinary Research* (Oxford University Press, 2015), pp. 383, 398–99; Dan Wielsch, 'Global Law's Toolbox: Private Regulation by Standards' (2012) 60 *American Journal of Comparative Law* 1075, 1088–91.

broader implications of the policy choice to allow parties to contract around what in other contexts are mandatory rules of law by using the express terms of the contract. The context of the cases means that judges are not engaging with any common law contract doctrine, except that of interpretation of standard forms.[57] The legal enforceability bestowed on the standard form by national contract law validates both the form *and the Association* as an institutional rival to national contract law. One effect of this is the 'embedding [of] private norms within national hard law'.[58] Legal validity bestows legitimacy on ISDA norms and ISDA as a rule-creating body that commands obedience.[59] The broader danger here is that the 'law' is whatever is accepted and promulgated by the relevant trade association or body whose rules are up for consideration. Agreements are not enforced by the power of the law but by the conventions of the relevant contracting and interpretative community that develops (or dictates) the rules. Thus, ISDA (and the British Bankers Association) have been described as the de facto 'regulators' of the OTC derivatives market.[60]

A system of contract law that defers to regimes of self-regulation created by others is easily captured by those regimes. Fewer opportunities are presented for legal development, since the law does not challenge, or will only challenge on very limited grounds, the commercial private ordering arrangements brought before it. Contract law capture by commercial interests compromises the judicial ability to scrutinise, criticise and evaluate standards in commercial activity from a position of independence. In addition, given the lack of differentiation in common law between contracting parties and contract types, a non-interventionist approach to one kind of contract is easily embedded as the general interpretative standard to be applied and transplanted across all contracts, including those to which such an approach is manifestly unsuited.

[57] Joanne P. Braithwaite, 'Law after Lehmans', LSE Law, Society and Economy Working Papers 11/2014, pp. 8ff and 16ff; see *Re Lehman Brothers International (Europe)* v. *Lehman Brothers Finance SA* [2013] EWCA Civ 188; Alireza M. Gharagozlou, 'Unregulable: Why Derivatives May Never Be Regulated' (2010) 4 *Brooklyn Journal of Corporate Financial and Commercial Law* 269, 271ff.

[58] Biggins and Scott, 'Public-Private Relations', 334; Donal Casey and Colin Scott, 'The Crystallization of Regulatory Norms' (2011) 38 *Journal of Law and Society* 76, 77.

[59] Biggins and Scott, 'Public-Private Relations', 333.

[60] Gabriel V. Rauterberg and Andrew Verstein, 'Assessing Transnational Private Regulation of the OTC Derivatives Market: ISDA, the BBA, and the Future of Financial Reform' (2013) 54 *Virginia Journal of International Law* 9, 11, see also p.19ff on how ISDA regulates the OTC derivatives market.

This serves only to reinforce the commercialisation of contract law and the primacy accorded to the autonomy norm.

4.3 Common Law and the Regulatory State

Regulation is a form of 'sustained and focused control' over economic activity 'by a public agency'.[61] The objective of this control is to modify the behaviour of individuals and firms to produce a particular set of outcomes.[62] Regulatory objectives will be many and diverse, not limited to market- or competition-oriented goals. A regulatory remit may encompass public-facing concerns with sustainability or the environment, or the promotion of aspirational goals and ethical commitments, such as equality and human rights protection. Though regulation usually emanates from state-created institutions exercising delegated powers conferred by legislation, regulation is increasingly undertaken by independent companies specially created by government for regulatory purposes.[63] Here, we are concerned with specific market regulation. This has assumed a primary role in contract enforcement and rule production, particularly in consumer contracting.

The rise of authoritative regulation via public agencies is inextricably linked to privatisation and the establishment of competitive markets for goods and services previously delivered by the state through public institutions.[64] The modern state has not diminished in consequence but rather evolved from direct provider to administrator and market overseer,[65] pursuing policy objectives at one remove through the work of regulatory agencies established by government. Privatisation has increased the importance of contracts as the mechanism for facilitating this market-based form of economic

[61] David Campbell, 'The "Market" in the Theory of Regulation' (2018) 27 *Social and Legal Studies* 545, 547; quoting Philip Selznick, 'Focusing Organisational Research on Regulation' in R. G. Noll (ed.) *Regulatory Policy and the Social Sciences* (University of California Press, 1985), p. 363; Anthony Ogus, *Regulation: Legal Form and Economic Theory* (Oxford University Press, 1994), p. 1.

[62] Julia Black, 'Decentring Regulation: Understanding the Role of Regulation and Self-Regulation in a "Post-Regulatory" World' (2001) 54 *Current Legal Problems* 103, 142.

[63] Terence Daintith, 'Government Companies as Regulators' (2019) 82 *Modern Law Review* 397, 406.

[64] John Braithwaite, 'The Regulatory State?' in Robert E. Goodin (ed.) *The Oxford Handbook of Political Science* (Oxford University Press, 2011), pp. 217, 220.

[65] John Braithwaite, 'The Regulatory State?', p. 220; Edward L. Rubin, 'From Coherence to Effectiveness: A Legal Methodology for the Modern World' in Rob van Gestel, Hans-W. Micklitz and Edward L. Rubin (eds.) *Rethinking Legal Scholarship: A Transatlantic Dialogue* (Cambridge University Press, 2017), pp. 310, 314.

organisation,[66] but regulation has ensured that the ideological trappings of traditional contract law – freedom of contract and party autonomy – have not been imported wholesale into the contracting process in these markets. Though predominantly established for consumer protection, any economic sector characterised by power imbalances between participants may be ripe for regulatory intervention. The intervention may restrict party autonomy and freedom of contract significantly. The Groceries Code Adjudicator,[67] for example, oversees the enforcement of the Groceries Supply Code of Practice between retailers (major supermarkets) and their suppliers.[68] The anti-competitive and exploitative supply-chain practices of the dominant supermarkets had long given rise to concern and complaints from suppliers and smaller retailers.[69] Retailer supply agreements must incorporate the Code and must not contain any provision inconsistent with the Code.[70] The Code includes obligations of good faith and places controls on contract terms, such as those dealing with a supermarket's power to vary the terms of its agreements with suppliers.[71] The regulator also administers a dispute resolution process.

On the face of it, there need be little overlap between common law and regulation. Nor should there be any problem with regulation eclipsing judicially created law. The animating ideals of regulation and the common law of contract are different and often incompatible. Regulators are not tasked with determining and enforcing individual legal rights but the pursuit of instrumental goals such as ensuring markets function fairly and competitively in the interests of participants, stakeholders and the public. Although operationally independent of government, regulation is a vehicle for implementation of government policy and objectives and thus not entirely free from government influence. Regulation is often presented as a supplement to the law, rather than a substantial legal alternative to it.[72] Judges adhere to this understanding, often

66 Ogus, *Regulation: Legal Form and Economic Theory*, pp. 1–2.

67 www.gov.uk/government/organisations/groceries-code-adjudicator established under the Groceries (Supply Chain Practices) Market Investigation Order 2009.

68 Available www.gov.uk/government/publications/groceries-supply-code-of-practice/groceries-supply-code-of-practice. See also Simon Whittaker, 'Unfair Terms in Commercial Contracts and the Two Laws of Competition: French Law and English Law Contrasted' in (2019) 39 *Oxford Journal of Legal Studies* 404.

69 Seely, *Supermarkets: The Groceries Code Adjudicator*, HC Briefing Paper 6124, p. 4.

70 Groceries (Supply Chain Practices) Market Investigation Order 2009 s 5(1).

71 See para 2 of the Code on good faith and para 3 on variation of the terms of supply agreements.

72 See, for example, Richard Samuel, 'Tools for Changing Banking Culture: FCA Are You Listening?' (2016) 11 *Capital Markets Law Journal* 129, 130.

ignoring the broader regulatory environment in which a dispute has arisen[73] or demonstrating reluctance to confer private law rights of action on individuals for breaches of regulatory requirements and rules.[74]

Unwillingness on the part of courts to regard the regulatory framework, where one exists, as an important element of the contractual context may reflect judicial appreciation of the different rationales behind law and regulation. Regulation is transparently concerned with the pursuit of collective goals, whereas in private (contract) law it is left to individuals to enforce the rights and obligations created by the contract. [75] Regulation is justified on the basis of functional criteria, not the moral theories within which we seek to locate and justify principles of law. Given these different rationales, divergence is unavoidable to a degree. It must be accepted that where regulation exists, and especially where the regulator has the power to force compliance and implement sanctions, the role of common law and the courts in promulgating general rules is much reduced. Clearly contract law operating and developing through litigated cases is rarely in a position to change or regulate entire markets,[76] although a judgment may answer a question of market-wide importance.[77] But divergence between law and regulation also produces problems. Regulators act according to the laws produced in courts and by statute, as well as their own rules developed under statutory authority. Given the possibility of occupation over substantially the same territory, there is potential for incoherence and inconsistency in how those laws are interpreted and applied by courts and regulators. Lack of attention to the regulatory scheme also reinforces the commercialisation of the common law of contract, endangering its generality. If consumers and other economically weaker parties are protected by legislative and regulatory schemes, there is little requirement for private law rights in contract to display a protectionist tendency. The values

[73] See Mr Justice Pelling in *TAQA Bratani Ltd* v. *RockRose UKCS8 LLC* [2020] 2 Lloyd's Rep 64, dismissing the broader regulatory context as irrelevant to the point of contract interpretation he had to decide: [39], [58]–[60]. Compare the regulatory emphasis on the need for collaboration in the industry: www.ogauthority co.uk/regulatory-framework/commercial-good-practice/

[74] See *Davis* v. *Lloyds Bank plc* [2021] EWCA Civ 557. The FCA is proposing that financial firms owe a duty of care to consumers, which would incorporate a duty to act in the customer's best interests: FCA, *Discussion Paper on a Duty of Care and Potential Alternative Approaches* DP 18/5 (July 2018).

[75] Ogus, *Regulation: Legal Form and Economic Theory*, pp. 2–3.

[76] Ogus, *Regulation: Legal Form and Economic Theory*, pp. 26–27; See also Andrei Shleifer, *The Failure of Judges and the Rise of Regulators* (MIT Press, 2012), p. 15.

[77] As seen recently with the business insurance test case: *Financial Conduct Authority* v. *Arch Insurance (UK) Ltd and others* [2021] 2 WLR 123.

underpinning the regulation, consumer protection for example, may make little impression on traditional contract law. In interpreting laws that bind regulators, or in determining the extent of regulatory powers and individual private law rights in a regulated field, courts can substantially undermine regulatory goals. We examine these issues below in relation to the main UK regulatory bodies with responsibility for consumer protection matters: the Financial Conduct Authority and the Competition and Markets Authority.

4.4 Divergence between Law and Regulation

The work of the CMA and FCA is administrative and market-oriented.[78] In keeping with their role as market overseers, neither the FCA nor the CMA offers dispute resolution or advice services to individual consumers or firms,[79] although they will receive information concerning lack of compliance in areas falling within their regulatory remit. Individual disputes with regulated businesses can be considered by various satellite organisations, such as the Financial Ombudsman Service. Regulators enjoy other powers to ensure compliance with the regulatory framework, which includes the relevant legislation on consumer rights (such as the Consumer Rights Act 2015) and competition law. Enforcement methods range from criminal sanctions (financial penalties) and reputational measures (negative publicity) to civil court actions seeking collective redress for consumers for breach of the rules[80] or to force businesses to comply with the rules. More conciliatory remedial outcomes are also available. In responding to unfair terms for example, the CMA and the FCA can seek undertakings from businesses to stop using unfair contract terms or to amend terms to achieve compliance.[81] The undertakings are a negotiated *contractual* settlement between regulator and business that need not involve any admission on the part of the business that its terms were unfair, nor an authoritative legal determination that the terms contravened legislation. Undertakings are an individualistic response to the problem of unfairness in contracts, and the precise nature of the undertaking will vary considerably between businesses. The terms of undertakings concerning future

78 The stated aim of the CMA is 'to make markets work well': Competition and Markets Authority, *Consumer Protection: Enforcement Guidance*, CMA 58, para 1.1.

79 See, for example, CMA *Consumer Protection: Enforcement Guidance*, para 2.10.

80 *Mastercard Incorporated* v. *Merricks* [2021] 3 All ER 285.

81 Consumer Rights Act 2015, Paragraph 6 Schedule 3; see also www.fca.org.uk/firms/unfair-contract-terms/library; and in relation to the CMA www.gov.uk/government/publications/consumer-enforcement-outcomes

conduct or the outcomes of investigations by the FCA may be kept confidential between the FCA and the business concerned.[82]

Enforcement of contractual rights and legal rights may vest in the regulator, as well as the individual consumer. However, the pursuit of action by regulators is concerned with the public interest in a way that may not encumber a court dealing with a contract dispute. Thus, CMA enforcement action is taken with regard to 'principles of good regulation', that is, 'proportionate; consistent; targeted; transparent and accountable'.[83] Regulators can also produce rules and enforceable codes of practice that impose standards on regulated firms that are quite alien to the common law. According to the FCA Handbook principles, a financial services firm must 'observe proper standards of market conduct'[84] and 'must pay due regard to the interests of its customers and treat them fairly'.[85] A regulated firm 'must act honestly, fairly and professionally in accordance with the best interests of its client'.[86] Although the duties owed under the FCA regime differ according to the financial sophistication of the client, responsibilities under the regulation are expressed in stronger terms than the more attenuated common law commitment that one contracting party may owe to the other in some circumstances: to act with *regard to* the counterparty's legitimate interests, which a contractor should take into account but is not required to prioritise.[87] Similarly, the CMA's proposed code of practice regulating the activities of powerful digital firms contains a suggested principle that their platforms 'trade on fair and reasonable contractual terms' in order to avoid exploiting platform users.[88] There is no corresponding general duty in the common law to trade on fair terms, only pockets of control on unfair terms exercised through doctrines such as incorporation, interpretation and implication. Regulators also enjoy widespread powers to investigate markets and to conduct research. Thus, the FCA has researched, amongst other things, the high-cost short-term credit market, which led to a cap on interest rates,[89] and how vulnerable consumers fare in

82 See *Davis* v. *Lloyds Bank plc*, above n. 74, [13].
83 CMA *Consumer Protection: Enforcement Guidance*, para 3.14.
84 Financial Conduct Authority, *Handbook – Principles for Business*, s 2.1.1, principle 5.
85 Financial Conduct Authority, *Handbook – Principles for Business*, s 2.1.1, principle 6.
86 Financial Conduct Authority, *Handbook – Conduct of Business Sourcebook* (COBS) 2.1.1.
87 *Barclays Bank PLC* v *Unicredit Bank AG & ANR* [2014] 2 Lloyd's Rep 59.
88 Competition and Markets Authority, *A New Pro-competition Regime for Digital Markets* CMA 135 (December 2020), para 4.35; and *Online Platforms and Digital Advertising: Market Study and Final Report* (1 July 2020), paras 7.76–7.77.
89 Financial Conduct Authority, *Detailed Rules for the Price Cap on High-cost Short-term Credit* PS14/16 (November 2014).

financial services markets.[90] The CMA has commissioned and published research into firms' understandings and attitudes to unfair terms,[91] as well as the operation of digital markets.[92] Such evidence is highly unlikely to find its way into a court's determination of legal rights.

Comprehensive regulation may reduce scope for the operation and enforcement of individual rights, but it does not render law redundant. Decisions of regulatory agencies are reviewable by courts under the ordinary principles of judicial review. Given the significance of administrative tribunals and regulation in modern economy, this judicial oversight is crucial. As some regulators readily acknowledge, the guidance they issue to firms on the law (on unfair terms in consumer contracts, for example) is based on their interpretation of what the law requires.[93] Authoritative determination of the legal position can usually only be given by a judge during legal proceedings. Counterintuitively, detailed and complex regulation is often limited and fragmented, leaving large gaps in the regulatory scheme that are plugged by default legal principles. The precise scope of regulation can be difficult to determine, and the distinction between the regulated and unregulated activities of firms (the 'regulatory perimeter') may be very fine, based on slender differences in fact that are unlikely to be appreciated or understood by a contracting counterparty or customer.[94] In terms of technique, regulation lacks the common law's capacity to generate broad principles that can be applied to novel situations by analogical reasoning.

In a number of respects therefore, the relationship between contract law and regulation is problematic. Regulation depends on pre-existing law while having a chilling effect on legal development. Regulatory controls may depart from general contract law in several important respects, giving rise to inconsistencies that are only partly explained by the differing purposes of vindicating individual rights in the common law and achieving policy objectives in the regulation. As a result, the common law and regulation can create an unpredictable legal background for contracting, conveying no clear and uniform educative message to society concerning acceptable standards of behaviour in markets. To illustrate this, we return to the mis-selling of interest rate hedging

[90] Financial Conduct Authority, *Understanding the Financial Lives of UK Adults* (2017, updated January 2020).

[91] BDRC Continental for the CMA, *SMEs & Unfair Contract Terms Qualitative Research Report* (11 January 2016); IFF Research, *Unfair Contract Terms Research* (19 October 2016).

[92] *Online Platforms and Digital Advertising: Market Study and Final Report* (1 July 2020) n. 88.

[93] For example, CMA, *Consumer Protection: Enforcement Guidance*, paras 1.4–1.5.

[94] See Dame Elizabeth Gloster, *Report of the Independent Investigation into the Financial Conduct Authority's Regulation of London Capital & Finance plc* (23 November 2020), Chapter 6.

products by banks to small businesses, noting the contrasting responses to this emanating from courts and regulators.

4.5 Swaps Mis-selling

Interest rate hedging products (swaps) are financial derivatives used to manage the risk posed by interest rate fluctuations in commercial borrowing. The sale of these products is regulated by the FCA. But the bank–client relationship is established by contract. Banks encouraged business customers with varying levels of sophistication to purchase swaps to manage the interest payable on underlying business loans. In some cases, entering into a swap agreement was a condition of obtaining finance, and the term of the swap could be longer than the underlying loan. The swap agreements were made with the expectation that interest rates would rise over the term of the swap. Following the series of base interest rate cuts in the wake of the global financial crisis of 2008–2009, purchasers often found themselves incurring heavy liabilities under the swap agreements and significant exit costs if they tried to end the agreements early. In 2012, after finding evidence of serious failings in the sector, the then regulator, the Financial Services Authority (succeeded by the FCA in 2013), announced a review of swaps selling to 'unsophisticated customers' by banks. The FCA's pilot review published its report in 2013.[95] In a test of 173 sales across various banks, the FCA found a failure to comply with regulatory requirements in 90 per cent of cases. In light of the FCA report, certain banks were required to review swap sales and identify possible instances of mis-selling. Out of approximately 20,000 customers identified by banks as possibly being affected by mis-selling, around 10 per cent of customers opted out of the review, 1,500 sales were reviewed and assessed as compliant and the remainder (approximately 16,500 non-compliant sales) have received 'determination of redress' letters, although in about 1,500 of these cases it has been established that there has been no loss to the customer from the mis-selling. Banks have since paid £2.2 billion in redress, including more than £500 million to deal with consequential losses.[96]

The FCA review has naturally generated its own stream of litigation concerning the conduct of the review.[97] Courts have been reluctant to afford

[95] Financial Services Authority, *Interest Rate Hedging Products – Pilot Findings* (May 2013).

[96] www.fca.org.uk/consumers/interest-rate-hedging-products

[97] *Suremime Limited* v. *Barclays Bank plc* [2015] EWHC 2277 (QB); *CGL Group Ltd* v. *Royal Bank of Scotland plc*, *Bartels* v. *Barclays Bank plc* and *WW Property Investments Ltd* v. *National Westminster Bank plc* [2017] EWCA Civ 1073.

private law rights and remedies to individuals arising out of the perceived failings of the review mechanism.[98] The operation of the scheme is itself currently under scrutiny.[99] Many of the original mis-selling claims that were not pursued against banks whilst customers waited for the outcome of the review are now statute-barred. One of the aims of the FCA action against banks was to keep claims out of the courts, but given the limitations on the FCA's redress system, private law claims were unavoidable.[100] The regulatory scheme presents limited opportunities to bring individual claims. Under section 138D of the Financial Services and Markets Act (FSMA) 2000 claims for breach of the regulatory regime can only be brought by 'private persons' (individuals who have not suffered the loss in the course of carrying on a business) and only in relation to some rule breaches. While 'retail customers' get the highest level of protection, more attenuated duties are owed to 'professional customers' and 'eligible counterparties', who are assumed to be more confident dealing with complex financial products and more comfortable with a higher level of risk exposure.[101] However, in all cases, financial institutions must ensure communications with clients are 'fair, clear and not misleading'.[102] Claimants ineligible for redress under the FCA review, usually because they were companies, brought various actions for negligent misstatement under *Hedley Byrne* principles, misrepresentation under common law and statute, breach of contract and breach of fiduciary duties. The claimants argued that they had been given false or no information, that they had been misled about the risks they were assuming or the level of break costs they would incur and that they had been advised negligently. Depending on the terms of the swap agreements, the legislation against unfair contract terms[103] and unfair relationships[104] was relevant. Breach of regulatory and statutory duties were asserted in some cases.

The treatment of the private law claims for swaps mis-selling in courts paints a contrasting picture to the FCA redress system. Despite the FCA finding of failings in the market, few of the private law claims dealing with

[98] See generally Samuel, 'Tools for Changing Banking Culture'.

[99] www.fca.org.uk/news/news-stories/update-irhp-final-report

[100] Samuel, 'Tools for Changing Banking Culture', 132.

[101] Iris H.-Y. Chiu and Alan H. Brener, 'Articulating the Gaps in Financial Consumer Protection and Policy Choices for the Financial Conduct Authority – Moving beyond the Question of Imposing a Duty of Care' (2019) 14 *Capital Markets Law Journal* 217, 219–20.

[102] Financial Conduct Authority, *Handbook*, COBS 4.2.

[103] Unfair Contract Terms Act 1977.

[104] Section 140A–D Consumer Credit Act 1974, replacing the previous jurisdiction to reopen an 'extortionate credit bargain' under s 137 of the Consumer Credit Act 1974.

aspects of swaps mis-selling brought before the courts have been successful.[105] These cases raise difficult issues concerning the interplay between the various legal sources that impinge on swaps mis-selling – legislation, common law, regulatory rules and contract terms. The decisions in courts usually turn on the distinction between a bank providing accurate information to the customer during the sale of the product and the bank *advising* on the sale. The identification of an advisory relationship is an important matter of fact for both the operation of common law duty of care (that the advice is given with reasonable care and skill[106]) and the financial services regulatory scheme.[107] As we saw in the last chapter, the terms of the contract may be crucial in determining whether a sale is advised, with stronger rights for the customer, or non-advised, where the bank's duties are generally limited to providing relevant information and not misleading the client.[108] The swaps contracts usually contained a contractual limitation on the bank's service, confining them to a 'sale only', 'execution only' or 'no advice' role.[109] Recall that, while ultimately the issue turns on the construction and context of each individual contract, these clauses have generally been interpreted as stipulating the 'basis of the contract', or the primary rights under the contract, rather than excluding or limiting liability.[110] In the context of swaps mis-selling, these terms render the sale of the swap as 'non-advisory',[111] with the effect that the customer is taken to rely solely on their own judgment in taking out the product, not on any advice or representations from the bank.[112] In claims coming before courts,

105 *Green & Rowley* v. *Royal Bank of Scotland plc* [2013] EWCA Civ 1197; *Crestsign Ltd* v. *National Westminster Bank plc & Anor* [2014] EWHC 3043 (Ch); *Thornbridge* v. *Barclays Bank plc* [2015] EWHC 3430; *Marz Ltd* v. *Bank of Scotland plc* [2017] EWHC 3618 (Ch); *Property Alliance Group* v. *Royal Bank of Scotland plc* [2018] 1 WLR 3529; *Carney & Ors* v. *NM Rothschild & Sons Ltd* [2018] EWHC 958 (Comm); *Parmar & Anor* v. *Barclays Bank plc* [2018] EWHC 1027 (Ch); *Fine Care Homes Ltd* v. *National Westminster Bank plc & Anor* [2020] EWHC 3233 (Ch).

106 Piers Reynolds and Anthony Collins, 'Non-advised Sales of Financial Products: An End to Caveat Emptor' (2018) 33 *Journal of International Banking Law and Regulation* 148.

107 Chiu and Brener, 'Articulating the Gaps', 224.

108 *Carney* v. *Rothschild*, above n. 105: the presence of a 'basis' clause in the contract can determine whether an advisory duty arises or not, at [346].

109 See *Green* & *Rowley* v. *RBS* above n. 105.

110 *Fine Care* v. *RBS*, above n. 105, from [117] ff, continues this trend of understanding 'no advice' and 'execution only' clauses as basis clauses, not reviewable under the unfairness legislation.

111 See *Thornbridge* [109]; *Carney* [346]; *Property Alliance Group* v. *RBS* [98]; contra, see *Thomas & Anor* v. *Triodos Bank NV* [2017] EWHC 314; Jo Braithwaite, '*Springwell*-watch: New Insights into the Nature of Contractual Estoppel', LSE Law Society and Economy Working Paper No 12/2017, p. 10–12.

112 *Parmar* v. *Barclays Bank plc*, above n. 105 [222].

therefore, the contractual scheme assumes paramount importance. Contract interpretation, rather than investigations of context or bank behaviour,[113] proved crucial to the determination of many of the legal claims. In effect, the courts were willing to enforce the contractual assertion made by the claimant that they did not rely on any representations, when other evidence may show representations were in fact made and relied upon.[114] Where the courts consider the position in an advisory relationship, it may be conceded that the parties cannot create 'an artificial basis for the relationship if the reality is different'.[115] In this situation the unfair terms legislation may apply to the no-reliance disclaimer, as the clause that 're-writes history' is an exclusion of liability that has arisen on the facts.[116] However, even if a claimant is successful in arguing that the protective legislation applies, the no-reliance term may be regarded as reasonable.[117]

It is tempting to dismiss these cases as simple instances of bad deals resulting from the global financial crisis. Of course it is trite that courts will not rescue parties from the unfortunate consequences of contracts freely made. Individual responsibility is a primary principle of contract law. But it is disingenuous to determine the existence of this 'individual responsibility' purely on the operation of contract terms. It also leads to perverse decision-making. *Crestsign Ltd* v. *National Westminster Bank* is a case in point. The no-reliance clause was interpreted as a basis clause and the Unfair Contract Terms Act 1977 was held inapplicable. This was notwithstanding the conclusion of the judge that the banker involved had given advice to the customer. Despite this finding of fact, the judge decided that the clause did not 're-write history'. He went on to say that had the Act been applicable, the no-reliance term would have been unreasonable,[118] but that test was rendered irrelevant on the spurious (and, as we saw in the last chapter, historically discredited) distinction between basis clauses and exclusion clauses.

The misalignment between law and regulation here is unacceptably wide and inconsistent. It is difficult to justify this discrepancy by appealing solely to the different rationales behind law and regulation, or to the principle of freedom of contract, or the slender differences between genuine consumer

[113] *Green & Rowley* v. *RBS* [2013] EWCA Civ 1197. [114] *Carney*, above n. 105, [79].

[115] *Parmar*, above n. 105, [133]; *Raffeisen Zentralbank* v. *Royal Bank of Scotland plc* [2011] 1 Lloyds Rep 123, [271]–[315].

[116] *Parmar*, above n. 105, [133]. See also *First Tower Trustees Ltd* v. *CDS (Superstores International) Ltd* [2018] EWCA Civ 1396; [2019] 1 WLR 637 [98].

[117] *Thornbridge*, above n. 105, [117]; *Carney* [347]–[348].

[118] *Crestsign*, above n. 105, [119]–[120].

contractors and small businesses. Part of the regulatory remit is to tackle endemic poor practice in banking and improve standards, but the common law does little to support the regulator in that endeavour. Instead, the law perpetuates the classical law value of the promotion of self-interest. This is unfortunate in the wake of regulatory failures.[119] Troubling too is the tendency for courts to interpret regulatory requirements through the lens of common (contract) law rules. This allows firms to use basis clauses to contract around the possibility of not only misrepresentation claims but also regulatory requirements. An illustration of the tendency to import traditional contract law values into regulation is found in *Russell Adams* v. *Options SIPP UK LLP (formerly Carey Pensions UK LLP)*.[120] The claimant, an unsophisticated retail client with limited assets, had suffered losses after he invested his pension funds (in the region of £52,500) in storage pods. He had followed the advice of an unregulated third-party firm (CLP) who introduced him to the defendant. He sued the defendant, who provided a self-invested pension plan (SIPP) as a wrapper for the investment, for negligence, breach of fiduciary duty and breach of statutory duty.

As part of the claim for breach of statutory duty, the claimant alleged that the defendant failed to act 'honestly, fairly and professionally in accordance with the best interests of its client' as set out in the FCA rules.[121] This allegation arose out of the defendant's failure to advise the claimant regarding the manifest unsuitability of the investment, given the claimant's modest means, and the defendant's connection to CLP. The defendant argued that they only established and administered the SIPP wrapper, and they had no regulatory authority to advise the claimant on the suitability of the SIPP or the underlying investment. Further, they stated that the contract terms and other documents supplied to the claimant made it clear the transaction was on an 'execution-only' basis and that the suitability of the investment was the sole responsibility of the claimant, who was aware it was a speculative and high-risk venture. The claimant had agreed to these terms by signing a declaration, notwithstanding that it was clear from his testimony that he did not pay much attention to what he was agreeing but was acting on the recommendation and advice of CLP.[122] The FCA, acting as intervener, argued that the regulatory

119 Dame Elizabeth Gloster, *Report of the Independent Investigation into the Financial Conduct Authority's Regulation of London Capital & Finance plc*, examining FCA failings in the wake of collapse of LCF.

120 [2020] EWHC 1229 (Ch).

121 Financial Conduct Authority, *Handbook*, COBS, r 2.1.1.

122 See the claimant testimony reproduced at [31]–[33] and [54] in the judgment.

rules could not be affected by any terms in the parties' contract.[123] The judge disagreed. The terms demonstrated that the claimant was responsible for his own investment decisions:[124]

> The provision requires the FCA, in securing an appropriate degree of protection for consumers to have regard to, among other things, 'the general principle that consumers should take responsibility for their decisions'. In this case those decisions, as between the claimant and defendant, are set out in the documents which comprise the contract between them.[125]

The regulatory duty to act honestly, fairly and professionally in the best interests of the client did not render the contract terms redundant or override the common law position of upholding freedom of contract.[126] The judge rejected the argument that the contract was an artificial attempt to alter the reality, since the relevant reality included contract terms.[127] In the appeal, the Court of Appeal did not discuss this issue, though it upheld the trial judge's decision on the operation of the regulatory rules on procedural grounds. Mr Adams succeeded, however, as the Court of Appeal regarded CLP realistically as having advised Mr Adams on the storage pod investment.[128] This was a breach of the 'general prohibition' against anyone except an 'authorised person' from carrying on a 'regulated activity'.[129] Under section 27 of FSMA 2000, this rendered the agreement between the claimant and the defendant unenforceable, a conclusion unaffected by the terms of the contract between the provider and the client. Lord Justice Newey observed that consumer protection was the animating value of FSMA 2000. While he conceded consumers had responsibility for their own decisions, regulation was motivated by the need to safeguard consumers from themselves, particularly in relation to high risk and speculative investments.[130] This is a welcome

[123] *Russell Adams,* above n. 120, [147].

[124] *Russell Adams* [150]. Cf. *Financial Conduct Authority* v. *Avacade Limited (In Liquidation)* [2020] EWHC 1673 where, in the context of a claim regarding Art 53 of FSMA 2000 (Regulated Activities) Order 2001/544 (unauthorised person advising on the buying or selling of investments), it was determined that whether a person had provided advice was a question of fact, irrespective of whether their assigned function was advisory or sales, or that the contract terms stated no advisory role had been assumed or that a duty of care did not arise: [350].

[125] *Russell Adams,* above n. 120, [149].

[126] *Russell Adams* [154].

[127] *Russell Adams* [152].

[128] [2021] EWCA Civ 474 at [131].

[129] Section 19 of FSMA 2000 provides the general prohibition. Article 53 of FSMA 2000 (Regulated Activities) Order 2001 is concerned with 'advising on investments'.

[130] *Russell Adams,* above n. 128, [115] (CA).

recognition of consumer vulnerability in markets, although it does not affect the general common law commitment to party autonomy.

The cases on the interaction of regulatory duties and contract terms reflects judicial reluctance to allow detailed contract terms to be destabilised by more general duties, whether those general duties arise under the common law or regulation.[131] Attempts in regulation to modify or encourage certain behaviour in markets is therefore substantially undermined by courts upholding contract terms. This position holds even when bank conduct is investigated and censured by the FCA.[132] In *Standish* v. *Royal Bank of Scotland plc and others,*[133] the claimant's business was transferred to the now discredited Royal Bank of Scotland (RBS) Global Restructuring Group (GRG) after running into difficulties caused by the global financial crisis. The GRG was the RBS division charged with turning around struggling firms. The GRG's aggressive practices in dealing with distressed business clients included engineering default to extract heavy fees and fines and appropriating company assets at undervalue for sale to the bank's property acquisition arm. An FCA investigation uncovered substantial failures in the way the GRG operated. Though critical of the conduct of the GRG, the FCA took no action against it because commercial lending was outside the scope of its regulatory remit and actions against individual senior managers within the group were unlikely to succeed.[134] The GRG was dissolved in 2014. While *Standish* was not a full trial of the issues (it was a successful application on part of RBS to strike out a claim for unlawful means conspiracy, breach of good faith and other equitable duties), it compounds and reinforces the judicial attitude that a dense set of contract terms are not to be undermined by broader umbrella duties couched in terms of good faith or commercial norms of reasonableness and fair dealing.[135] This outcome also reflects the problem of lack of access to justice in financial cases.[136] Potential claimants cannot litigate because of their

[131] *Adare Finance DAC* v. *Yellowstone Capital Management SA and another* [2020] EWHC 2760 at [101].

[132] Financial Conduct Authority, *Report on the Financial Conduct Authority's Further Investigative Steps in Relation to RBS GRG* (June 2019) 31.

[133] [2018] EWHC 1829.

[134] For a brief history of the RBS GRG and the regulatory response to its conduct, see HC Treasury Committee, *SME Finance* HC 805 (26 October 2018), paras 52–64.

[135] *Standish* v. *RBS*, above n. 133, [38]–[39].

[136] The FCA has recognised that small businesses are often on the receiving end of 'poor outcomes' in financial services. Financial Conduct Authority, *Our Approach to SMEs as Users of Financial Services* DP 15/7 (November 2015).

straitened financial circumstances, and the complexity of the legal and factual issues generates considerable risk in undertaking legal proceedings.[137]

The case of swaps mis-selling provides only a snapshot of one area where law and regulation intersect. But the outcomes from the cases seem supportive of the general trend towards upholding party autonomy in contract. As far as courts are concerned, regulation occupies a distinct territory and one that does not necessarily intrude on the application of the individualistic contract values reflected in the common law. Regulation rarely affects the consideration of legal or contract rights by courts, which are determined primarily by reference to the contract terms.[138] Regulatory rules could be implied into contracts in some circumstances if the traditional tests under English law are met, but the detailed documentation that accompanies financial transactions is likely to preclude a finding that additional terms are to be implied.[139] An individual contract law claim arising out of breach of the rules will occur only if the rules are incorporated into the contract, and this will not be automatic.[140] Similarly, a direct action by a 'private person' for breach of FCA rules may lie under section 138D of FSMA 2000, but this is separate and distinct cause of action from any common law rights that may arise.[141] Thus, regulation (with its own remedies and schemes of enforcement) and private law rights are fundamentally distinct forms of obligation and remedy. That such regulations are not treated as part of the context according to which the contract is interpreted is particularly problematic, given that regulators may rely on laws produced by courts in order to determine whether enforcement action is warranted and can be pursued under the current legal and regulatory framework. The judicial attitude towards regulatory controls augments the discreteness of contract law, allowing the imposition of contract's individualistic value system even where relational norms (such as the need for collaboration in a sector or the imperative to reverse damaging market culture or enhance consumer protection) inform the regulatory approach.

The exclusion of regulatory purposes from judicial decision-making may be motivated by the desire to keep contract law free from policy considerations that would impact negatively on the certainty and predictability of contract

137 Beale, 'Access to Financial Justice: Three Financial Services Conduct Scandals, and a Proposal for Reform', 153, 157–58.

138 *Flex-E-Vouchers Ltd* v. *Royal Bank of Scotland plc* [2016] EWHC 2604 [18].

139 *Marks and Spencer plc v BNP Paribas Securities Services Trust Co Ltd* [2016] AC 742.

140 See *Target Rich International Ltd* v. *Forex Capital Markets Ltd* [2020] EWHC 1544 [95], emphasising that 'regulatory obligations are distinct from contractual rights'.

141 *Green & Rowley*, above n. 105.

law as it applies to commercial contractors transacting at arm's length. This assures contract law will operate on an ever-diminishing canvas. One response to the misalignment between courts and regulators is to cut out courts altogether, enlarging regulatory powers to include traditional judicial functions of interpreting and applying the law, supported by more robust enforcement methods that can be utilised without going through courts.[142] Alternatively, the establishment of specialist tribunals to enforce law and regulation under a unified scheme could be considered.[143] These kinds of measures would contribute to the further fragmentation of the legal sphere, relegating common law principles to an even smaller subset of transactions.

4.6 Conclusion

In relation to the growth of private ordering, and law's role as its vindicator, it might be argued that the law is simply ceding control over merchant practice in a reversal of the incorporation process associated with Lord Mansfield's development of common law in the eighteenth century. One might regard this as a form of denationalisation or decentralisation, in keeping with privatisation of other aspects of society and economy.[144] Private ordering entails that parties may eschew legal enforcement in favour of a range of formal and informal alternatives whose authority and legitimacy do not derive from legal imprimatur. Lack of effective legal oversight of private ordering regimes is nonetheless problematic. It suggests common law is relinquishing a role as general regulator of contractual activity in favour of a more limited function as enforcer of commercial contracts. This is unfortunate for the contracts that are still subject solely to common law control and to which the application of a formal law may be wholly inappropriate. We explore some of these contracts in the next chapter.

It is apparent that the growth of regulation has had little substantive impact on the rules of the common law of contract. Given the different rationales between law and regulation,[145] this might be regarded as inevitable. But courts called upon to determine the scope of regulatory authority, or to interpret

142 See John Penrose MP, *Power to the People* (February 2021) recommending that the CMA should be able to decide consumer cases without recourse to courts: 16. See also Department for Business, Energy and Industrial Strategy, *Reforming Competition and Consumer Policy* CP 488 (July 2021), para. 3.15.

143 Samuel, 'Tools for Changing Banking Culture', 138; Beale, 'Access to Financial Justice', 160.

144 Cooter, 'Decentralized Law for a Complex Economy'.

145 Ogus, *Regulation: Legal Form and Economic Theory*, pp. 26–27.

regulatory principles, may reach outcomes that undermine regulatory goals, increasing the risk that regulation simply bypasses the law. Reliance on informal dispute resolution to enforce regulatory duties does not require attention to legal rules or legal validity but abjures them, accelerating legal decline. Regulation entails there is less for contract law to do and little need for the common law to consider how its rules can support the functioning of markets. As with private ordering, the regulatory state shrinks the operational scope of contract law rules, and judicial attitudes mean courts may refuse to allow regulatory duties to penetrate the contractual scheme, or replace the contract as the governing framework, or even influence contract reasoning. The result is that the general principles of contract law are likely to become even more focused, and even more functionally irrelevant.

5

Contracts through the Gaps

Specific consumer legislation and regulation, and the inclination of commercial contractors to create their own contractual governance regimes, may reduce the demand for the kind of general contract law principles that the common law produces. This does not mean that ordinary contract problems with a common law dimension, and where judicial attention might usefully be directed, simply disappear. Instead, the problems may be shunted into private and cheaper fora for settlement and disposal. Or, more likely, they are simply not addressed at all, and certainly not by a contract law focused on furthering commercial interests and wary of disturbing commercial expectations. The contractualisation of society and economy produces ongoing challenges for contract regulation, but a formal law designed to appeal to commercial contractors is unable to provide an adequate response. Legislation and market regulation may not necessarily fill the gaps either. These forms of rule-making are usually specific and selective, applying only to certain contracts or contracting parties (protective legislation applicable to consumers may not extend to small businesses or sole traders, for example). The rhetoric around contract law's default status, the importance of party autonomy and legal support for business obscures the practical significance that contract law rules have to the conduct of many routine contracts that do not fit with the commercial paradigm.

In this chapter we consider the disadvantages arising from the reduced capacity of contract law to serve as a general regulator of contracts. We examine four areas of ordinary (non-commercial) contracting activity that raise substantial questions of contract law principle. However, judicial engagement with these questions has been minimal or non-existent. The examples show how little influence some common problems in consumer contracting, or other contracts involving inequality of bargaining power, have had on the development of contract law rules. The law's lack of exposure to some common issues generated by its rules only serves to compound the hold that commercial contracting has over legal development. The dearth of legal engagement with these issues also closes off an important forum for the debate, development and communication of contract's deeper normative values, including the general standards of conduct that are, or should be, inherent in contracting. This accelerates the process of contract law impoverishment.

5.1 Consumer Debt Management and Consideration

Rules concerning consideration are reckoned to cause little practical difficulty in the commercial context. The fluidity of consideration, particularly in light of the decision that practical benefits can constitute good consideration, means that judges can take a flexible approach to the requirement.[1] Given this, debates about consideration may appear of limited interest: a diversion for academics but lacking in any real-world importance. Lord Sumption, giving the leading judgment in *Rock Advertising Ltd* v. *MWB Business Exchange Centres Ltd*,[2] appeared to subscribe to this view, choosing not to deliver an opinion on the implications of the 'practical benefit' approach to consideration for the operation of the part payment rule.[3] Though conceding that the case 'raises truly fundamental issues in the law of contract',[4] Lord Sumption considered it unwise to deliver an obiter dictum, recommending that the point be reserved for determination by an enlarged Supreme Court.[5] Lord Sumption chose to direct his judicial attention to the enforceability of a 'no oral modification' clause in the contract. His conclusion that the clause was effective to prevent informal contract variations provided clarity for commercial contractors, though it failed to remove a source of controversy in the law.

Why might it be valuable to have an authoritative determination of the role of practical benefit in agreements involving the part payment of a debt? It is likely that creditors will take a pragmatic approach to problem debtors, preferring to accept a proportion of the debt in settlement rather than attempt enforcement of the whole. It could be assumed that clarity on the legal implications of the arrangements that individuals make in order to manage indebtedness and financial distress would be beneficial. Evidence appears to bear this out. A 2018 report indicated that approximately eight million people

[1] *Williams* v. *Roffey Bros & Nicholls (Contractors) Ltd* [1991] 1 QB 1; *Simantob* v. *Shavleyan* [2019] EWCA Civ 1105.

[2] [2019] AC 119.

[3] *Foakes* v. *Beer* (1884) 9 App Cas 605.

[4] *Rock* v. *MWB*, above n. 2, [1].

[5] *Rock* v. *MWB* [18].

in the United Kingdom struggle with debt.[6] The vast majority of these do not seek advice on managing their debt and are unlikely to enter into personal bankruptcy proceedings or seek other formal solutions, such as Debt Relief Orders and Individual Voluntary Arrangements. Instead debtors may attempt to reach informal deals with creditors, most usually through Debt Management Plans but also self-negotiated agreements or 'full and final settlement' offers.[7] Even if agreed by creditors, these may not be legally binding and enforceable unless all the requirements for a contract, including consideration, are present. Self-negotiated debt management plans are also most likely to fail, due to unsustainable repayment levels.[8] It may provide some much-needed stability and reassurance to debtors, and also creditors, that the arrangement creates a legally enforceable agreement if it confers practical benefits on the creditor, without the debtor having to depend on the operation of estoppel.

Consideration is still, therefore, a doctrine with ramifications for the operation of many informal debt repayment arrangements. The potential of the part-payment rule to impinge on the validity of these informal arrangements was recognised, if only obliquely, in the Court of Appeal decision in *CFL Finance Ltd* v. *Laser Trust and Gertner*.[9] The case concerned whether a structured settlement agreement that deferred payments due under a personal guarantee for a company debt was a form of 'credit' regulated by the Consumer Credit Act 1974. It was noted that 'debt deferment must take place pursuant to an agreement ... Absent consideration, a creditor's agreement to delay could not effect a contractual variation and would be binding on the creditor, if at all, only by way of promissory estoppel.'[10] The possibility of practical benefit constituting good consideration is not discussed. Admittedly, it may be relatively straightforward to recognise the presence of consideration,

[6] Peter Wyman, *Independent Review of the Funding of Debt Advice in England, Wales, Scotland and Northern Ireland* (Money Advice Service, 2018), at para 6.

[7] Given the informal nature of these processes, it is difficult to find data on how many people rely on self-negotiated or other non-binding measures of debt management: see *Review of the Literature Concerning the Effectiveness of Current Debt Solutions: Final Report for the Money Advice Service* (Money Advice Service, 2017), para 1.2.4. However, there is some evidence that these informal measures are utilised more often than the various formal insolvency processes: Wyman, *Independent Review of the Funding of Debt Advice*, 118; *Final Report for the Money Advice Service*, 10; Financial Conduct Authority, *Consumer credit and Consumers in Vulnerable Circumstances* (April 2014), p. 34.

[8] FCA, *Consumer Credit and Consumers in Vulnerable Circumstances*, p. 34.

[9] [2021] EWCA Civ 228. See also *Collier* v. *P & M J Wright (Holdings) Ltd* [2008] 1 WLR 643

[10] *CFL Finance Ltd* per Lord Justice Newey at [36].

given the inherent flexibility of the doctrine. The debtor's forbearance to pursue an arguable defence against the creditor (that interest payments under an agreement constitute a penalty, for example) is good consideration for any agreement on the part of the creditor to extend time for payment or other debt compromise.[11] Nevertheless, the uncertainty around this question has the potential to heap pressure on already vulnerable debtors. Debt Management Plans or other forms of informal debt restructuring do not prevent creditor actions to enforce debts. The plans may include elements, such as freezing interest and other charges, that are acceded to by the creditor as a matter of goodwill, not legal obligation.[12] The Financial Conduct Authority (FCA) has noted the problem of lack of transparency in the sector, notably in the way that debt management firms market themselves to debtors and in the advice given to the customer about alternative forms of debt relief, fees charged in administering the Debt Management Plans by commercial firms and the degree of creditor willingness to freeze interest and other charges on the debt.[13] The fact that any informal agreement to freeze debt is not binding can lead to unfortunate results, such as a debt of £1,000 increasing to £20,000 in the course of a year.[14]

More broadly, debt relief is an area where private ordering increasingly supersedes state-administered insolvency procedures. Individual Voluntary Arrangements (IVAs), for example, are the privatised face of insolvency management. The procedural framework for IVAs is found in statute,[15] but the legal basis for the operation of an IVA is contract. A competitive market has emerged for providers of IVAs.[16] Walters observes that '[a]n IVA is essentially a private deal between the debtor and the creditors with very few legal limits on what can be agreed which is subject to professional regulation and limited oversight by the court'.[17] IVAs are legally binding. They are

[11] *Simantob* v. *Shavleyan* above n. 1.

[12] Financial Conduct Authority, *Quality of Debt Management Advice: Thematic Review* (June 2015), 2.16.

[13] Financial Conduct Authority, *Quality of Debt Management Advice*, 3.3.

[14] Financial Conduct Authority, *Consumer Credit Research: Payday Loans, Logbook Loans and Debt Management Services* (ESRO Ltd, April 2014), p. 40.

[15] Insolvency Act 1986, Part VIII.

[16] See Katharina Möser, 'Making Sense of the Numbers: The Shift from Nonconsensual to Consensual Debt Relief and the Construction of the Consumer Debtor' (2019) 46 *Journal of Law and Society* 240, 246–47.

[17] Adrian Walters, 'Individual Voluntary Arrangements: A "Fresh Start" for Salaried Consumer Debtors in England and Wales?' (2009) 18 *International Insolvency Review* 5, 19 footnote omitted.

generally made on standard conditions that preclude a creditor pursuing the debtor for any other remedy. The conditions may state that the composition is 'in full and final satisfaction of the Debtor's Debts'[18] and that when a certificate of completion is issued 'the Debtor shall be released from all Debts which are subject to the arrangement'.[19] The risk of further enforcement action against a debtor is very low, given that many creditors in IVAs are large institutional lenders and repeat players who may have little to gain.[20] Nevertheless, it cannot be ruled out. The IVA is, ultimately, a contract, and the extent to which the debtor is discharged from the debt is a question of the interpretation of the IVA, including the terms of any underlying trust in favour of the creditors and the assets specified as the subject of the IVA. The combined effect of the legal analysis on these matters is that although the IVA may end, the debt is not extinguished.[21] In *Green* v. *Wright*, a certificate of completion of an 'all assets' IVA had been issued to the debtor stating that he had no further liability to his creditors. The Court of Appeal held that notwithstanding the certificate of completion, which made no mention of what was to happen to the trust created by the IVA, the trust continued with the creditors as beneficiaries, and any additional funds received by the debtor could be paid over to the creditors. The debts remain unpaid, and the creditors still existed. There are plans to change the system of debt relief, but it may be that the changes simply reproduce the same uncertainties.[22] Thus a debtor who believes they are discharged may still face legal proceedings with no clear indication of when their liability to the creditor ends. Clearly, these problems are not just the result of the operation of contract law principles. But a determinative ruling on consideration may at least remove one source of uncertainty for the parties and provide contractual finality for the debtor.

[18] Association of Business Recovery Professionals, *Standard Conditions for IVA* (version 4, 2018) condition 4.

[19] *Standard Conditions for IVA*, condition 9.

[20] Walters, 'Individual Voluntary Arrangements', 29.

[21] *Green (Supervisor of the Voluntary Arrangement of James Patrick Wright)* v. *Wright* [2017] EWCA Civ 111 [32].

[22] In May 2021, the Debt Respite Scheme (Breathing Space Moratorium and Mental Health Crisis Moratorium) (England and Wales) Regulations 2020 came into force. These will give eligible problem debtors meeting the criteria identified in the Regulations a moratorium period against certain actions by a creditor. See H. M. Treasury, *Breathing Space Scheme: Response to Policy Proposal* (June 2019), Chapters 4 and 5.

5.2 Payday Lending and Judicial Powers

Problems of personal indebtedness can be aggravated by the contract practices of predatory firms taking advantage of vulnerable individuals. Aspects of payday lending illustrate the widespread abuse of contract norms that contract law did little to curb. High-cost credit is nothing new (more traditional forms being pawnbroking, door-step lending and hire purchase), but the growth of the high-cost short-term loan market during the first decade of the 2000s was unprecedented. By 2012, the market for high-cost short-term credit had reached a peak, providing over ten million loans, with a total value of £2.8 billion, to around 1.8 million people in the United Kingdom.[23] Lack of access to affordable credit was exacerbated by restrictions on lending imposed by banks following the global financial crisis. This led to an expansion in the number of short-term lenders promising quick access to credit facilitated through user-friendly and automated online application platforms. Using aggressive marketing across a variety of media to target a younger demographic, purveyors of short-term loans were able to extend their reach beyond the local communities in which their predecessors operated.[24] Lenders promised easily available credit to subprime borrowers at eye-watering interest rates. When expressed in terms of equivalent annual percentage rate (APR), some of these rates reached several thousand per cent.[25] Lenders maintained the APR was not necessarily a reliable guide to fairness or the amount that would be repaid.[26] They stressed that the loans were designed to be for modest amounts, taken over a short term (usually extending to the borrower's next payday) and offered to customers at a high risk of defaulting.

The attempt by payday lenders to defend their activities was disingenuous. The combination of high credit charges, a lending business model predicated on pressure-selling, quick customer turnover, fast online decision-making

[23] Competition and Markets Authority, *Payday Lending Market Investigation: Final Report* (24 February 2015), para 9–10.

[24] Abdul Karim Aldohni, 'The UK New Regulatory Framework of High-Cost Short-Term Credit: Is There a Shift towards a More "Law and Society" Based Approach?' (2017) 40 *Journal of Consumer Policy* 321, 324.

[25] 'The payday lender that charged 16,734,509.4 per cent', *The Guardian* 16 March 2013, www.theguardian.com/money/2013/mar/16/payday-lender

[26] An argument with strong antecedents: *Blair* v. *Buckworth* (1908) 24 TLR 474, 476. See also Office of Fair Trading, *Review of High-cost Credit* OFT 1232 (June 2010), 2.12. Other positive aspects of payday lending have been identified, such as anonymity, retention of dignity, speed and ease: Karen Rowlingson, Lindsey Appleyard and Jodi Gardner, 'Payday Lending in the UK: the Regul(aris)ation of a Necessary Evil?' (2016) 45 *Journal of Social Policy* 527, 534ff.

with minimal attention to affordability and, crucially, deliberately engineered loan rollovers compounded the financial misery of distressed and vulnerable debtors. Market justification also played a role. In a consumer society manifesting increasing reliance on credit, payday loan companies were able to exploit a gap by catering to a section of borrowers with poor credit histories locked out of more reasonably priced credit available from banks or other mainstream lenders.[27] Lending practices in the sector drew censure from debt charities, poverty campaigners and consumer associations alike.[28] Following an initial period of non-intervention, motivated by the expectation that competition amongst lenders would lead to a degree of self-regulation, the sector was first investigated in 2010.[29] Regulators found serious problems in the market, including little evidence of direct price competition amongst the credit providers[30] and widespread non-compliance with consumer credit legislation regarding pre-contract information and affordability checks.[31] However, no direct action was taken until the beginning of 2015, when the FCA introduced price caps on high-cost short-term credit.[32] This has seen many loan providers exit the market.[33]

The rise of payday lending resulted from a period of economic austerity in the 2010s, increasing precarity in the labour market,[34] and the operation of neo-liberal market ideology.[35] The freedom of contract dogma and relative

27 Office of Fair Trading, *Review of High-cost Credit,* at 5 and para 3.5. The report recognised the problems in the market but did not recommend price controls (at 9 and para 2.29ff).

28 Office of Fair Trading, *Payday Lending Compliance Review: Final Report* OFT 1481 (March 2013) found that lenders tended to compete on speed of approval rather than price (3) and that loan rollovers accounted for 50 per cent of revenue (11). The report also noted that some of the worst payday loan providers were members of the appropriate trade association (5).

29 See generally, Aldohni, 'The UK New Regulatory Framework'', 321, 328–29.

30 Office of Fair Trading *Review of High-cost Credit* 3.62; Competition and Markets Authority, *Payday Lending Market Investigation Final Report,* at paras 31 and 35. The CMA report found that 'customer demand responded weakly to prices', para 34.

31 Office of Fair Trading, *Payday Lending: Compliance Review Final Report* OFT 1481 (March 2013).

32 Financial Conduct Authority, *Proposals for a Price Cap on High-Cost Short-Term Credit* CP 14/10 (July 2014), p. 6. The price cap was introduced in January 2015. The rules are contained in CONC 5A.2.3R (currently the interest cap is 0.8 per cent per day). The total cost cap is 100 per cent of the amount borrowed, including all interest, fees and charges. The loan can be rolled over on only two occasions. See also Aldohni, 'The UK New Regulatory Framework' 334–35.

33 Competition and Markets Authority, *Payday Lending Market Investigation: Final Report,* 2.74. See also Andrea Fejős 'Achieving Safety and Affordability in the UK Payday Loans Market' (2015) 38 *Journal of Consumer Policy* 181.

34 Rowlingson et al., 'Payday Lending in the UK', 528.

35 Aldohni, 'The UK New Regulatory Framework', 326–27.

ease of assuming contractual liability, coupled with lack of effective legal oversight, contributed to an economic environment where payday lending could proliferate. Very little in contract law changed in response to the rapid growth of high-cost short-term lending. The encouragement of individual responsibility for decision-making entailed that only the most manifest inequality and clear advantage-taking would be controlled by law. This attitude has been reflected in the general legal approach to credit dating back to the first usury laws of 1487.[36] Contract law doctrine has played a part here too. Forbearance from interfering in prices is part of the traditional contract law rules on consideration. This doctrinal limitation manifested itself in a judicial reluctance to interfere with interest rates, even when provided with a statutory authority to do so.[37] Statutes enacted over a century ago sought to address the kind of problems that re-emerged during the peak of payday lending in the 2010s. The Moneylenders Act of 1900 followed a report detailing money lending transactions with interest rates as high as 3,000 per cent. Renewals with compounded interest were also a problem, leading to a lifetime of indebtedness in the unfortunate borrower.[38] Section 1(1) of the 1900 Act gave judges a broad discretion to reopen transactions made at excessive rates of interest, where the transaction was harsh or unconscionable or where equity would have given relief. In *Wilton & Co* v. *Osborn* an agreement with an equivalent 60 per cent annual interest rate was held not to be harsh and unconscionable under the 1900 Act.[39] Mr Justice Ridley noted, '[i]t appears to be established by a series of decisions that a Court of Equity will not grant relief in such cases just because the charges or interest are excessive . . . neither excess of interest nor exorbitance of charge will suffice unless the element of unfair dealing is found to have existed.'[40] While the interest rate was high and the 'bargain was improvident and foolish', the judge found 'no pressure was put upon him which can be called undue or unfair'.[41] This interpretation substantially undermined the purpose of the Act by limiting the judicial discretion to reopen the credit bargain to occasions when equity would previously have intervened. The decision was reversed by the House of

[36] Karen Fairweather, 'Redressing Inequality in Personal Credit Transactions: 1700–1974' in Kit Barker, Simone Degeling, Karen Fairweather and Ross Grantham (eds.) *Private Law and Power* (Hart Publishing, 2016), pp. 53, 62–63.

[37] Notably the power to reopen extortionate credit bargains under s 137 Consumer Credit Act 1974. Previous powers to adjust were given under the Moneylenders Acts of 1900 and 1927.

[38] Fairweather, 'Redressing Inequality in Personal Credit', p. 68.

[39] [1901] 2 KB 110.

[40] At p. 113. See also Fairweather, 'Redressing Inequality in Personal Credit', p. 70.

[41] *Wilton* v. *Osborn*, above n. 39, at 114.

Lords in *Samuel* v. *Newbold* who held that excessive interest was sufficient for a transaction to be harsh and unconscionable.[42] The Moneylenders Act 1927 went further, imposing an effective ceiling on the annual interest rate for loans by creating a rebuttable presumption that a transaction at interest in excess of 48 per cent annually was harsh and unconscionable. Both the 1900 and the 1927 Acts were repealed by the Consumer Credit Act 1974.

Notwithstanding that the 1971 Crowther Report on Consumer Credit accepted the reality that 'freedom of contract has little meaning in consumer transactions',[43] the Consumer Credit Act 1974 was premised on the policy 'that the state should interfere as little as possible with the consumer's freedom to use his knowledge of the consumer credit market to the best of his ability and according to his judgment of what constitutes his best interests'.[44] In a similar sentiment, the report identified 'the first principle of social policy should be to treat the users of consumer credit as adults who are fully capable of managing their own financial affairs and not to restrict their freedom of access to it in order to protect the relatively small minority who get into difficulties'.[45] A balance between consumer freedom and protection from exploitation was sought to be achieved not by directly intervening in the price of credit but through procedural controls. These included information disclosure duties, licensing pre-requisites for creditors, formalities in the creation of the credit agreement, greater transparency over the charge for credit and measures such as cooling-off periods.

Notwithstanding the tendency of the 1974 Act towards instituting fair procedures, the discretion to reopen harsh and unconscionable lending agreements was retained by section 137 of the Act. Under this provision, judges were empowered to reopen the 'extortionate credit bargain' and do 'justice between the parties' where the debtor was required to make payments that were 'grossly exorbitant'[46] or that 'otherwise grossly contravene[d] ordinary principles of fair dealing'.[47] In making this assessment, regard was to be had to the age, experience, business capacity and health of the debtor as well as the extent to which they were under financial pressure.[48] From the creditor side, the risks accepted by the creditor having regard to any security provided, and any relationship to the debtor, were material factors.[49] Prevailing interest rates

42 [1906] AC 461.

43 *Consumer Credit: Report of the Committee* (Cmnd 4596, 1971) ('Crowther Report'), para 6.1.12.

44 Crowther Report, para 3.9.1.

45 Crowther Report, para 3.9.9.

46 Section 138(1)(a) Consumer Credit Act 1974.

47 Section 138(1)(b) Consumer Credit Act 1974.

48 Section 138(3) Consumer Credit Act 1974.

49 Section 138(4) Consumer Credit Act 1974.

also had to be considered, which could work to either the debtor's or the creditor's advantage.[50]

Most of the case law under section 137 concerned mortgages. The risks to the creditor were often the decisive factor in determining whether to grant relief to the debtor. Thus, a short-term bridging loan at 48 per cent per annum, granted in a hurry ('a matter of hours') by a creditor without any security or investigation, to a debtor who had not been entirely honest about his financial circumstances was held not to be extortionate.[51] Prevailing interest rates were also very influential in the assessment, although courts tended to examine the rates charged for similar loans, rather than compare rates on high-cost loans with those available from mainstream lenders.[52] If the creditor could demonstrate they acted in a way that an ordinary commercial lender would be expected to act, that is, in accordance with the market standards, the claim that a bargain was extortionate would usually fail.[53] The courts were not generous in utilising the discretion to reopen credit agreements,[54] and the judicial preference to uphold loan terms was manifest. It has been maintained that the legislation did not favour debtors,[55] and that it did little to discourage loan-sharking.[56] The influence of freedom of contract was not easily overcome, even when judges were given legislative license to interfere. Judges displayed a similar tendency to import familiar common law considerations around unconscionability into their assessment of the credit bargain (such as whether the creditor had taken advantage of the debtor's inequality of bargaining power[57] or the transaction was to the debtor's 'manifest and unfair disadvantage'[58]) arguably against the wording of the section and certainly against the underlying policy of the Consumer Credit Act.[59]

The judicial reluctance to intervene was not necessarily an admission that they lacked the expertise to control contract fairness or interest rate levels but

50 Section 138(2)(a) Consumer Credit Act 1974.

51 *A Ketley Ltd* v. *Scott* [1999] GCCR 543 (ChD 1980). In *Wills* v. *Wood* [1999] GCCR 709 (CA 1984), in allowing an appeal against a finding of an extortionate credit bargain, the judge remarked that 'the word is "extortionate" not "unwise"' per Sir John Donaldson MR, 716.

52 *Davies* v. *Direct Loans* [1999] GCCR 795 (ChD 1985).

53 *Coldunell Ltd* v. *Gallon* [1986] 1 QB 1184 per Lord Justice Oliver, 1202.

54 Geraint G. Howells and Lionel Bently, 'Judicial Treatment of Extortionate Credit Bargains: Part 1' (1989) *Conveyancer and Property Lawyer* 164, 173.

55 Geraint G. Howells and Lionel Bently, 'Loansharks and Extortionate Credit Bargains: Part 2' (1989) *Conveyancer and Property Lawyer* 234.

56 Howells and Bently, 'Loansharks', 236.

57 *Wills* v. *Wood*, above n. 51.

58 *Woodstead Finance Ltd* v. *Andreas Petrou and Androuilla Petrou* [1999] GCCR 925 (1986 CA).

59 Howells and Bently, 'Loansharks', 237.

reflected the sentiment that it formed no part of the judicial role to address questions of market failure represented by the extortionate credit bargain. Nor was it part of the judicial remit to consider the public interest consequences or social desirability of high-cost credit.[60] There were also problems with the test itself, chiefly that it was the credit bargain that had to be shown to be extortionate. Other elements of the credit provided, such as the cost of optional payment protection insurance, the level of default payments and the power to vary interest rates after the agreement was entered into, were not reviewable under the statute. [61] The limitations on the discretion to reopen extortionate credit bargains were apparent. In proposals for reform, the Department of Trade and Industry noted the paucity of cases reaching trial, the lack of success of debtors[62] and the focus of the 'extortionate' test on interest rates (with which courts were reluctant to interfere) rather than ancillary unfair terms or other agreements not forming part of the 'credit bargain'.[63] In 2007, the power to reopen credit bargains was replaced with a broader 'unfair relationships' test.[64] Early decisions on this new power were not promising. Judges tended to rely on the earlier case law under section 137. Thus where the creditor was a lender of last resort and the debtor presented a high risk due to a poor credit history, a higher interest rate was justified. The debtor's awareness of the interest and charges, and what would happen in the event of missing instalments, was also relevant.[65] In one early decision, the court considered that a relationship could not be unfair if the creditor had followed the standards set out by the regulatory authorities.[66]

The decision in *Plevin* v. *Paragon Personal Finance Ltd*[67] appeared to indicate a more debtor-friendly interpretation of the 'unfair relationships' test. The case concerned the undisclosed commission paid by an insurer to a lender when the customer took out payment protection insurance alongside the loan. In that case, 71.8 per cent of the claimant's insurance payment was commission paid to the lender. The Supreme Court found that the relationship was

[60] Howells and Bently, 'Loansharks', 236.

[61] *Brookman* v. *Welcome Financial Services Ltd* [2015] GCCR 13267.

[62] See Department of Trade and Industry, *Fair, Clear and Competitive: The Consumer Credit Market in the 21st Century* Cm 6040 (December 2003), para 1.62. The Department of Trade and Industry noted there were thirty cases in thirty years (1974–2003), only ten of which were successful, para 3.43.

[63] DTI, *Fair, Clear and Competitive: The Consumer Credit Market in the 21st Century*, para 3.31.

[64] Section 140A Consumer Credit Act 1974 amended by the Consumer Credit Act 2006.

[65] *Nine Regions t/a Logbook Loans* v. *Sadeer* [2008] GCCR 8501 at [41]. Contra, see Mr Justice Leggatt in *Patel* v. *Patel* [2009] GCCR 9801.

[66] *Harrison* v. *Black Horse Ltd* [2012] Lloyd's Rep IR 521 [58].

[67] [2014] 1 WLR 4222.

unfair because of the 'extreme inequality of knowledge and understanding' between the parties.[68] It was immaterial that the lender had not breached any part of the regulatory framework by failing to disclose the level of commission. The Supreme Court determined that the fairness of the relationship involved a broader range of considerations than an enquiry into whether a lender had complied with regulations.[69] However, the problem identified was the failure to disclose, not the level of commission charged. Lord Sumption recognised the inherent inequality between lender and debtor, but the relationship could not be assessed for unfairness on that ground alone.[70] This interpretation tends to reinforce the traditional contract law approach of responding to procedural over substantive unfairness.[71] Despite the outcome in *Plevin*, the unfair relationships test under section 140A has had little impact on lending practices. Notably, it has not been successfully deployed against the use of basis clauses to defend claims of mis-selling made against banks.[72]

While a causal connection is difficult to establish, it is not hard to infer that these judicial attitudes towards credit agreements contributed to a liberal credit environment where payday lending could proliferate largely unchecked. Even in 2010, the problematic element of payday lending was not necessarily thought to be interest rates per se but the advantage-taking involved in rolling over the loan, offering additional credit to a borrower already in financial difficulty and taking payments via continuous payment authorities (sometimes emptying a customer's bank account in the process). The regulatory view was that these could be solved with consumer education rather than price controls.[73] The common law did develop tools to tackle some aspects of the problem. The unilateral power to vary interest rates is controlled at common law through the implied term that rates will 'not be set dishonestly, for an improper purpose, capriciously or arbitrarily'[74] and a 'lender will not exercise his discretion in a way that no reasonable lender, acting reasonably, would do'.[75] Similarly, any unexpectedly onerous obligation must be clearly expressed and notice provided. Nevertheless, interest rates themselves are not usually the subject of court control unless lacking transparency. Under the Consumer Rights Act 2015 such rates are the 'price' of the credit and hence not subject directly to the unfairness controls. Ancillary matters covered by

68 *Plevin* [18]. 69 *Plevin* [17]. 70 *Plevin* [10]. 71 *Plevin* [20].
72 *Carney* v. *N M Rothschild & Sons Ltd* [2018] EWHC 958 (Comm).
73 Office of Fair Trading, *Review of High-cost Credit* (2010), pp. 6 and 4.4ff.
74 *Paragon Finance plc* v. *Nash (and others)* [2002] 1 WLR 685, per Lord Justice Dyson [36].
75 *Paragon Finance plc* v. *Nash (and others)* per Lord Justice Dyson [41].

contract terms, such as those relating to the circumstances in which rates can be varied or the ways in which charges can be imposed, may be subject to the unfairness test contained in the Act.

It might be denied that judges have any responsibility in relation to high-cost credit. Senior courts hear so few cases on consumer contracts that it is difficult to reflect the consumer interest in contract law in a coherent and principled fashion. This is only a partial response. We noted earlier that judicial decision-making in consumer contract cases tends to draw upon the same commercial contract principles that might be applied in a dispute between businesses. We have seen in this section that judges can be reluctant to use the legislative authority conferred on them to control unfairness and pursue a policy of protection for weaker parties. The limited way in which judges interpret the doctrines and powers available to them exacerbates the use of contract as a tool of exploitation. Equitable doctrines are similarly subject to restrictive interpretation. Deliberate advantage-taking of the debtor's weakness or of the debtor's financial distress (but where there were promising future prospects as an 'expectant heir') is a necessary condition in order for equity to intervene in contracts on grounds of unconscionability.[76] General vulnerability of the debtor is not enough; they must have suffered some abuse or victimisation from the creditor.[77] In *Multiservice Bookbinding Ltd* v. *Marden* Mr Justice Browne-Wilkinson remarked, 'a bargain cannot be unfair and unconscionable unless one of the parties to it has imposed the objectionable terms in a morally reprehensible manner, that is to say, in a way which affects his conscience ... the court can and should intervene where a bargain has been procured by unfair means.'[78] Similarly the Privy Council in the case of *Boustany* v. *Piggot*[79] stressed the need for 'moral culpability' on the part of the stronger party. The court observed that 'unequal bargaining power or objectively unreasonable terms provide no basis for equitable interference in the absence of unconscientious or extortionate abuse of power where exceptionally, and as a matter of common fairness, "it was not right that the strong should be allowed to push the weak to the wall"'.[80] This requirement of moral culpability on the part of the lender and weakness on the part of the borrower is a limitation on the viability of the unconscionability doctrine, given the

[76] Fairweather, 'Redressing Inequality in Personal Credit', p. 62.

[77] Lord Justice Lindley in *Allcard* v. *Skinner* (1887) 36 ChD 145, 182 (although here dealing with undue influence). See also Fairweather, 'Redressing Inequality in Personal Credit', p. 61ff.

[78] [1979] 1 Ch 84 at 110.

[79] (1995) 69 P & CR 298.

[80] *Boustany*, 303, quoting *Alec Lobb (Garages) Ltd* v. *Total Oil (Great Britain) Ltd* [1985] 1 WLR 173, 183.

judicial reluctance to impute bad faith motives to contracting parties. Such an approach does little to discourage the pursuit of contract abuses through the operation of contract terms.

In some respects, English law is an outlier here. In deciding whether an agreement is unconscionable, other common law jurisdictions have abandoned the requirement that the weaker party display some vulnerability – special disadvantage or disability – that the stronger party has exploited. In Australia, an action for unconscionability in a consumer contract is founded on statute. A recent decision has recognised that acting in ways that were 'systematically dishonest, entirely in bad faith in undermining a bargain, involving misrepresentation, commercial bullying or pressure and sharp practice, using a superior bargaining position, behaving contrary to an industry code, using significant market power in a way to extract an undisclosed benefit that will harm others who are commercially related to the counterparty' could also be instances of unconscionability, irrespective of whether the claimant displayed any specific vulnerability.[81] It is difficult to see English judges following this path and addressing these potential sources of contract misuse, even if given a direct legislative power to do so. Though contract law does have doctrines that can be turned to tackling abuses in the lending market, it appears highly unlikely courts will use them.

5.3 Student Loans and Unfair Terms

Consumer contracts falling within the ambit of the operation of the Consumer Rights Act 2015 are subject to various rules concerning the transparency and fairness of the terms. The statutory scheme does not provide a general power to review contract terms however. There are agreements characterised by complete inequality of bargaining power, and an effective monopoly in supply, where the contractual powers conferred on one party are subject neither to the legislative scheme nor effective judicial oversight. The student loan regime in England is an example. The aim of this section is not to investigate the politics and economics of university financing in England,[82] nor to unpack how changes in student funding have contributed to the marketisation of tertiary

[81] *Australian Competition and Consumer Commission* v. *Quantum Housing Group Pty Ltd* [2021] FCAFC 40, following *Australian Securities and Investments Commission* v. *Kobelt* [2019] HCA 18; 267 CLR 1.

[82] See generally Dr Philip Augar, *Independent Panel Report to the Review of Post-18 Education and Funding*, CP 117 (May 2019) ('Augar Review').

education.[83] Our interest is in the obligations imposed on loan recipients under the terms of the student loan contract and the paucity of regulation controlling the content of these obligations.

The student loans scheme in England has undergone various iterations since first introduced by the Education (Student Loans) Act 1990. The system was radically overhauled and extended by section 22 of the Teaching and Higher Education Act 1998. University tuition fees were introduced in the same year. The Act authorised the Secretary of State for Education to give income-contingent repayment loans to students to finance their higher or further education. This change formed the beginning of a larger and longer term project of expansion and marketisation of higher education in England. The obligations under the student loan agreement arise between the citizen (student) and state (more specifically the Secretary of State for Education) and are inherently a matter of public law rather than private law. As such, how the Secretary of State exercises their powers under the enabling legislation may be subject to judicial review. Notwithstanding that, the choice of the paradigmatic private instrument – contract – as the tool for implementing higher education policy, as well as the outsourcing of student loan administration to various independent organisations, also makes contract law an appropriate tool for analysis of the liabilities created under the student loan agreement. Elements of the student loan contract would raise questions in other contracting contexts. While harnessing the ideological aspects of freedom and party autonomy through the contract mechanism, the student loan agreement contains few of the safeguards that are a feature of other contracts involving long-term financial commitments, such as mortgages.

The liabilities created under the student loans scheme are considerable. One in ten UK adults has a student loan.[84] The total loan balance at the end of financial year 2018–2019 was in the region of £121 billion, and was predicted to rise further.[85] The system is administered through the Student Loans Company (SLC), a not-for-profit government organisation, acting as an agent on the government's behalf. Though styled a loan, higher education financing

83 A good overview of the issues is contained in the HC Treasury Committee Report, *Student Loans* HC 478 (February 2018).

84 Figures from Financial Conduct Authority, *The Financial Lives of Consumers Across the UK: Key Findings from the Financial Lives Survey 2017* (20 June 2018), 74.

85 Student Loan Company, *Student Loans in England: Financial Year 2018–2019*, SP 01/2019 (June 2019), p. 6. By 2021, the loan balance had risen to £160 billion, and only 25 per cent of students were expected to repay in full, Paul Bolton, *Student Loan Statistics*, HC Library CBP01079 (23 June 2021), p. 5.

is not comparable to other forms of consumer credit.[86] Unlike more conventional forms of debt, repayments are administered as a tax on future graduate earnings and commence only when an earnings threshold is reached.[87] Repayments vary with income, as does the interest payable on the outstanding balance under the current loans regime. The interest rate charged is notionally lower than commercial loans and, in perhaps the biggest distinction from conventional borrowing, any outstanding debt is written-off after a number of years (currently thirty). A high proportion of write-off is anticipated. Only 55 per cent of loan value is expected to be repaid,[88] and only 30 per cent of students are expected to repay loans in full.[89] The shortfall is funded out of general taxation.

Under the terms of the Student Loan Contract, the student's obligations are many, varied and variable. The terms state that 'any loan(s) made to me by the Secretary of State for Education, "the lender" (which includes any persons exercising functions on behalf of the Secretary of State . . .) will be on the terms set out in these declarations and in Regulations . . . as amended from time to time'. The applicant agrees 'that any loan(s) made to me . . . is a/are contract(s) between me and the lender which binds me from the payment to me of the first loan advance and that the repayment of any such loan(s), together with all and any interest, penalties and charges which apply, will be due by me to the lender as a debt'. Further, breach of the terms results in an obligation to pay 'penalties which may apply under the Teaching and Higher Education Act 1998 and the regulations made under that Act, as amended from time to time or successor legislation and/or regulations'.[90] The power to vary the terms of the student loan contract is granted by the enabling legislation, the Teaching and Higher Education Act 1998 under sections 22(2)(g) and 22(3). Using these powers, variations have been made to the interest rate charged, the threshold income repayment level and the overall duration of the loan.[91]

[86] See HC Treasury Committee, *Student Loans*, para 103.
[87] See Augar Review, 169.
[88] *Student Loan Forecasts, England: 2017 to 2018* www.gov.uk/government/statistics/student-loan-forecasts-england-2017-to-2018 (p. 5); Augar Review, 169.
[89] Paul Bolton, *Student Loan Statistics* HC Briefing Paper 1079 (28 June 2019), 3. For obvious reasons, repayment rates are difficult to predict over the long term. See also HC Treasury Committee, *Student Loans*, para 6.
[90] Student Finance England, *Form PN1 Application for Student Finance for New Students* (2019/20), Loan Contract Conditions b, e, and m (p. 25).
[91] HC Treasury Committee, *Student Loans*, para 48; s 76 of the Education Act 2011 (changes to interest rates); www.gov.uk/guidance/how-interest-is-calculated-plan-2

Notwithstanding that the student receives a considerable benefit from the loan, from a contract law perspective the student loan system has a number of problematic features. Most notably, the government has sweeping powers to make unilateral, unpredictable and retrospective amendments to repayment terms through the enabling legislation and subsequent regulations.[92] The 'terms' operating when the student takes out the loan will not be stable over the loan lifetime. From the point of view of the relationship between citizen and state, this power to vary regulations is unremarkable. But a commitment from a young adult to a sizeable debt with a thirty-year repayment period from a single provider in a non-competitive market, and where the terms can be altered at will by the provider, would be of questionable validity in almost every other contract context. Tranches of the student loan book have been sold off to private companies.[93] No detriment to the borrower is supposed to follow from this,[94] but problems have been reported concerning previous sales of the loans where private companies have reneged on various parts of the original SLC commitment, including notifying non-payment to credit reference agencies and harassing graduates for repayment.[95]

What contract law rules are applicable to the student loan agreement? The SLC is not regulated by the FCA, so the consumer credit rules promulgated by the FCA are not applicable.[96] The only other unregulated lenders identified by the FCA are family and friends, and unregistered moneylenders (loan sharks).[97] Neither the Consumer Credit Act 1974 nor the Consumer Rights Act 2015 is applicable to student loans. The Consumer Rights Act 2015 does not apply because the contract is not one between consumer and trader (that is, a contractor acting in the course of a trade, business, craft or profession).[98] The SLC is exempt from regulatory controls applying to most other forms of credit under the Consumer Credit Act 1974. The Sale of Student Loans Act 2008 reiterates that the loans are regulated neither by the FCA nor under

[92] HC Treasury Committee, *Student Loans*, para 47.

[93] The current legislation is in the Sale of Student Loans Act 2008; Sue Hubble and Paul Bolton, *Update on the Sale of Student Loans*, HC Briefing Paper 8348 (9 January 2019).

[94] Section 5(6) of the Sale of Student Loans Act 2008; Department for Education, *Second Sale of Pre-2012 (Plan 1) Income Contingent Student Loans* HC 1843 (December 2018), para 12.

[95] See *The Guardian* report www.theguardian.com/money/2016/apr/08/student-loans-firm-erudio-leaves-graduates-fuming-over-latest-error 8 April 2016.

[96] Schedule Part 4, para 57 Financial Services and Markets Act 2000 (Exemption) Order 2001 (as amended 2015).

[97] FCA, *The Financial Lives of Consumers Across the UK: Key Findings from the FCA's Financial Lives Survey 2017*, 58, 127.

[98] Section 61(1) Consumer Rights Act 2015.

consumer credit legislation.[99] The lack of legislative oversight of what is in effect a 'contract of adhesion' reflects the desire to regard the student as a consumer vis-à-vis the university[100] but not the funder.

What of the common law? Common law doctrines that might be applied to the loan contract include the limits on the unilateral power to vary contract terms, the jurisdiction against penalties and rules on incorporation and interpretation of standard terms. It is highly unlikely that any of these rules could be deployed in a successful legal challenge to the validity of terms in the student loan contract. At common law, the discretion to unilaterally vary contract terms is governed by an implied term that the power to vary will be exercised 'honestly and in good faith, but, having regard to the provisions of the contract by which it is conferred ... not ... arbitrarily, capriciously or unreasonably'.[101] 'Unreasonableness' has since been interpreted to mean irrationality; that is, something more than a failure to act reasonably is required before intervention would be contemplated.[102] The government can mount a strong defence by arguing that the right to vary is pursued through regulations, rather than an exercise of a contractual discretion. Hence the power to vary is a matter of government fiat and legal imposition, to which questions of good faith and reasonableness are simply irrelevant. The SLC also has the power to impose potential liabilities ('penalties') whose exact quantification is unpredictable. However, unless unconscionable (a finding that seems unlikely unless it can be established that the SLC has behaved in a morally reprehensible manner), such penalties are unlikely to fall foul of the *Cavendish* v. *Makdessi* test as the government (or the SLC) will face little difficulty manifesting a legitimate interest in seeking performance of the repayment and other obligations that arise under the student loan contract. Incorporation of the terms is unlikely to be problematic as the prospective student must sign a declaration indicating that they have read and understood the terms. Nor do the terms appear onerous on their face, only in their potential effect. Individual agreements may be challenged for unconscionability in equity, but, as we saw above, some element of victimisation of the weaker party, or moral culpability on the part of the stronger, is required.

[99] Sale of Student Loans Act 2008 (as amended 2013), s 8.

[100] See, for example, Competition and Markets Authority, *Higher Education: Undergraduate Students – Your Rights Under Consumer Law* (12 March 2015).

[101] *Abu Dhabi National Tanker Co* v. *Product Star Shipping Ltd (The Product Star) (No 2)* [1993] 1 Lloyd's Rep 397, 404 per Lord Justice Leggatt; *British Telecommunications Plc* v. *Telefónica O2 UK Ltd and Others* [2014] 4 All ER 907 at [37].

[102] *Braganza* v. *BP Shipping Ltd* [2015] 1 WLR 1661.

The student loan contract, therefore, is subject to few regulatory controls, although proposed changes to the loan regime are open to parliamentary scrutiny. Common law doctrines may be applicable to the loan agreement but are unlikely to render any practical assistance in challenging the terms for fairness. We are left with a situation where the age group concerned is required to make a complex decision with long-term implications at a relatively young age.[103] Research undertaken by the FCA has found that the eighteen to twenty-four age group is the least financially resilient, the least confident in managing money and the least knowledgeable about financial matters.[104] It must be doubted how far the student has the financial literacy assumed of the 'average consumer'[105] to be aware of the effect of these terms and assess their likely implications. The House of Commons Treasury Committee noted the lack of student awareness about the terms on which loans are supplied. They recommended ending the practice of retrospective change to the conditions of the loan.[106] The government's response focused predictably on the information available to prospective students about the possibility of future amendments to the loan terms and the requirement that students sign a declaration that they have read and understood the terms and conditions.[107] The use of the contract framework to administer the loan means the loan regime can be presented as a private arrangement – a debt – procured and advanced though an exercise of autonomy, for which the student bears individual responsibility, but without any substantive contract law protections.

5.4 Non-disclosure Agreements and Public Policy

Many legitimate contract terms can be manipulated to serve illegitimate ends. The use of confidentiality or non-disclosure agreements (hereafter NDAs) in contracts provides a timely example. More disapprovingly referred to as hushing or gagging clauses, the use of NDAs to silence victims of crime and prevent whistle-blowers from disclosing wrongdoing has garnered much

[103] HC Treasury Committee, *Student Loans*, para 100ff.

[104] Financial Conduct Authority, *Understanding the Financial Lives of UK Adults: Findings from the FCA's Financial Lives Survey 2017* (October 2017, updated January 2020), p. 29.

[105] Section 64(5) Consumer Rights Act 2015 defines the 'average consumer' as 'a consumer who is reasonably well-informed, observant and circumspect'.

[106] HC Treasury Committee, *Student Loans*, paras 47–49.

[107] *Student Loans: Government and Office for National Statistics Responses to the Committee's Seventh Report* HC 995 (May 2018), para [11].

media attention and criticism.[108] The policy questions surrounding the use of contractual NDAs in these contexts have received scant attention from courts, though academics have begun to examine the legality of these terms.[109] This is an area that would benefit from the articulation of a clear common law position, yet it also raises doubts concerning the capacity of a law heavily wedded to autonomy to tackle the abuse of NDAs. Having positioned themselves away from considering the public interest concerns that flow from the use of contracts, unless clearly engaging traditional areas for the operation of policy, such as illegality or restraint of trade, the courts may have difficulty regulating such clauses under common law principles. The prevalent use of NDAs counterpoised with the lack of case law examining their legitimacy exposes the serious public interest and social welfare concerns raised by contracts that are conveniently buried by an undifferentiated appeal to the principle of freedom of contract. We review the law on NDAs here, considering how the common law default of non-intervention may have contributed to the proliferation of these clauses.

The legal landscape of NDA control is complex and multi-layered.[110] Here, we concentrate mainly on the use of NDAs in the employment context. NDAs may serve a variety of legitimate functions, such as preventing employee disclosures of trade secrets, customer details, and other sensitive or confidential information acquired during the course of employment. Non-disclosure terms are also a standard feature of compromise agreements reached between an employer and employee as part of dispute settlement. The terms will usually mandate that matters concerning the grievance and settlement payment are kept confidential.[111] There are strong incentives in law for the employee to comply with confidentiality clauses. The legal challenges faced if an employee discloses information covered by an NDA include an action for damages for breach of contract; damages for breach of the common law duty

[108] Particularly in the light of the revelations of Zelda Perkins concerning Harvey Weinstein, 'Former Weinstein Assistant Seeks Reform of Nondisclosure Deals' *Financial Times* (8 March 2018); Jeffrey Steven Gordon, 'Silence for Sale' (2020) 71 *Alabama Law Review* 1109, 1177ff.

[109] Catharine MacMillan, 'Private Law and Public Concerns: Non-disclosure Agreements in English Contract Law' in Paul S. Davies and Magda Raczynska (eds.) *Contents of Commercial Contracts: Terms Affecting Freedoms* (Hart Publishing, 2020), p. 315; Richard Moorhead, 'Professional Ethics and NDAs: Contracts as Lies and Abuse' in Davies and Raczynska (eds.), *Contents of Commercial Contracts: Terms Affecting Freedoms*, p. 339; David A. Hoffman and Eric Lampmann, 'Hushing Contracts' (2019) 97 *Washington University Law Review* 165.

[110] See MacMillan, 'Private Law and Public Concerns', p. 317ff; Gordon, 'Silence for Sale', 1123ff.

[111] ACAS COT3: *Settlement Where No Tribunal Claim*; *Duchy Farm Kennels* v. *Steels* [2020] EWHC 1208 (QB).

of confidentiality to the employer; proceedings for an injunction to prevent intended disclosures; or the enforcement of remedies set out in the contract, such as claw-back of payments made under the settlement, or other financial penalties. Protecting the employer's interest in confidentiality has led to innovations in contract remedies designed to vindicate the employer's rights and encourage compliance.[112]

Despite having legitimate functions, NDAs have gained notoriety for deterring employees from exposing unlawful or unethical conduct in the workplace. The abuse of NDAs in contracts has been derided as 'the triumph of contract over speech'[113] and as an interference with human rights.[114] Of particular concern is the use of confidentiality terms in compromises of employee complaints concerning harassment or discrimination at work or to conceal incidents of serious sexual assault by high-profile individuals. The use of NDAs in contracts is subject to legal control, but in practice many of the laws are ineffective to protect victims who have signed NDAs. Under legislation designed to protect whistle-blowing employees, some 'qualifying disclosures' are protected by law, irrespective of any contractual attempt to mandate secrecy.[115] To gain the legislative protection, the disclosure must be in the public interest and the information must relate to serious misconduct. A range of disclosures is covered, including those relating to criminal offences and the failure to comply with a legal obligation, or concealment of either of these.[116] There are a number of regulatory or other interested bodies to whom protected disclosures can be made, such as the Equality and Human Rights Commission and the FCA, but the disclosures must relate to matters falling within their regulatory remit (for example, money laundering or other financial crime for disclosures to the FCA).[117]

The requirement that a disclosure be in the public interest was added to the legislation in 2013, precisely to forestall use of the legislation to protect disclosures concerning purely private matters or individual grievances.[118]

[112] The development of restitutionary damages in *Attorney General* v. *Blake* [2001] 1 AC 268.
[113] Gordon, 'Silence for Sale', 1114. [114] MacMillan, 'Private Law and Public Concerns', p. 328.
[115] Part IVA of the Employment Rights Act 1996, as amended by the Public Interest Disclosure Act 1998.
[116] Section 43B of Employment Rights Act 1996.
[117] A list of prescribed persons/bodies to whom protected disclosures can be made is available at www.gov.uk/government/publications/blowing-the-whistle-list-of-prescribed-people-and-bodies–2/whistleblowing-list-of-prescribed-people-and-bodies
[118] The additional requirement that the disclosure be in the 'public interest' was added to the Employment Rights Act by the Enterprise and Regulatory Reform Act 2013.

The criticism levelled at this state of affairs prompted the government to announce legislation to strengthen the law on NDAs in the context of claims for workplace discrimination and sexual harassment.[119] The chief recommendation is that legislation should provide that no contract can prevent a disclosure to the police, regulated health and care professionals, or a lawyer. Further recommendations are that improvements should be made to legal advice and that NDAs should be more clearly drafted, including a transparent statement in the contract concerning their limitations.[120] However the overall tone of the government proposals is placatory. NDAs are regarded as having a 'legitimate place in the employment context' particularly when used to protect confidential information gained as part of employment and as part of a settlement 'to allow both sides of an employment dispute to move on with a clean break'.[121]

What of contract law? As with the phenomenon of payday lending, it is arguable that our current contract law has contributed to the creation of a permissive contracting environment in which NDAs are tolerated. Moorhead has argued that complexity in whistle-blowing law, uncertainty regarding the legality of some NDAs and the influence of contract norms in supporting freedom of contract have combined to create powerful disincentives for lawyers to act in the public interest over the use of NDAs, notwithstanding their professional ethical commitments. Lawyers are encouraged to put the client's interest first and attempt to 'get way with' NDAs that are of questionable legality.[122] Contract law has the requisite doctrines to invalidate exploitative NDAs,[123] but this is precisely an area where courts may be reluctant to use the rules for these purposes, for fear of disturbing commercial expectations about the enforceability of agreements. In prioritising the express contract terms, the law arguably takes too narrow a view, overlooking the effect that unchallenged discrimination and harassment has on overall social welfare beyond the immediate victims and the circumstances in which the NDA is executed. Victims may be legally advised or other procedural requirements met before the NDA is signed, but legal advice is not all of the same quality.

[119] Department for Business, Energy and Industrial Strategy, *Confidentiality Clauses: Response to the Government Consultation on Proposals to Prevent Misuse in Situations of Workplace Harassment or Discrimination* (July 2019), pp. 4–5.

[120] Department for Business, Energy and Industrial Strategy, *Confidentiality Clauses*, pp. 10–12.

[121] Department for Business, Energy and Industrial Strategy, *Confidentiality Clauses*, p. 6.

[122] Moorhead, 'Professional Ethics and NDAs', p. 350.

[123] See MacMillan, 'Private Law and Public Concerns', for a review.

Though notionally subject to controls on the grounds of public policy in contract, the various considerations in play means that public policy arguments are not straightforwardly harnessed to invalidate NDAs except in the most serious cases. The use of NDAs in contracts engages with a number of different and competing aspects of the public interest and individual rights: the public interest in settling disputes and discouraging litigation; the need to maintain privacy for both parties and give them the ability to move forward; the victim's right to autonomy in agreeing not to disclose; the public interest in maintaining freedom of expression and exposing unlawful or unethical conduct by employers or other authority figures; the public interest in maintaining confidentiality obligations;[124] and the public interest in the general reliability of contractual undertakings and in maintaining freedom of contract. In some cases it may be obvious that an NDA has been included as part of a legitimate settlement, not as an attempt to evade accountability for illegal behaviour. In other cases it may be much more difficult to distinguish whether a payment to a complainant is compensation as part of a compromise or a bribe intended to buy silence. The multiplicity of interests makes the relevant test of proportionality between the public interest in disclosure and maintaining confidentiality (and the efficacy of confidentiality agreements) very difficult to apply. However, it is arguable that the legal minefield around NDAs only contributes to a culture of confidence that they will be effective in discouraging disclosure, even in circumstances where the legal validity of the NDA is questionable. If so, this culture should be dismantled by the law as a matter of urgency. A starting point would be to rethink the priority accorded to contract in these cases.

The reluctance to engage with policy explains the common law tendency to treat contract duties of confidentiality as decisive in the face of countervailing considerations concerning freedom of expression or arguments about whether disclosure is in the public interest. Doubtless, courts would depart from this position in cases of serious illegality or where clear public policy concerns arise. Other cases may require a more difficult balancing exercise to be undertaken. Nevertheless, the desire to maintain freedom of contract is likely to exert an irresistible influence over the decision. An indication of this is

[124] Charles Phipps, William Harman and Simon Teasdale, *Toulson and Phipps on Confidentiality*, 4th ed. (Sweet & Maxwell, 2020), para 6-075, 'respect for confidentiality is itself a matter of public interest'; *Attorney General v. Observer Ltd* [1990] 1 AC 109, per Lord Keith of Kinkel, 256.

provided in *ABC* v. *Telegraph Media Group Ltd.*[125] The case concerned allegations of sexual harassment brought against a prominent businessman by five of his employees. The claims had been settled and the complainants had signed NDAs. The complainants had received legal advice, and crucially, the NDAs did not prevent disclosure of the allegations to regulatory and statutory bodies.[126] A national newspaper became aware of the allegations and proposed to run the story. The businessman sought an interim injunction to prevent publication on the grounds that the information had been obtained by the newspaper in breach of confidence. The trial judge refused to grant the injunction on the basis that the public interest in publication outweighed the duty of confidentiality. The Court of Appeal reversed this and remitted the case back to the High Court for a speedy trial of the substantive issues. At this point the businessman was identified in parliament and the proceedings were dropped.

In reaching its decision, the contractual basis of the NDA weighed heavily with the Court of Appeal. After conceding that there was a clear public interest in disclosure of criminal behaviour or other wrongdoing, the court remarked that any contractual basis for the obligation of confidence strengthened it, particularly where 'the obligation in question is contained in an agreement to compromise, or avoid the need for, litigation, whether actual or threatened'.[127] The court continued:

> Provided that the agreement is freely entered into, without improper pressure or any other vitiating factor, and with the benefit (where appropriate) of independent legal advice, and (again, where appropriate) with due allowance for disclosure of any wrongdoing to the police or appropriate regulatory or statutory body, the public policy reasons in favour of upholding the obligation are likely to tell with particular force . . .[128]

The priority accorded to contract was clear. The court went on:

> We accept . . . as a general proposition [that there could be no reasonable expectation of privacy or confidentiality in some of the particular misconduct alleged] but it does not meet the point that *the complainants had entered into particular obligations of confidence in this*

[125] [2018] EWCA Civ 2329, [27] and [47]ff; see also *Mionis* v. *Democratic Press SA* [2017] EWCA Civ 1194, [67].

[126] Moorhead, 'Professional Ethics and NDAs', p. 354.

[127] Above n. 125 at [24]. See also *Saab* v. *Angate Consulting Ltd* [2019] EWHC 1558: 'the court is looking to protect not only the public policy in favour of confidentiality, but also the well acknowledged public policy in favour of upholding freedom of contract' [151].

[128] Above n. 125 at [24].

> *case, including in the NDAs.* The real issue is whether, in the light of all the relevant facts, breach of that confidentiality is justified as a matter of public interest.[129]

The Court of Appeal noted 'the important and legitimate role played by non-disclosure agreements in the consensual settlement of disputes, both generally but in particular in the employment field'.[130] Ultimately, contract was king. While the NDA in the *ABC* v. *Telegraph* maintained the employee's right to make protected disclosures, this was substantially diluted by other provisions in the agreement. These included a declaration that the complainant 'warrant[s] ... that [they] do not know of any circumstances which would lead [them] to making a disclosure in the form of or in the circumstances referred to in this clause'.[131] The wording of this term has overtones of the 'basis clause' that we examined in Chapter 3. That is, the clause requires the signatory to acknowledge that certain past events have not actually occurred. As we have seen, judges have upheld basis clauses in other commercial contexts, utilising a doctrine of 'contractual estoppel', although these clauses supposedly will not be permitted to 'rewrite history'.

The Court of Appeal in *ABC* acknowledged the importance of debate about standards of conduct in public and commercial life. Nevertheless, the reasoning in the case does little to discourage the pernicious use of NDAs to conceal objectionable conduct and shield wrongdoers from accountability. Nor did the court consider the implications of its endorsement of freedom of contract over the public interest for ending workplace harassment and discrimination. The contract created a rarefied context that rendered these considerations irrelevant. In *Saab* v. *Angate Consulting Ltd*, it was maintained that public interest alone was not sufficient to justify disclosure. The public interest in disclosure must also outweigh the public interest in respect for confidentiality and freedom of contract.[132] Far from acting as a brake on the abuse of contract powers, law is becoming its enabler.[133] There are various common law doctrines, however, that can be used to constrain the use of NDAs. Courts could turn to interpretation, the doctrine of illegality and rules against the use of improper pressure (duress and undue influence) to control

129 Above n. 125 at [34] emphasis added. 130 Above n. 125 at [41].

131 See related case of *Arcadia* v. *Telegraph Media* [2019] EWHC 223 (QB) appendix; Moorhead, 'Professional Ethics and NDAs', pp. 356–57. On the public policies of upholding freedom of contract and encouraging settlement, see *Printing and Numerical Registering Co* v. *Sampson* (1875) LR 19 Eq 462, per Sir George Jessel MR 465; and *Simantob* v. *Shavleyan* [2019] EWCA Civ 1105, [50]–[51].

132 *Saab* v. *Angate Consulting Ltd*, above n. 127, [132].

133 Hoffman and Lampmann, 'Hushing Contracts', 171.

excessive NDAs.[134] Nevertheless, these doctrines are fact-dependent and ineffective to condemn the abuse of confidentiality agreements more generally. Judicial reluctance to engage with social welfare concerns and matters of the public policy as they impinge on contracts – the question of what is a permissible use of contract – has created the perfect conditions for NDAs to thrive.

In earlier case law on confidentiality, upholding freedom of contract was not the overriding concern.[135] Wood VC in *Gartside* v. *Outram* maintained that there could be 'no confidence as to disclosure of iniquity ... no private obligations can dispense with that universal one which lies on every member of society to discover every design which may be formed contrary to the laws of the society, to destroy the public welfare'.[136] It is hard to imagine courts making such a statement today. While a public interest in disclosure may be made out in cases of harassment and discrimination, the contract mandate of confidentiality may be sufficient in many cases to outweigh any wider policy considerations. Given the power of contract norms, the argument for upholding the NDA may seem particularly compelling if the defendant can assert some legitimate interest in confidentiality (if the allegations are contested, for example, and the truth has not been established) or if the NDA is included as part of settlement proceedings and the complainant has received a generous payment in return. This interprets the NDA as a simple private transaction, downplaying its social welfare implications or public interest dimension.

In addition, the changing view of the role of public policy in contracts reflects the attitude of modern courts that the operation of policy is fundamentally a matter for legislators. This militates against declaring any type of agreement (unless clearly illegal or falling within the existing categories of contracts voided by policy) as contrary to the public interest.[137] A further consideration is that notions of public policy change over time. Interventions in contracts on grounds of policy that seemed acceptable decades ago may no longer seem appropriate in the modern context. The advent of contractualisation, which emphasises individual autonomy and benefit, creates a contracting environment and culture hostile to interventions in contracts based on the

134 See further MacMillan, 'Private Law and Public Concerns', p. 321ff.

135 *Neville* v. *Dominion of Canada News Co Ltd* [1915] 3 KB 556; *Initial Services* v. *Putterill* [1968] 1 QB 396, 405.

136 (1857) 26 LJ Ch 113.

137 See Warren Swain, *The Law of Contract 1670–1870* (Cambridge University Press, 2015), pp. 245–46; *Multiservice Bookbinding Ltd* v. *Marden* [1979] 1 Ch 84, 104; *Johnstone* v. *Bloomsbury Health Authority* [1992] 1 QB 333, 346–47.

public interest. Evidence of this shift can be seen in relation to another area of public policy: contracts in restraint of trade. In *Peninsula Securities Ltd* v. *Dunnes Stores (Bangor) Ltd* the Supreme Court considered the circumstances in which the doctrine of restraint of trade could be raised against covenants restricting the use of land.[138] The Supreme Court supported Lord Wilberforce's 'trading society' test, determining that the restraint of trade doctrine was not engaged with restrictions that 'have become part of the accepted machinery of a type of transaction which is generally found acceptable and necessary, so that instead of being regarded as restrictive they are accepted as part of the structure of a trading society'.[139] It was held that a covenant that restrains the use of land did not engage the restraint of trade doctrine if it is part of the 'normal currency of commercial or contractual or conveyancing relations'.[140] Naturally, a test that takes its lead from what is regarded as 'accepted as part of the structure of a trading society' is liable to promote the individual interest of commercial contractors in protecting their contracts from intrusive judicial inquiries into whether freely agreed terms are justified in the public interest. Lord Wilson thought such a development was entirely in keeping with the common law tradition of rules 'generated from below, not imposed from above'.[141] Lord Carnwath echoed this attitude against the public interest when he remarked that the doctrine of restraint of trade 'is an exception to the ordinary principles of freedom of contract, and should not be extended without good justification beyond those categories already established by the case law, or indistinguishable in principle from them'.[142]

These sentiments give a good indication of the current direction of travel of English contract law. The partiality of the courts in according primacy to commercial considerations and interests is demonstrable. This militates against the deployment of public policy to invalidate any but the most egregious uses of NDAs. In the employment context, the fact that NDAs are normally included either in the contract of employment or in a settlement agreement following a dispute is particularly problematic for any public policy argument. Every settlement agreement may tend to oust the jurisdiction of the

[138] [2020] 3 WLR 521; [2020] UKSC 36.

[139] *Esso Petroleum Co Ltd* v. *Harper's Garage (Stourport) Ltd* [1968] AC 269 per Lord Wilberforce, 335.

[140] *Esso Petroleum Co Ltd*, per Lord Wilberforce 333, quoted by Lord Wilson in *Peninsula Securities Ltd* at [46].

[141] *Peninsula Securities Ltd*, per Lord Wilson [45].

[142] *Peninsula Securities Ltd*, per Lord Carnwath [61].

court, yet courts continue to encourage settlement over litigation or other court proceedings. Courts are unlikely to take a course of action perceived as encouraging litigation or that jeopardises chances of settlement. As far as courts are concerned, the combination of the private nature of the compromise and the allegations at the root of it, together with a commitment to freedom of contract, may prove too powerful to resist, inhibiting a court from applying public policy arguments to invalidate the NDA.

More specific doctrines, such as economic duress, may be ineffective against confidentiality clauses. There is evidence that victims, women in particular, are often pressurised into agreeing to settle claims for sex discrimination and sexual harassment in the workplace and to keep the allegations secret.[143] Employees may feel they have little choice but to accept when faced with the potential cost implications of refusing settlement and taking a claim to an Employment Tribunal.[144] Victimisation and intimidation and long, arduous negotiation meetings may intensify the victim's anxiety and distress.[145] If illegitimate pressure was placed on the victim in agreeing to the NDA, then the agreement may be voidable for duress or undue influence. A claim for duress may be hampered by the requirement to demonstrate that the pressure exerted is in excess of what is normally experienced as part of the contract bargaining process. The classical law model of the contractor assumes that a party can take care of themselves in negotiating, and the fact that the contract involved is not a commercial one is no guarantee of a moderated approach. Since the settlement marks the end of the employment relationship, an employer may refuse to compromise a claim unless the settlement agreement includes confidentiality clauses.[146] Extrapolating from the commercial context, courts may be likely to regard the employer as justified in using whatever bargaining chips they have during the negotiations. In another recent decision on restraint of trade, Lord Wilson in the Supreme Court remarked, '[h]igh-ranking employees can do particular damage to the legitimate interests of their employers following termination of their employment; and it may be that,

[143] Evidence of Melanie Newman to HC Women and Equalities Committee, *The Use of Non-disclosure Agreements in Employment Cases* HC 1720 (11 June 2019).

[144] HC Women and Equalities Committee, *The Use of Non-disclosure Agreements,* para 59.

[145] HC Women and Equalities Committee, *Sexual Harassment in the Workplace* HC 725 (25 July 2018), paras 110–11; and evidence of Zelda Perkins at para 122. See also HC Women and Equalities Committee, *The Use of Non-disclosure Agreements,* paras 23 and 24.

[146] HC Women and Equalities Committee, *Sexual Harassment in the Workplace,* para 109.

when they enter into their post-employment covenants, they are able to negotiate with their employers on nearly an equal footing.'[147]

In the midst of a difficult dispute where settlement has been offered, presented with a contract with all the appearances of validity or sanctioned by an independent and impartial third-party organisation, such as the Advisory, Conciliation and Arbitration Service (ACAS),[148] and the fundamental imbalance between employer and employee, agreement to NDAs is easy to procure. In addition, if the threat is one the employer is entitled to make, such as withholding a reference, then the illegitimacy of the pressure may be hard to establish. Even where an employer seeks to exploit the victim's weakness in forcing them to agree to confidentiality, courts may be reluctant to intervene and to make a judgment that the employer has acted in bad faith. As in the commercial context, identifying the point at which the pressure, though involving a lawful act, becomes illegitimate is difficult. The bar is generally set very high.[149] Courts do not lightly make the determination that pressure has been unlawfully applied, taking the view that negotiations are an arena for the operation and promotion of self-interest and that 'rough and tumble' must be expected in all forms of negotiation.[150] A victim may find mounting this sort of claim, and the allied one of undue influence, difficult especially where they have had the benefit of legal representation and advice.[151]

The common law commitment to freedom of contract is not absolute. Nevertheless, judicial reticence to expand public policy into areas not already recognised in the case law is manifest. The public interest in disclosure may be difficult to establish when set against the private interests of individuals to agree to a compromise that includes confidentiality. Striking out an NDA on the basis of the public interest may expose judges to the criticism that they are usurping legislative authority in making assessments of how public welfare is best served. It may be better to perceive this not as judges assuming legislative powers but as fulfilling an educative role. Hoffman and Lampmann point out that one of the functions of law is to communicate to society what is

147 *Egon Zehnder Ltd* v. *Tillman* [2020] AC 154 at [82]. Ian Ayres, 'Targeting Repeat Offender NDAs' (2018) 71 *Stanford Law Review Online* 76, makes a similar point, although he questions its legitimacy in relation to NDAs, at 77.

148 For example, COT3 standard settlement form used by ACAS includes confidentiality clauses, at paras 7 and 8.

149 *Times Travel (UK) Ltd* v. *Pakistan International Airlines Corporation* [2019] 3 WLR 445; *CTN Cash and Carry Ltd* v. *Gallaher Ltd* [1994] 4 All ER 714.

150 *DSND Subsea Ltd* v. *Petroleum Geo-Services ASA* [2000] BLR 530.

151 MacMillan, 'Private Law and Public Concerns', p. 323.

important, what is permitted and what kind of behaviour will be censured. They note that 'when courts choose to enforce a contract, or pick a particular default rule as the basis for bargaining, or adopt a damages limitation, they are in effect sending out a message about which (of a competing set of values) our political-legal order privileges'.[152] The law's unequivocal message is that NDAs are acceptable. It is yet another example of commercial interests dominating the contract law field, eclipsing other considerations in the process.

5.5 Conclusion

It is natural that much contracting activity takes place beyond the reach of effective legal oversight. Making and performing agreements is central to our participation in markets. Most of these agreements – even when legally enforceable – are trouble-free. If problems do arise, they can usually be resolved quickly and easily through informal methods. Nevertheless, the four areas examined here demonstrate how contract law principles remain highly relevant to the operation of some common contracts, either in bestowing notional legal validity to some problematic terms or denying legal enforceability. The examples illustrate the inadequacy of current contract law in recognising the problems raised within these contracting contexts (amongst others). These are not new problems in contract law, but the law has not engaged with these issues to any great extent, nor is it likely that current law is well equipped to do so. Importantly, the examples illustrate that the rules of contract law are not just relevant to commercial contractors. A supposed default or gap-filling law that only responds to commercial contract environments has substantially disabled itself from a role in responding to the use of contracts to perpetuate injustice.

Evidently, the likelihood of disputes over these matters reaching senior courts is vanishingly remote. This is a general problem within common law, but it is not just a matter of bringing cases before judges. NDAs, for example, raise complex and multi-layered issues of public policy. The law in this area would benefit from detailed judicial analysis and the development of principles governing the validity of confidentiality clauses. Judicial engagement would provide guidance on the permissibility of these terms and also communicate a broader message concerning the limits on the operation of freedom of contract. However, such analysis is effectively excluded by a contract law centred

[152] Hoffman and Lampmann, 'Hushing Contracts', 207.

primarily on upholding party autonomy and that disavows public policy considerations. Exposure to the problems that these contracting scenarios represent would provide clarity in the common law rules and could influence common law development along more generalist lines. It would also reinvigorate the basic principles of contract law as tools against contract manipulation and abuse.

6

Future Challenges for Contract Law

In previous chapters we have examined the recent history of contract law in order to support a claim that the law is diminishing in scope and normative substance. The judicially created rules of contract law have little impact on current contract problems as they affect large sections of society, leaving us without a general authoritative voice that speaks to the core values of, and limits on, contractual liability. Ultimately, common law principles may become devoid of principle because these are no longer necessary for contract law to fulfil its self-directed mission of facilitating commerce, validating and legitimising a commercialised model of contract law in the process. There are many drivers of this process, such that further commercialisation of contract law may be unavoidable. It is no less regrettable for that.

In this chapter we explore some of the current and future pressures on contract law that are likely to reinforce its formalist and commercialist tendencies. The first of these is the recasting of contract law as a commodity that should primarily serve the interests of commercial contractors (usually by upholding the terms of the contract), at the expense of doctrinal development. The second is the declining use of adjudication to resolve disputes, rooted in lack of support for litigation and the emphasis on non-adjudicative dispute resolution within courts themselves. A third factor can be identified that is likely to impact significantly on contract law, although the precise effects of it cannot yet be predicted with any certainty. This is the increasing automation of contract processes, manifest in the development of 'smart contracts' and algorithmic contracting. These innovations are likely to require revision of the foundational understandings upon which contract law is built, notably around how contracts are created, by whom and for what purposes. We examine these three factors in this chapter, as the likely influences over contract law's future development.

6.1 Law as Commodity

It is clear that English courts are keen to capture a significant share of the market in international commercial dispute resolution. Commercial law incorporates many areas of domestic law, not just contract, but nevertheless certain features of English contract law – such as the attenuated role for the operation of subjective intent, a plain meaning interpretation method, resistance to a general doctrine of good faith, a strong commitment to party autonomy and scant role for policy – confer a certain distinctiveness on English law as a product in the market for laws.[1] The accompanying claim that we should reorient our understanding of domestic contract law as a commodity operating in a market that must be adapted to suit market needs, and that this mandates a more formal style of law,[2] appears to resonate amongst some judges and legal practitioners. Statements of the importance of international business to the courts appear regularly in literature produced by the Courts and Tribunal Service, along with the aspirations for English law to remain the law of choice with regard to new developments in artificial intelligence and smart contracting.[3] Judges are sensitive to whether English contract law accommodates the requirements of commercial contractors and whether it compares favourably with the offerings of other legal systems in the market for commercial dispute resolution.[4] The prioritisation of business interests is demonstrated by the creation in 2015 of the specialist Financial List in the High Court. Cases commenced in the Commercial Court or Chancery Division are allocated to the list where the claim requires judicial expertise in financial markets, or the value of the dispute exceeds £50m, or where an issue of general importance for the operation of financial markets is raised.[5] The creation of the list might be regarded as an attempt to see off competition from an increasing number of rivals in the international market

[1] Ilias Bantekas, 'The Globalisation of English Contract Law: Three Salient Illustrations' (2021) 137 *Law Quarterly Review* 330, 330.

[2] Jonathan Morgan, *Contract Law Minimalism: A Formalist Restatement of Commercial Contract Law* (Cambridge University Press, 2013), pp. 87–89.

[3] Lord Burnett, *The Lord Chief Justice's Report 2020* (Judicial Office, 2020), p. 24; Law Commission, *Smart Contracts: Call for Evidence* (December 2020), para 1.5.

[4] Lord Thomas, 'Keeping Commercial Law Up to Date', Jill Poole Memorial Lecture, Aston University (8 March 2017) [8]. Perhaps a benign indication of the way this is viewed appears in Lord Justice Briggs, *Civil Courts Structure Review: Final Report* (July 2016), paras 5.18 and 9.3.1.

[5] Civil Procedure Rules, part 63A.1. The most noteworthy case to start in the list is *Financial Conduct Authority* v. *Arch Insurance (UK) Ltd and others* [2021] 2 WLR 123. This case determined various issues around business interruption insurance claims in the light of the Covid-19 pandemic.

for law and legal services. The push to establish specialist commercial courts and tribunals is manifest in Asia[6] but also in the closer market of the EU 27, notably the Netherlands, France and Germany.[7]

The conceptualisation of national law as a product with an export market is appealing and enduring. English common law gained a foothold throughout many areas of the world thanks to Britain's colonial past, and it continues as a dominant force in international dispute resolution. In 2019–2020, non-domestic disputes accounted for 75 per cent of case load in the Commercial Court, although the number of cases heard remains relatively small.[8] Legal services contributed approximately £5.6 billion to the United Kingdom's export economy in 2018.[9] The Commercial Court is itself a commercial entity, keen to develop competence in areas of future legal significance. There is a clear aspiration within the UK government that English law attracts new business into the domestic legal system.[10] This pressure to bring in business has intensified in light of the negative consequences of Brexit for traditionally strong sectors of the economy that call upon legal expertise, such as financial services.[11] Brexit may render UK legal services a less attractive option, certainly for users in the European Union and potentially for clients in the non-EU international environment. Regulatory divergence from the European Union is likely, as the United Kingdom attempts to find new outlets for its legal and financial services to replace those lost to Brexit.[12] Brexit is likely to influence legal development in other ways. English judges were largely

[6] The Singapore International Commercial Court was established in 2015, the Chinese first and second International Commercial Court and the Chamber in 2018.

[7] The Netherlands Commercial Court was established in 2019, the International Chamber of the Court of Appeal of Paris in 2018 and the Frankfurt Chamber for International Commercial Disputes at the beginning of 2018.

[8] *The Commercial Court Report* 2019–2020, pp. 18–19.

[9] According to figures from the Office for National Statistics, the international trade in legal services was worth £5.6 bn in 2018; the figure was £3.2 bn in 2013, www.ons.gov.uk/businessindustryandtrade/internationaltrade/datasets/internationaltradeinservicesreferencetables Table C5 2013–2018 Professional, Scientific and Technical Support industry analysed by product 2013–2018; see also KPMG, *Contribution of the UK Legal Services Sector to the UK Economy: A Report for the Law Society* (January 2020), p. 15; Ministry of Justice, *Plan for Growth: Promoting the UK's Legal Services Sector* (2012).

[10] See the 'Legal Services Are Great' campaign, www.gov.uk/government/publications/legal-services-are-great

[11] John Armour, 'Brexit and Financial Services' (2017) 33 *Oxford Review of Economic Policy* S54; Oliver Wyman/TheCityUK, *The Impact of the UK's Exit from the EU on the UK-Based Financial Services Sector* (2016).

[12] Rishi Sunak, *Mansion House Speech* (1 July 2021) www.gov.uk/government/speeches/mansion-house-speech-2021-rishi-sunak

equivocal about importing into English contract law legal concepts from continental Europe during the EU membership era. Brexit allows English judges to mould contract law rules without regard to EU initiatives towards legal harmonisation or convergence. Though not yet extinguished entirely, recourse to the Court of Justice of the European Union for questions of interpretation will be much more limited, notwithstanding that much EU-derived law remains on the UK statute book.[13] The contract jurisprudence of the European Union, particularly its manifest commitment to open-ended concepts such as good faith, is likely to have much-reduced significance for domestic legal development.

The concern with the attractiveness of English law in the market is not new.[14] As with trends we have observed elsewhere, the perception of law as a product reflects a shift from justificatory arguments stressing the community benefits of adjudication to those according value only to the private interest in dispute resolution. Emphasis on private interests and benefits also brings considerations concerning the costs of resolving disputes to the fore. Equating the worth of the legal system with its financial viability marginalises the largely unquantifiable public advantages derived from the role of courts in developing legal principle. An economic rationale for the system becomes all important, with the result that the production of public rules through the litigation process is regarded not as a social good but as an instance of free-riding.[15] National law that does not accommodate alternative governance systems is castigated as a state monopoly that should be broken up.[16] Litigation itself becomes just one option in an increasingly overcrowded dispute resolution market whose (commercial) users are acutely sensitive to price. The 'contract law as commodity' view has not escaped criticism, although judicial pushback is generally directed towards government for cutting legal aid funding and channelling disputes into cheaper, informal resolution procedures. Lord Scott remarked that a 'policy which treats the

[13] Catharine MacMillan, 'The Impact of Brexit upon English Contract Law' (2016) 27 *King's Law Journal* 420, 427–28. See also www.commonslibrary.parliament.uk/brexit-next-steps-the-court-of-justice-of-the-eu-and-the-uk/

[14] Lord Devlin, 'The Relation between Commercial Law and Commercial Practice' (1951) 14 *Modern Law Review* 250.

[15] William M. Landes and Richard A. Posner, 'Adjudication as a Private Good' (1979) 8 *Journal of Legal Studies* 235, 238–39 and 249.

[16] Thomas Ackermann, 'Private Production of Transnational Regulation through Standard Form Contracts' in Horst Eidenmüller (ed.) *Regulatory Competition in Contract Law and Dispute Resolution* (Verlag C H Beck, Hart Publishing, Nomos, 2013), pp. 142, 145.

civil justice system merely as a service to be offered at cost in the market place, and to be paid for by those who choose to use it, profoundly and dangerously mistakes the nature of the system and its constitutional function'.[17] In his Keating Lecture in 2010, Lord Neuberger observed that the 'civil justice system exists for all citizens. It provides a benefit for all and should be properly accessible by all. If it is not it cannot properly provide a general public benefit; it cannot properly be a public good.'[18] Similarly, Lord Reed has denied that bringing a claim before the court is entirely a private activity with no social benefit.[19] These warnings are apt. Even if we are not likely to run out of legal principles, it is likely that those principles will increasingly reflect the concerns of those who can afford to litigate their disputes to trial and judgment.

Lawyers in commercial practice have been influential too in the commercialisation and commodification project. Moorhead and Hinchly observe that 'the practice of law as a profession is increasingly being replaced with the practice of law as a business' and that this 'represents an escalation of commercial and business logics within practice' to the detriment of professional ethics.[20] The authors conclude from their empirical study of professional attitudes that the 'professional ethical consciousness of commercial lawyers in-house or in private practice is minimalistic'.[21] They found that lawyers regarded law as setting the technical limits that they worked around in order to satisfy their client. There was little concern with any wider professional or social responsibilities.[22] This attitude was particularly marked amongst lawyers in private practice, who tended to rank the firm's commercial interest higher than the public interest.[23] These views about commercial law and practice reflect a wider view about the fundamentally self-serving nature of commerce held by some senior members of the judiciary: recall Lord Sumption's remark that 'fairness has nothing to do with commercial

[17] Quoted in Lord Neuberger, 'Has Mediation Has Its Day?' Gordon Slynn Memorial Lecture (10 November 2010), at [10]. The quote appears in Michael Zander, *The State of Justice* (Sweet & Maxwell, 2000), at p. 39 n. 49, where it is attributed to a transcript of a speech made by Lord Scott to the County Court Advisers' Group, May 16, 1997. See also Lord Neuberger, 'Equity, ADR, Arbitration and the Law: Different Dimensions of Justice' Fourth Keating Lecture (19 May 2010) at [6].

[18] Lord Neuberger, 'Equity, ADR, Arbitration and the Law', [24].

[19] *R (on the application of UNISON)* v. *Lord Chancellor* [2020] AC 869 [66]–[72].

[20] Richard Moorhead and Victoria Hinchly, 'Professional Minimalism: The Ethical Consciousness of Commercial Lawyers' (2015) 42 *Journal of Law and Society* 387.

[21] Moorhead and Hinchly, 'Professional Minimalism', 389.

[22] Moorhead and Hinchly, 'Professional Minimalism', 396.

[23] Moorhead and Hinchly, 'Professional Minimalism', 399.

contracts . . . [c]ommercial parties can be most unfair and entirely unreasonable, if they can get away with it.'[24] The negative social effects of perpetuating this mindset, and allowing it to permeate the development of the legal rules, are rarely identified, still less commented on.

The pressure to win market share suggests contract law's commercial turn is likely to become only more entrenched. The bias towards the commercial contract in contract law has a distorting effect on common law development. First, the concentration of the law on high-value and high-stakes litigation claims, and the desire to facilitate the efficient disposal of these claims, generates principles that are taken to express some universal and inviolable truth about contract that is taken to apply across the whole range of contracting activity. An aggravating factor is that many complex commercial contract cases involve reactive decision-making in the wake of a crisis. Attention to the interests of the dominant group results in litigation that tends to cluster around unique, disruptive events. This scenario generally yields single-issue solutions not readily transferable across different contracting contexts, and with possibly unpredictable long-term effects.[25] Alternatively, the rules derived from such decisions are applicable only in a reductive fashion that concentrates on the operation of express terms to the exclusion of almost all other considerations.[26] A recent example is provided by the litigation arising out of the global financial crisis, particularly the collapse of Lehman Brothers Holdings Inc.[27] Most of the disputes in these cases turned on contract interpretation. The individualistic and terms-based reasoning adopted naturally has a tendency to seep into the determination of other disputes displaying only superficial levels of factual similarity.[28] Second, the dominance of commercial parties in contract law tends to reinforce the archetype of the non-co-operative

[24] Lord Sumption, 'A Question of Taste: The Supreme Court and the Interpretation of Contracts' (2017) 17 *Oxford University Commonwealth Law Journal* 301, 310.

[25] Michael Bridge and Jo Braithwaite, 'Private Law and Financial Crises' (2013) 13 *Journal of Corporate Law Studies* 361, 366.

[26] Emily Strauss, 'Crisis Construction in Contract Boilerplate' (2019) 82 *Law and Contemporary Problems* 163, 164.

[27] *RAB Capital Plc* v. *Lehman Brothers International (Europe)* [2008] EWHC 2335 (Ch); *Belmont Park Investments PTY Ltd* v. *BNY Corporate Trustee Services Ltd and Lehman Brothers Special Financing Inc* [2011] 3 WLR 521; *Re Lehman Brothers International (Europe)* [2011] EWCA Civ 1544; [2012] 2 BCLC 151; *Lehman Brothers International (Europe) Ltd* v. *CRC Credit Fund Ltd* [2012] 3 All ER 1; *Lomas & Ors* v. *JFB Firth Rixson Inc* [2012] EWCA Civ 419; *BNY Mellon Corporate Trustee Services Ltd* v. *LBG Capital No 1 plc* [2016] 2 Lloyd's Rep 119; Bridge and Braithwaite, 'Private Law and Financial Crises', 365.

[28] See further Chapter 3 on operation of 'basis of contract' and 'no reliance' clauses.

and adversarial contractor, who is already over-represented throughout contract doctrine. As we saw in the previous chapter, non-commercial contractors affected by the rules remain outliers. Their interests are at the margins of contract law's central concerns. This displays a poor legal grasp of the profound social welfare issues generated by formal contract enforcement. The orientation of contract law towards the interests of its immediate users confuses the demands of a litigating class of contractors with a much wider group affected by the resulting law.

6.2 Privatising Justice

Concerns over the ascription of product-like characteristics to law mirror wider uneasiness about the privatisation of justice.[29] This refers to the tendency to dispose of legal disputes through private methods such as settlement and alternative dispute resolution (ADR). Arbitration has long been favoured over litigation as the main method of dispute resolution in the area of commercial contracts.[30] Nevertheless, fears have been expressed that common law is stagnating in areas of commercial law where arbitration is the preferred forum for hearing disputes.[31] The proliferation of ADR is not confined to commercial disputes but has become a feature of the civil justice landscape more generally. Various civil procedure initiatives from the Woolf reforms onwards have facilitated ADR through the mechanism of judicial case management powers.[32] Since 1996 the consistent message from courts has been

[29] See Owen M. Fiss, 'Against Settlement' (1984) 93 *Yale Law Journal* 1073; David Luban, 'Settlements and the Erosion of the Public Realm' (1995) 83 *Georgetown Law Journal* 2619, 2622; Judith Resnik, 'Diffusing Disputes: The Public in the Private of Arbitration, the Private in Courts, and the Erasure of Rights' (2015) 124 *Yale Law Journal* 2804; Margaret Jane Radin, *Boilerplate: The Fine Print, Vanishing Rights and the Rule of Law* (Princeton University Press, 2013), pp. 133–34. For the UK concerns see Robert Dingwall and Emilie Cloatre, 'Vanishing Trials?: An English Perspective' (2006) 7 *Journal of Dispute Resolution* 51; Hazel Genn, *Judging Civil Justice* (Cambridge University Press, 2010); Linda Mulcahy, 'The Collective Interest in Private Dispute Resolution' (2013) 33 *Oxford Journal of Legal Studies* 59. For the judicial reservations see Lord Reed in *R (on the application of UNISON)* v. *Lord Chancellor* [2020] AC 869 [66]–[67]; Lord Thomas, 'Developing Commercial Law through the Courts: Rebalancing the Relationship between the Courts and Arbitration' BAILII Lecture (9 March 2016).

[30] Walter Mattli, 'Private Justice in a Global Economy: From Litigation to Arbitration' (2001) 55 *International Organization* 919–20; Vijaya Kumar Rajah, 'W(h)ither Adversarial Commercial Dispute Resolution?' (2017) 33 *Arbitration International* 17, 24–25.

[31] Lord Thomas, 'Developing Commercial Law through the Courts: Rebalancing the Relationship between the Courts and Arbitration', para 5.

[32] Under Civil Procedure Rules 1.4(2)(e) (overriding objectives) and 3.1(2)(m) (case management powers).

that litigation is a last resort.[33] Judges seek to discourage litigation by channelling disputes into mediation and other similar processes in an attempt to broker settlement over trial, with the possibility of adverse cost consequences for any unreasonable refusal to participate.[34] The pressure on parties to resolve their dispute through methods other than litigation is likely to intensify given the recent conclusion of the Civil Justice Council that parties can lawfully be compelled to engage in ADR.[35] Anti-adjudication sentiments have been reinforced by the Covid-19 pandemic. Despite the numerous and novel contract legal issues raised by the Covid outbreak, contracting parties have been directed to avoid litigation in favour of conciliatory methods of dispute resolution when confronting the contract problems generated by the crisis.[36] Only disputes raising matters of sector-wide importance, such as the insurance industry response to the pandemic, have found their way to the highest courts.[37]

Judges bear only some responsibility for generating an anti-adjudication climate. The significant practical impediment to common law development is the lack of financial support for small businesses, consumers and other weaker contracting parties litigating the type of case that might moderate the court bias towards commercial disputes and help to restore balance to contract law. The question is one of distributive justice in allocating finite resources. The period of austerity following the global financial crisis of 2008–2009 saw a sharp reduction in public funding for the Ministry of Justice generally.[38] An overhaul of the legal aid system in 2013 removed most non-family private law

[33] Lord Woolf, *Access to Justice: Final Report to the Lord Chancellor on the Civil Justice System in England and Wales* (HMSO, 1996), s 1, para 9.

[34] *Dunnett* v. *Railtrack plc (in railway administration)* [2002] 1 WLR 2434; *Halsey* v. *Milton Keynes General NHS Trust* [2004] EWCA Civ 576; *PGF II SA* v. *OMFS Co 1 Ltd* [2014] 1 WLR 1386. Refusal to mediate might be justified if the dispute is complex or a party is justified in seeking vindication of their rights in court or where mediation has no reasonable prospect of success: *Gore* v. *Naheed and Ahmed* [2017] EWCA Civ 369 [49]–[50].

[35] Civil Justice Council, *Compulsory ADR* (June 2021), para 7.

[36] See, for example, Cabinet Office, *Guidance on Responsible Contractual Behaviour in the Performance and Enforcement of Contracts Impacted by the Covid-19 Emergency* (7 May 2020).

[37] *Financial Conduct Authority* v. *Arch Insurance (UK) Ltd and others* [2021] 2 WLR 123.

[38] Research conducted for the Bar Council indicated a 27 per cent cut in real terms to Ministry of Justice funding between 2008 and 2018, www.barcouncil.org.uk/resource/new-research-questions-link-between-austerity-and-legal-aid-cuts.html. This was the largest budget cut in a government department: *The Guardian* 26 December 2018, www.theguardian.com/law/2018/dec/26/legal-aid-how-has-it-changed-in-70-years

claims from eligibility for financial support from the state,[39] including consumer and contract matters.[40] Contract claims may generate little sympathy in the debate over access to civil justice until one appreciates that many employment disputes, debt matters, housing cases and consumer rights problems rest ultimately on a contractual relationship and engage with an element of traditional contract law. The cuts to civil legal aid funding are unlikely to be reversed. The government has recognised the problem of unmet need for legal services but looks to find the answer in ADR rather than litigation funding, which is regarded as wasteful and excessive.[41] The result is that, as Dingwall and Cloatre observe, the 'state is tending to withdraw and leave civil justice to the market'.[42]

Court-ordered ADR is only the tip of a very large iceberg of dispute disposal by various non-trial methods conducted in private.[43] On the commercial side, specialist dispute resolution may be offered by industry representative bodies and organisations. Claims may be handled through complaints procedures for customers or expert determination panels for members. Such informal measures are administrative rather than quasi-legal in function. The International Swaps and Derivatives Association (ISDA), for example, offers a service to users defining terms in the Master Agreement through its Credit Derivatives Determinations Committee (DC). The role of the committee is described as 'to apply the terms of market-standard credit derivatives contracts to specific cases, and make factual determinations on Credit Events, Successor Reference Entities and other issues, based on information provided to the

39 Legal Aid, Sentencing and Punishment of Offenders Act 2012 (LASPO); Law Society of England and Wales, *Access Denied? LASPO Four Years On: A Law Society Review Report* (June 2017); Government statistics show a fall in civil representation costs met by the Legal Aid Agency in non-family matters from £79 m in 2010–2011 to £40 m in 2018–2019 (Legal Aid Statistics England and Wales, Tables October to December 2019, Table 6.5).

40 Although falling outside the scope of LASPO, consumer and contract cases may be eligible for Legal Aid through Exceptional Case Funding (ECF). Government statistics show that out of twenty-eight applications for ECF made between 2013 and the end of 2019 and falling within the Debt/Consumer/Contract category, only two received grants (Legal Aid Statistics England and Wales Tables October to December 2019, Table 8.2).

41 Ministry of Justice, *Legal Support: The Way Ahead – An Action Plan to Deliver Better Support to People Experiencing Legal Problems* CP 40 (February 2019), p. 3.

42 Dingwall and Cloatre, 'Vanishing Trials?', 70.

43 Gillian K. Hadfield, 'Where Have All the Trials Gone? Settlements, Nontrial Adjudications, and Statistical Artifacts in the Changing Disposition of Federal Civil Cases' (2004) 1 *Journal of Empirical Legal Studies* 705, 705; Chris A. Carr and Michael R. Jencks, 'The Privatization of Business and Commercial Dispute Resolution: A Misguided Policy Decision' (1999) 88 *Kentucky Law Journal* 183.

DCs by credit default swap . . . market participants'.[44] Regulatory bodies may also offer arbitration or other dispute resolution services. An example is the Groceries Code Adjudicator,[45] who is charged with enforcing the Groceries Supply Code of Practice between retailers (primarily major supermarkets) and their suppliers. The adjudicator is empowered to arbitrate disputes between retailers and suppliers under the Code.[46] Details of the arbitration and its outcome are confidential unless the parties agree to disclosure,[47] although confidentiality will normally be mandated by the contract between the retailer and the supplier.

Individual claimants and consumers may be directed towards various complaints procedures instituted by administrative bodies or regulators charged with overseeing the operation of a particular market or sector. Such procedures tend towards complaint disposal, rather than dispute resolution in a genuine sense. The Financial Ombudsman Service,[48] for example, does not determine legal entitlements but renders decisions 'based on what [they] think is fair and reasonable, accounting for the unique circumstances of each case'.[49] Ombudsman systems were originally developed to respond to complaints concerning administrative failures in the public sector. It has been observed that the contemporary office of ombudsman increasingly reflects the managerialist model of public administration. This is manifest in the use of managerialist language, the emphasis on efficiency and consumer satisfaction in public services, and reliance on informal complaint resolution (taking its lead from complaints management in the private sector) rather than full investigation and report.[50] The managerialist shift is reflected in civil justice more generally,[51] augmenting a change in ethos in public service dispute handling away from 'law-like' values – upholding the rule of law, due process and public adjudication – and towards the same efficiency and value for money goals that underpin much modern regulation.[52]

[44] www.cdsdeterminationscommittees.org/

[45] www.gov.uk/government/organisations/groceries-code-adjudicator

[46] Groceries Code Adjudicator Act 2013 s 2.

[47] Groceries Code Adjudicator Act 2013 s 18. See also para 43 of Groceries Code Adjudicator, *Arbitration Policy* (April 2014); the *Annual Report and Accounts* HC 256 (2020–2021) noting the importance of confidentiality in raising complaints and taking action (19).

[48] www.financial-ombudsman.org.uk/

[49] www.financial-ombudsman.org.uk/data-insight/ombudsman-decisions

[50] Chris Gill, Tom Mullen and Nial Vivian, 'The Managerial Ombudsman' (2020) 83 *Modern Law Review* 797, 798.

[51] Gill, Mullen and Vivian, 'The Managerial Ombudsman', 829–30.

[52] Gill, Mullen and Vivian, 'The Managerial Ombudsman', 801.

Supplementing these relatively formal methods of dispute resolution are the goodwill gestures, pay-offs and other mollification measures that form the mainstay of complaint handling by firms. These methods do not necessarily resolve the dispute in the sense of tackling the source of the problem directly and conclusively but dispense with trouble privately and usually in secret. Confidentiality in reporting disputes and consequent proceedings is justified in many contexts, such as to protect whistle-blowers and others who may fear retaliation after making a complaint to a regulator or other official body. But privacy also shields decisions and procedures from scrutiny, forestalls criticism and conceals matters of public interest that might prompt reform if revealed and debated. The use of non-disclosure agreements in settlements of work-place harassment claims that we examined in the last chapter is an apt example. Private dispute disposal can usually dispense with detailed reasons for an outcome, can prevent the exercise of any further right of recourse or appeal, and, if reliant on negotiation, will be controlled (and manipulated) by the economically stronger party.[53] Evidently many of these claims – often small – are not suitable for litigation to judgment. Similarly, the vast majority of disputes may raise no wider issues of public importance. Nevertheless, the shift towards disposal of disputes through private administrative procedures and away from adjudication according to law cannot be presented as a wholly positive development. Private processes do not contribute to publicly available rules that might serve the interests of a potential class of future disputants, and there is no requirement to observe the basic tenet of justice to treat like cases alike.[54] Specialist dispute resolution by regulators or specialist courts and tribunals risks capture by the interests represented. It also contributes to the loss of generalist judicial skills in favour of managerial competence.[55]

The shift to private and alternative dispute resolution poses an existential threat to legal development, particularly in the common law. It is also likely to compound issues of the commercialisation of contract law. ADR is often lauded for promoting access to justice, overlooking that the procedures

[53] See Trevor C. W. Farrow, *Civil Justice, Privatization and Democracy* (University of Toronto Press, 2014), pp. 62–68. For a judicial defence of open courts as a requisite of justice see Lord Shaw of Dunfermline in *Scott* v. *Scott* [1913] AC 419, 477 (HL).

[54] Farrow, *Civil Justice, Privatization and Democracy*, Chapter 3, p. 251ff; Dame Hazel Genn, 'Why the Privatisation of Civil Justice is a Rule Of Law Issue', 36th F A Mann Lecture (19 November 2012).

[55] Owen M. Fiss, 'The Bureaucratization of the Judiciary' (1983) 92 *Yale Law Journal* 1442, 1466; Judith Resnik, 'Managerial Judges' (1982) 96 *Harvard Law Review* 376; Luban, 'Settlements and the Erosion of the Public Realm', 2624.

involved do not always tend to produce justice in the sense of vindicating legal rights. Rather, ADR elides justice with efficiency measured in terms of speed and cost. Genn observes that ADR solves a problem but rarely upholds a legal entitlement and manifests little concern with substantive justice.[56] The role of contract here should not be overlooked. Contract terms may attempt to place various limitations on remedies available to a party and to keep disputes out of public courts.[57] ADR prosecuted through contract mechanisms accentuates the individualistic approach to dispute resolution, accentuates the importance of negotiating skills and aggravates problems of inequality of bargaining power.[58] As with any contract, an agreement to submit to ADR, or to settle, can be procured through acquiescence or inertia and can be a source of exploitation and imbalance.

Shunting dispute resolution into secret fora is an ad hoc form of resolution that contributes nothing to legal development. Neither does it communicate anything about the values inherent in contracting nor do anything to protect and uphold those values. Naturally, the public nature of the trial also demonstrates that law and the legal process are flawed, contingent and controversial. But in the same way that dissenting judgments have value in presenting an alternative view of the law, the exposure of these negative traits is significant in stimulating debate and raising questions, and opportunities to answer them, about the nature of justice and legal authority. Ultimately, public decisions are important forms of *data* that can be analysed, assessed, evaluated and theorised. While one can obtain raw figures on the number of disputes resolved by private means, one gets little indication of the process of decision-making, or the reasoning behind the outcome, that can contribute to informing the public about the expectations they are entitled to have concerning contract conduct when participating in markets. Crucially, judges are aware of the public nature of adjudication and this transparency gives rise to certain constraints on legal reasoning and decision-making that do not restrain private decision-makers. Judicial decisions are open to criticism, not least by other judges. Trials and judgments, and the discussion and controversy that often result from judgments, open up opportunities for a form of dialogue between judges,

56 Genn, *Judging Civil Justice*, p. 116.

57 In consumer contracts such provisions may be automatically unfair under the Arbitration Act 1996 s 91(1), and the Unfair Arbitration Agreements (Specified Amount) Order 1999, or under the Consumer Rights Act 2015.

58 Fiss, 'Against settlement', 1075, 1076ff; Luban, 'Settlements and the Erosion of the Public Realm', 2639 footnote omitted.

academics, practitioners and the public more generally.[59] As Fiss notes, adjudication is enclosed by 'adherence to the strictures of public reason'.[60]

The ADR and justice privatisation project has received a fillip from the increasing use of online methods of dispute resolution.[61] Some judges already look to the online dispute handling systems of businesses with a certain degree of admiration. Amazon and eBay reportedly resolve sixty million disputes a year satisfactorily through online processes, compared with three million formal disputes resolved through civil courts, ombudsmen and the like.[62] The establishment of online courts is perhaps a more ambitious manifestation of platform-based dispute resolution. As with other ADR imperatives, online courts are motivated by the desire to cut costs, reduce delay and ensure English legal services retain market share in the competition for commercial clients.[63]

To the extent that 'online court' merely indicates that the work of courts is transferred away from a physical space to an online environment, as was necessary during the Covid-19 pandemic, there may be few implications for common law development. Judgments on legal questions will still be delivered, although without the magisterial court buildings that represent a potent symbol of legal authority and are the 'physical expression of our relationship with the ideals of justice'.[64] This may be a positive or negative development depending on what access to justice means and how we measure success in improving it. The shift to online courts is more problematic when 'online' refers not just to the environment in which cases or disputes are heard and resolved but to an entirely different mechanism for producing decisions bearing little resemblance to traditional courts engaged in conventional adjudication. That is, a system where substantial decision-making is undertaken by computers producing the kind of outcomes normally regarded as the preserve of judgment. Susskind observes that 'online courts . . . are a clear illustration of

59 Joanne P. Braithwaite, 'Standard Form Contracts as Transnational Law: Evidence from the Derivatives Markets' (2012) 75 *Modern Law Review* 779, 801–02.

60 Owen M. Fiss, 'The History of an Idea' (2009) 78 *Fordham Law Review* 1273, 1276.

61 Lord Sales, 'Algorithms, Artificial Intelligence and the Law', The Sir Henry Brooke Lecture for BAILII (12 November 2019), p. 9.

62 Sir Geoffrey Vos, 'Technological Challenges for English Law and Jurisdiction' ISDA Virtual Annual Legal Forum (10 March 2021), para 27. See also Sir Geoffrey Vos, 'The Relationship between Formal and Informal Justice', Hull University (26 March 2021), at para 24.

63 Lord Justice Briggs, *Civil Courts Structure Review: Final Report*, paras 9.3 and 5.18.

64 Linda Mulcahy, *Legal Architecture: Justice, Due Process and the Place of Law* (Routledge, 2011), p. 1.

transformation and not automation'.[65] That is to say, online courts are not just a new way of facilitating existing legal processes but herald a radical change to our ideas of what courts are, what their function is, and to our ways of thinking about justice. For Susskind, embracing the potential of online courts involves 'outcome-thinking' about the law. This means understanding that what the public wants from the law is not lawyers, courts and judges, or even necessarily the law itself. These are only a means to the real ends, which are justice, vindication and resolution.[66] For Susskind, these outcomes can be divorced from the current legal and adjudicative processes that we identify as necessary to achieving them.

Should we embrace this vision of case determination that dispenses with legal rules and legal reasoning as an unnecessary and expensive distraction from achieving a satisfactory (for whom?) result? This wholly instrumental view of law (or not-law) that sees dispute resolution as the entire point of the legal (or not-legal) process no doubt has some appeal. But it renders the concept of judgment obsolete as an expression of community values, the culmination of a transparent reasoning process and a conduit for censure and explanation. Whereas Susskind is enthusiastic about this development, Zuckerman is more circumspect, pointing out the dangers of decline in the judicial skill set. Not only do we risk the loss of formal legal reasoning proficiency but the disappearance of empathy, emotion, an innate sense of fairness and justice, an understanding of context and nuance when dealing the existing legal canon and, occasionally, a recognition of human frailty, which are part and parcel of the (admittedly not perfect) human process of delivering a judgment.[67] There are practical difficulties too. An initial rule-set must be programmed into the online platform that delivers the decision. The normative complexity of a judgment or rule (particularly one emanating from the common law) may be a stretch for a programmer to code and for a machine to apply to a different fact-scenario. The rote determinations that come with computational judging on the basis of past cases and previous outcomes may also render judging an excessively backward-looking enterprise, mired in the past, with no immediate mechanism to institute a complete break with tradition and certainly not a break based on any moral or value-based criteria,

65 Richard Susskind, *Online Courts and the Future of Justice* (Oxford University Press, 2019), p. 35.

66 Susskind, *Online Courts*, p. 48.

67 Adrian Zuckerman, 'Artificial Intelligence – Implications for the Legal Profession, Adversarial Process and Rule of Law' (2020) 136 *Law Quarterly Review* 427, 428.

such as the 'reasonable expectations of honest people'. This will undoubtedly please formalists who would like to eliminate any trace of judicial activism and discretion ('bias') from cases in favour of the operation of fixed and determinate rules delivering predictable and consistent outcomes. Ultimately, however, it may not be the code that is required to change. If our aim is to deliver efficiency over justice then if the machine cannot adapt to our ideas about law, then the rules may have to adapt instead to what can be produced in code. This will change our ideas not only of legal practice but what law is. We explore these issues in the next section, when we consider the implications for contract law of 'smart' or 'algorithmic' contracts, that is, contracts created or performed by computer software with a relative degree of autonomy from human programmers and without human intervention or agency.

6.3 Contract Law and Contract Automation

Online courts and automated dispute resolution may exert a profound influence on some of our foundational ideas about law. Contract law will not be immune. Innovations in information and communication technology have radically altered the ways we make and perform voluntary agreements. Automation is likely to reduce further the role of state institutions in facilitating certain transactions, ushering in methods of computer-driven contract creation and enforcement that are subject to minimal legal scrutiny. To the extent that these processes depend on law to generate confidence amongst users that computers can create valid obligations, they cannot dispense with legal regulation entirely. Whether current contract law is an effective regulator, however, remains to be seen. Practical changes in contracting methods frequently put some of contract law's assumptions under strain: face-to-face dealing is replaced with electronic communications; meaningful negotiation is replaced with instantaneous agreements; lengthy legal proceedings are replaced with automatic and immediate enforcement. Despite the considerable gap that often exists between legal expectations and contracting reality, the prevailing common law strategy has been to accommodate innovation within existing rule frameworks, taken to the relevant degree of abstraction.[68] Thus a mouse click on 'accept' on a screen can be likened to a signature on a document, and provided there is reasonable notice of terms (and subject to any controls on unfairness of terms) a contract will be created. This fits with

[68] Mark Giancaspro, 'Is a "Smart Contract" Really a Smart Idea? Insights From a Legal Perspective' (2017) 33 *Computer Law & Security Review* 825, 829.

the common law instinct towards coherence and 'leisurely change … not geared to a world of rapidly emerging and highly disruptive technologies'.[69]

As the technology becomes more complex, and smart or algorithmic contracting encroaches further into the legal and contract space,[70] it is not clear that 'forcing the facts' to fit the legal rules will be an effective strategy.[71] This may not matter too much, since the strengths of English contract law in tackling the challenges presented by the technological age are not to be found in its doctrinal rules but in its support for party autonomy.[72] Appeals to party autonomy alone, however, will not be sufficient to head off the questions presented by new ways of making and performing agreements. In relation to the sharing and gig economy, for example, transactions are facilitated through electronic platforms where relationships are created and mediated through detailed standard contracts. These new systems produce novel legal problems, such as the status of the electronic platform that facilitates peer-to-peer supply of goods and services. Courts realise that these issues cannot be resolved by appealing to the bootstrap quality of the terms themselves that may dictate the platform is an 'agent', and not, say, an employer, of the user offering their services via the platform.[73] Common law solutions can be fashioned from the existing concepts, but programmers and coders will find ways to neutralise unfriendly interventions, much in the way that lawyers may react to an unfavourable legal precedent or a controversial statutory rule by changing the contract small print. Understandably, law reform bodies have taken a much clearer lead than judges here. The Law Commission has developed legal statements and proposals on aspects of electronic contracting as a response to

[69] Roger Brownsword, 'Smart Contracts: Coding the Transaction, Decoding the Legal Debates' in Philipp Hacker, Ioannis Lianos, Georgios Dimitropoulos, and Stefan Eich (eds.) *Regulating Blockchain: Techno-Social and Legal Challenges* (Oxford University Press, 2019), pp. 311, 312.

[70] Smart contracts can be distinguished from algorithmic contracting in that smart contracts are a method of automating aspects of traditional contracting whereas algorithmic contracting describes a process of contract creation between machines acting autonomously with no human involvement, see Lord Sales, 'Being a Supreme Court Justice in 2030', Law and the Digital World Cour de Cassation Seminar (16 April 2021).

[71] *New Zealand Shipping Co Ltd* v. *A M Satterthwaite & Co Ltd (The Eurymedon)* [1975] AC 154, per Lord Wilberforce 167.

[72] Sir Geoffrey Vos, 'Cryptoassets as Property: How can English Law Boost the Confidence of Would-be Parties to Smart Legal Contracts?' Joint Northern Chancery Bar Association and University of Liverpool Lecture (2 May 2019), at para 13.

[73] See *Uber BV and others* v. *Aslam and others* [2021] UKSC 5, [2021] ICR 657.

the numerous, overlapping rules produced by the common law, the European Union and domestic legislation.[74]

The impact of automation on contract law is hard to predict, since developments in information and communication technologies may impinge on contracting in different ways. Computer-based automation may facilitate the performance of what is in all other respects a traditional written contract. Using technology to facilitate aspects of contract creation or performance is not problematic from a contract law point of view. Similarly, there are many traditional contract law functions that might be usurped by technology without fundamentally altering the nature of the rules. It is conceivable that a contract interpretation problem could be run through a computer primed with empirically derived information on the meaning of certain words and phrases and a result on liability delivered in a few seconds, rather than months or years.[75] This capacity to transform selected contract law tasks may risk redundancy for some practical aspects of the legal profession and the judicial role but not necessarily contract law itself. The technology may simply mirror the result a judge would reach if they had infinite time, resources and the requisite cognitive capacity to process a mass of evidence and empirical data.

That said, even relatively benign uses of technology to facilitate aspects of the contracting process are likely to disrupt some established legal principles. We noted earlier that judges have tended to reconfigure contract practice to fit the existing legal rules. The use of innovative technologies to streamline legal procedures and reduce costs may prompt a reversal of this particular dynamic. Cautious judges may be reluctant to undermine the benefits of the technology by subjecting its slick processes to the unpredictable operation of contract law. This would constitute a shift in contract law thinking whereby the rules are sacrificed to maintain the efficiencies of the automated system. An indication of this can be seen in a string of cases involving the Ministry of Justice Claims Portal. The portal is an online platform used by claimants, defendants, their lawyers and insurers for processing and settling personal injury claims up to £25,000.[76] The cases have adopted the line that the law of unilateral mistake is inapplicable when low settlement offers erroneously entered into the portal's

[74] See, for example, Law Commission, *Electronic Commerce: Formal Requirements in Commercial Transactions: Advice* (2001); Law Commission, *Electronic Execution of Documents* Law Com No 386 (2019); Law Commission, *Smart Contracts: Call for Evidence*; Law Commission, *Digital Assets: Electronic Trade Documents – A Consultation Paper* CP 254 (30 April 2021).

[75] Betsy Cooper, 'Judges in Jeopardy! Could IBM's Watson Beat Courts at Their Own Game?' (2011) 121 *Yale Law Journal Online* 87, 95ff.

[76] www.claimsportal.org.uk/

electronic forms are 'snapped-up' by the defendant.[77] In *A* v. *B*[78] the claimant's legal representatives mistakenly entered a settlement figure of £550 into the portal instead of the intended £5,550. The lower figure was accepted by the defendant and payment made immediately. The settlement agreement was upheld notwithstanding that the defendant was aware the figure in the offer was a mistake. Under the common law rules this is a ground to avoid the resulting contract.[79]

The decisions prioritising the Claims Portal over common law mistake reflect the analogous position concerning offers to settle under Part 36 of the Civil Procedure Rules. In *Gibbon* v. *Manchester City Council*, the Court of Appeal determined that Part 36 was a self-contained procedural code containing its own rules, to be read without importing aspects of the general law.[80] This legal justification is supplemented by a more pragmatic reason for refusing to intervene. Mistakes in online processes are very easy to make but can be difficult to reverse. Courts may take the view that allowing the mistaken party to avoid the resulting contract at common law will only lead to complex satellite litigation that undermines the purpose of the online process: to settle relatively low-value personal injury claims with a summary form of justice that offers quick resolution, cost savings and certainty.[81] This justification is disingenuous given that satellite litigation is not necessarily prevented, only shifted onto the hapless professional pressing the wrong button or entering the wrong figure who must now deal with a claim from a short-changed client. Ultimately, the function of the portal is not legal or adjudicative but administrative and managerial – to dispose of the primary dispute. The anti-interventionist approach to online systems indicates a degree of legal deference towards the technology. The Claims Portal is regarded as a contained system, self-justifying on the basis of norms of speed, efficiency and finality. The general legal norms of contract are external, superfluous and obstructive, like so much 'grit in the oil'.[82]

[77] *Zommers* v. *Litham* and *Lis* v. *Rogers* [2020] 6 WLUK 499 Liverpool County Court (23 June 2020); see also *Purcell* v. *McGarry* [2013] 12 WLUK 237; *Draper* v. *Newport* [2014] 9 WLUK 74; *Fitton* v. *Ageas* [2018] 11 WLUK 703; contra, *Harris* v. *Browne* unreported HHJ Davey, Bradford County Court (18 June 2019); (2020) Law Society Gazette (14 September), p. 11.

[78] *AKA Mahoney* v. *Royal Mail* unreported DDJ Doman, Truro County Court (26 May 2020). See also *Zommers* v. *Litham* at [35].

[79] Cf. *Hartog* v. *Colin & Shields* [1939] 3 All ER 566.

[80] [2010] EWCA Civ 726, per Lord Justice Moore-Bick [6].

[81] *Draper* v. *Newport* [5]; *Fitton* v. *Ageas* [36]–[37]; *Zommers* v. *Litham* [32].

[82] Lord Goff, 'Commercial Contracts and the Commercial Court' (1984) *Lloyd's Maritime and Commercial Law Quarterly* 382, 391.

The operation of the Claims Portal gives one indication of how the law may respond to technological innovations. The law's existence is acknowledged, but its regulatory force is moderated to avoid incompatibility with the technology. This is problematic in relation to potentially the most disruptive use of the technology for contract law: to create an alternative contract enforcement system. Emerging information and communication technologies, such as distributed ledgers, blockchains and 'smart contracts', may remove the requirement for state institutions to enforce certain kinds of transaction, replacing them with private and autonomous forms of control facilitated electronically through computer software and cryptography.[83] There isn't space here to deal with all the ramifications of smart contracts for contract law. Notably, we leave aside the vexed question of whether smart contracts are contracts at all.[84] We deal here only with the smart contract's potentially rupturing effect on the idea that contract law is essential to the facilitation and effective enforcement of the market transaction.

One key technology here is the distributed ledger (blockchain is perhaps the most well-known example), which is a method of recording transactions or data that are shared without variation across a network of computers who 'agree' that they are accurate.[85] Peer-to-peer transactions can be recorded, stored, executed and validated in the ledger. There are different types of public and private ledgers (permissioned-less or permissioned), but the ledger will be accessible to anyone who has the necessary permissions and digital key. It is supposedly tamper-proof. Unlike, say, an individual bank, which ultimately may be the arbiter of whether a transaction goes ahead depending on the state of the payer's account, the ledger is not held or administered by any individual or central organisation but is instead subject to a network-consensus verification system. The ledger dispenses with the need for third-party intermediaries, or 'authorities', that might perform functions of logging, enforcing and otherwise enabling the transfers and transactions undertaken via the ledger. As an alternative to the general law of contract, these systems may be less costly,

[83] Kevin Werbach and Nicolas Cornell, 'Contracts *Ex Machina*' (2017) 67 *Duke Law Journal* 313; Kevin Werbach, 'Trust, But Verify: Why the Blockchain Needs the Law' (2018) 33 *Berkeley Technology Law Journal* 487; Karen Yeung, 'Regulation by Blockchain: The Emerging Battle for Supremacy between the Code *of* Law and Code *as* Law' (2019) 82 *Modern Law Review* 207.

[84] Doubts are expressed by Eliza Mik, 'The Resilience of Contract Law in Light of Technological Change' in Michael Furmston (ed.) *The Future of the Law of Contract* (Routledge, 2020), pp. 112, 114; 'Smart Contracts: A Requiem' (2019) 36 *Journal of Contract Law* 70.

[85] Michèle Finck, 'Blockchains: Regulating the Unknown' (2018) 19 *German Law Journal* 665, 667.

more efficient and more responsive to the individual features of the parties' contracting environment. Distributed ledger technology (DLT) enables cryptocurrencies such as Bitcoin and Ether and the phenomena of smart contracts. Giancaspro explains smart contracts as 'a computer program which verifies and executes its terms upon the occurrence of predetermined events. Once coded and entered into the blockchain the contract cannot be changed and operates in accordance with its programmed instructions.'[86] The potential in smart contracts is for 'contracting parties [to] deal directly with one another without banks, without offline registries and, potentially, without lawyers'.[87]

There cannot be a single contract law response to these technological developments, as the extent to which they rely on legal contracts and legal enforcement will vary.[88] Smart contracts may operate within legal parameters by being predicated on a legal and 'natural language' traditional contract between users of the technology. Somewhere in this process will be an agreement, and coders, that the law can latch onto, deploying the usual rules about interpretation and so on when dealing with problems generated by the agreement.[89] Thus a 'smart contract' might turn out to be wholly conventional in legal terms, notwithstanding the novel way in which the obligations under the agreement are performed.[90] Other smart contracts may embody a different balance between natural language and code, rendering legal intervention and enforceability more doubtful. Either way, the current consensus amongst judges, legal professionals and law reform bodies is that while these technologies will raise significant questions for law, English law is sufficiently adaptable to cope. Where the law is unable to adapt, the prevailing view is that the law should not impede the use of the technology. The *Legal Statement on Cryptoassets and Smart Contracts* produced by the Law Tech Delivery Panel's UK Jurisdiction Taskforce (UKJT) states that while smart contracts may not need interpreting in the traditional sense, 'in principle, a smart contract can be identified, interpreted and enforced using ordinary

86 Giancaspro, 'Is a "Smart Contract" Really a Smart Idea?', 826.

87 Sarah Green and Adam Sanitt, 'Smart Contracts' in Paul S. Davies and Magda Raczynska (eds.) *Commercial Contracts: Terms Affecting Freedoms* (Hart Publishing, 2020), pp. 191, 192.

88 See Law Commission, *Smart Contracts: Call for Evidence*, para 2.32.

89 Eliza Mik, 'From Automation to Autonomy: Some Non-existent Problems in Contract Law' (2020) 36 *Journal of Contract Law* 205, 222–23.

90 Pierluigi Cuccuru, 'Beyond Bitcoin: An Early Overview on Smart Contracts' (2017) 25 *International Journal of Law and Information Technology* 179, 185 footnote omitted; Alexander Savelyev, 'Contract Law 2.0: "Smart" Contracts as the Beginning of the End of Classic Contract Law' (2017) 26 *Information & Communications Technology Law* 116, 127.

and well-established legal principles'.[91] The UKJT also asserts that where computer code allows for automatic enforcement there is still no reason 'for treating smart contracts as being different in principle from conventional contracts ... there will always be a risk that performance is affected by an event external to the code ... and in such cases any dispute must be capable of adjudication ... In principle, therefore ... the ordinary rules of contract law will apply to smart contracts.'[92] The *Legal Statement* exudes confidence that English law can respond appropriately to technological advances and that 'it has an impressive track record of doing so'.[93] The statement was developed by expert lawyers in the field after extensive consultation with regulators, financial services firms and technology specialists. While not an authoritative statement of legal principles, it is likely to set the tone of the English law response to technological innovation.[94]

This view about the adaptability of the law is not necessarily universally shared. Some judges have made extra-judicial statements expressing doubts about the common law role at least in regulating smart contracts.[95] The Law Commission is also more circumspect about the relationship between law and smart contracts, taking the view that not all smart contracts will be amenable to legal regulation. Thus, the Commission confines its analysis of the law as it affects, and is affected by, smart contracts to those agreements facilitated by DLT that are 'legally enforceable'.[96] The Commission anticipates that smart contracts and DLT may be used to circumvent the possibility of legal intervention but predicts that the parties will make clear in their agreement that they have no intention to create a legal relationship.[97] In cases of complete automation via the DLT, an assessment of the parties' intentions to create legally enforceable agreements would depend on an assessment of all the circumstances.[98] The smart contract that seeks to exclude legal enforceability is therefore removed from the law's field of vision by the familiar operation of

[91] UK Jurisdiction Taskforce, *Legal Statement on Cryptoassets and Smart Contracts* (November 2019), para [19].

[92] UKJT, *Legal Statement on Cryptoassets*, [136].

[93] UKJT, *Legal Statement on Cryptoassets*, [22].

[94] Mr Justice Bryan in *AA* v. *Persons Unknown and others* [2019] EWHC 3556 (Comm) relied on the statement in determining that cryptocurrencies could be treated as property, [57] and [61].

[95] Lord Hodge, *Technology and the Law*, Dover House Lecture (10 March 2020), pp. 12, 16.

[96] Law Commission, *Smart Contracts: Call for Evidence*, para 2.4.

[97] Law Commission, *Smart Contracts: Call for Evidence*, para 3.45.

[98] Law Commission, *Smart Contracts: Call for Evidence*, para 3.49.

intent. The general desirability of code superseding the possibility of legal oversight and control of these contracting methods is not addressed.

Though falling outside the Law Commission's field of interest, the possibility of smart contract methods dispensing with law altogether has been observed by some commentators on the smart contract phenomenon. Wright and De Fillipi note:

> To the extent that a blockchain allows for the implementation of self-executing transactions, parties can freely transact with one another, without the technical need to enter into a standard contractual arrangement.[99]

This encapsulates an idea of the smart contract as capable of autonomous creation and execution, not premised upon an underlying natural language contract. Evidently such a system would need to be coded by humans but it need not be done with any particular parties or specific contract in mind. Unlike a paper contract text in natural language, which is the outward expression of some antecedent agreement, the smart contract is the antecedent agreement, the text and performance combined into a single stage.[100]

Does this form of smart contract render contract law redundant?[101] On the face of it, the smart contract and automated execution seems to dispense with many contract problems that generate legal claims. An action for breach would seem to be precluded since the point of a smart contract is that it is self-executing and thus obviates the possibility of breach in favour of guaranteed performance. Clauses for the payment of damages could be coded into the agreement, although an unenforceable penalty payment may be executed by the computer code regardless of its legal validity.[102] However, such self-help measures are designed to encourage performance, and since performance of the agreement is automated, liquidated damages provisions appear superfluous.[103] The definition of a penalty in English law is that it is a payment triggered by breach, but in a smart contract breach cannot occur (unless, it seems, if there is human intervention in the transaction to reverse it), so there is no need for an incentive to perform. Similarly, some varieties of boilerplate, the legal effect of which occasionally requires court determination, would be unnecessary. The entire agreement clause or the no-oral modification clause

[99] Aaron Wright and Primavera De Filippi, 'Decentralized Blockchain Technology and the Rise of Lex Cryptographia' (2015) www.ssrn.com/abstract=2580664, 11 (footnote omitted).

[100] Jason G. Allen, 'Wrapped and Stacked: "Smart Contracts" and the Interaction of Natural and Formal Language' (2018) 14 *European Review of Contract Law* 307, 310.

[101] See generally Werbach and Cornell, 'Contracts *Ex Machina*', 338.

[102] Werbach and Cornell, 'Contracts *Ex Machina*', 373.

[103] Cuccuru, 'Beyond Bitcoin', 187.

would be redundant. Termination of the agreement outside of the parameters set by the code would be impossible. As McKinney et al. have written, '[s]mart contracts are purposefully designed to be inflexible.'[104] Similarly the smart contract will not contain gaps and will be 'complete', at least for the purposes of executing the transaction according to the code, seemingly dispensing with the possibility of implying terms. Neither could normative reasoning form any part of the smart contract's process of enforcement, nor would there be any interpretative difficulty or even room for interpretation.

Although it has been observed that the autonomous character of smart contracts challenges the state monopoly on the use of force,[105] contract law may still be necessary.[106] Smart contracts may 'close off the possibility of breach of contract and the resultant litigation to enforce',[107] but contract law responds to much more than breach. Undoubtedly the technology can be used to create reliable exchange systems that do not depend on authoritative institutions such as national legal systems and fiat currency. Public blockchains in particular are decentralised systems accessible to all. However, the blockchain is a method of performance. It does not regulate the transaction, in the sense of scrutinising it for external grounds, independent of the code, that justify intervention in the transaction and the prevention or reversal of its effects. The smart contract simply executes (enforces) the agreement automatically in line with the underlying contract code. External grounds may still exist to challenge legally the transactions undertaken via the ledger. There may be errors in the code, malicious interference in the ledger and other problems. Given this, there must be the possibility of an authoritative legal response. Although contract law may have little role to play in enforcement, vitiating factors attaching to the transaction executed via DLT – fraud, mistake,

[104] Scott A. McKinney, Rachel Landy and Rachel Wilka, 'Smart Contracts, Blockchain, and the Next Frontier of Transactional Law' (2018) 13 *Washington Journal of Law, Technology and Arts* 313, 322.

[105] Florian Möslein, 'Legal Boundaries of Blockchain Technologies: Smart Contracts as Self-Help?' in Alberto De Franceschi and Reiner Schulze (eds.) *Digital Revolution – New Challenges for Law* (C H Beck Nomos, 2019), pp. 313, 317.

[106] The present general consensus is that the law is still necessary: see Yeung, 'Regulation by Blockchain'; Giancaspro, 'Is a "Smart Contract" Really a Smart Idea?'; Werbach and Cornell, 'Contracts *Ex Machina*'; Möslein, 'Legal Boundaries of Blockchain Technologies'; Mik, 'From Automation to Autonomy'; Phillip Paech, 'The Governance of Blockchain Financial Networks' (2017) 80 *Modern Law Review* 1073, at 1110: 'There is a general understanding that blockchain-based financial networks should operate within the reach of the law, courts and supervisors.'

[107] Werbach and Cornell, 'Contracts *Ex Machina*', 353.

illegality – will remain relevant. Remedial claims are likely to shift from expectation damages, specific performance and other performance-enhancing measures to those focused on restoring the status quo ante.[108] On this basis there may be less recourse to contract law and more reliance on unjust enrichment to reverse any impugned transactions.

Even if the existing rules are notionally applicable to the automated contract, a more interesting question is whether English law will deploy its traditional doctrines in responding to problems with the smart contract. We saw earlier that contract law principles have limited applicability to the operation of the Claims Portal. An anti-interventionist stance may be adopted in relation to algorithmic contracting more generally. Notwithstanding the considerable value that lies in exposing new methods of making contracts to contract law scrutiny, and generating guiding public rules in the process, it appears traditional court adjudication will be eschewed in favour of speedier dispute resolution through expert panels or arbitration. The UKJT have produced a set of Digital Dispute Resolution Rules for incorporation into smart contracts and on-chain digital relationships. Dispute resolution under the Rules adopts arbitration rather than an adjudication as the preferred method of dispensing with trouble. The Rules propose the use of expert arbitrators to ensure quick decision-making directly on-chain using a private key (although precise methods and procedures will be variable according to the nature of the dispute and the facts).[109] It is anticipated that decisions will be delivered within thirty days of the arbitrator's appointment.[110] The Rules also provide for any automatic dispute resolution process – that is, dispute resolution 'by the automatic selection of a person or panel or artificial intelligence agent whose vote or decision is implemented directly within the digital asset system' – to be legally binding.[111] The parties will have the choice to maintain anonymity between themselves, in line with the original transaction, although not with the arbitrator.[112] There is provision for awards or decisions in the general interest to be published in an anonymised form.[113] But it seems tolerably clear from these developments that reasoning around smart contracts may not lead to any lasting transformation in contract law principles. If

[108] Werbach and Cornell, 'Contracts *Ex Machina*', 376.

[109] UK Jurisdiction Taskforce *Digital Dispute Resolution Rules* Version 1.0 (2021); Sir Geoffrey Vos, 'Technological Challenges for English Law and Jurisdiction' Speech to ISDA Virtual Annual Legal Forum (10 March 2021), para 9.

[110] DDRR rule 12. [111] DDRR rule 4. [112] DDRR rule 13. [113] DDRR rule 15.

anything, contract law is likely to be bypassed to ensure the benefits of the technology are fully realised.

Even if lacking a direct impact on common law development, smart contracts may affect contract law indirectly. Given the autonomy-driven focus of English contract law, if the parties have consented to algorithmic methods of contracting, then this will be enforceable (subject to consumer protection or other bespoke regulation that might be developed). It is entirely possible that a contract law that is content to enforce terms in a formal manner may find a competitive edge in relation to advances in technology. Smart contracts favour the kind of transaction that can be coded and performed with 'if-then' commands. There is no need for a human interpreter to give meaning to these commands.[114] This makes these methods suitable only for certain forms of transaction, notably those involving obligations that are relatively fixed and certain, that can be coded for performance on a blockchain or other similar computer system. This includes deals such as those involving transfer or exchange of assets in digital form,[115] or where payment is triggered on the occurrence of some specified action, or where it is necessary to track the movement of goods to destination and facilitate payment mechanisms.[116] In other words, scenarios where obligations can be rendered in precise terms with little ambiguity.[117]

A formalistic and plain-meaning approach to contract interpretation in English law, together with an attenuated commitment to any overriding standard of good faith and reasonableness, seems conducive to the endeavour to reduce obligations to machine-readable code, rendering contract context marginal or irrelevant.[118] While the law may not have a role in enforcing such agreements – since that is automatic – there may be some reassurance for the smart contractor in the low likelihood of the smart contract being subjected to a serious legal challenge in a formalistic legal system. After all, the software simply executes the terms in the same way a formalist legal system might enforce the plain meaning of an unambiguous contract text. Smart contract technology appears less suited to facilitating complex, more uncertain and longer term contracts involving ongoing collaboration, co-ordination or repeat

[114] UKJT *Legal Statement on Cryptoassets*, states that smart contract in code can 'be seen as an extreme example of a contract whose language is clear, with the result that there is no justification to depart from it', [150].

[115] Green and Sanitt, 'Smart Contracts', 196.

[116] Finck, 'Blockchains: Regulating the Unknown', 672.

[117] Kevin Werbach, *Blockchain and the New Architecture of Trust* (MIT Press, 2018), p. 125.

[118] Werbach and Cornell, 'Contracts *Ex Machina*', 43.

commitments (such as infrastructure projects, strategic alliances or in areas of innovation). Parties here may avoid legalistic express terms in favour of more reassuring, informal norms. Soft obligations to co-operate, act in a spirit of trustworthiness, or partnership, can be written into a traditional contract text straightforwardly, but their open-ended and value-laden nature makes them difficult to interpret and, one assumes, more difficult to capture in computer code that can judge reliably whether these standards have been reached or not.[119] Relational contracts, for example, demand engagement with the underlying human elements of the exchange, and to the expectations generated by contract context, rather than strict, to-the-letter (of the code), performance.[120] Coding seems precisely designed to remove relational elements of co-operation, conciliatory action and flexibility from the contracting environment, reducing the agreement to the purest form of transaction.[121] However, the more formal and clear the wording/code, the less likelihood that it requires legal interpretation, or any legal intervention at all. In a world of automated enforcement, it is interesting to conjecture that, insofar as contract law is still required, its main role will be to interpret and enforce vaguely expressed contract commitments that cannot be captured in code. Contract law may not be able to ignore those relational qualities (good faith, reasonableness, co-operation) to which it has so long resisted ascribing meaning and effect in its legal reasoning.

In dealing with the effects of technological innovation, we can expect legal institutions to vie for commercial business by presenting themselves as non-obstructive towards the use of the technology. The UKJT is already attempting to create a hospitable legal environment for these methods. It is likely to face competition however. The desire to attract business may augment the formalist tendency in contract law, at least initially. This possibility is borne out to an extent by the decision from the Singapore Court of Appeal in *Quoine Pte Ltd* v. *B2C2 Ltd*.[122] The court in the case demonstrated manifest reluctance to subject the operation of innovative technology to traditional contract law

[119] See Werbach, 'Trust, But Verify', 527; Giancaspro, 'Is a "Smart Contract" Really a Smart Idea?', 831–33. Contra, see Eliza Mik, 'Smart Contracts: Terminology, Technical Limitations and Real World Complexity' (2017) 9 *Law, Innovation and Technology* 269, 288–89, arguing that all contracts involve natural language and hence all are vulnerable to interpretative difficulty. Any kind of contract would be difficult to translate into code.

[120] Sally Wheeler, 'Modelling the Contracts of the Future' (2017) 26 *Griffith Law Review* 593, 606.

[121] Jeremy M. Sklaroff, 'Smart Contracts and the Cost of Inflexibility' (2017) 166 *University of Pennsylvania Law Review* 263, 284–86.

[122] [2020] (I) SGCA 02.

rules, resolving the case by attention to the underlying written agreement. Quoine ran a cryptocurrency exchange platform operated through algorithms developed by them. The transactions between traders on the platform were executed without any direct human intervention. One of the users of the platform, B2C2, traded Ether and Bitcoin using their own trading software. As a result of Quoine's failure to make some necessary changes to several critical operating systems, the platform, following its software protocols, erroneously concluded that two traders were in a margin sell-out position. This autonomously triggered the sale of their Bitcoin for Ether in circumstances matching the instructions coded into B2C2's trading software intended to deal with extreme market conditions (which were not actually expected by B2C2 to occur). The trades between B2C2 and the traders were at 250 times the market rate. The trades were automatically settled by the platform. When a Quoine programmer discovered the error, he cancelled the trades and reversed the amounts paid.

B2C2 claimed the reversals were a breach of contract and breach of trust, since the terms of use between Quoine and the platform's users stated that 'once an order is filled, you are notified via the Platform and such an action is irreversible'. The Singapore International Commercial Court ruled that it was a breach of contract for a human programmer to reverse the trades. The argument that the computers were legal agents of human principals was rejected. Nor were the trades held void for mistake.[123] The Singapore Court of Appeal upheld the judgment of the lower court that 'there were no terms in the various contractual documents, whether express or implied, which entitled Quoine to unilaterally cancel the Disputed Trades'.[124] A relevant finding was that the anonymity of the platform, with contractor identities only revealed after the sale, did not prevent a contract arising between the buyer and the seller through offer and acceptance by algorithm.[125] This finding on formation influenced the conclusion that the trades were not void at common law, nor voidable in equity, on the grounds of unilateral mistake. Although the mistake might have voided the trades had the parties met in person on a trading floor to conduct the exchange, this was irrelevant, since the parties had chosen to contract via deterministic algorithm and not face to face.[126] The case gives an indication that the brave new world of computer-created contracts is not assimilable with face-to-face dealing. As with the Claims Portal, the algorithm and the terms upon which it operates creates a self-contained system. Notably, the mechanics of automated enforcement on the platform meant the

[123] [2019] SGHC(I) 03. [124] Above n. 122 at [7].
[125] Above n. 122, per Chief Justice Sundaresh Menon at [96]. [126] Above n. 122 at [97].

intentions of the contracting parties were irrelevant to the issue of mistake. For the operation of mistake, the relevant state of mind was that of the software programmers, and it could not be shown that B2C2's programmer had actual or constructive knowledge of the counterparties' error. The resulting contract may have been between the human buyer and seller, but its creation by deterministic algorithm, rather than the parties personally, rendered their actual intentions immaterial.[127] Pre-eminence was accorded to the algorithm.

In his dissent, Lord Mance took the view that the contract was created ultimately between human buyers and sellers, and it was obvious to them that a fundamental error had occurred. For Lord Mance, this was clearly a case where equity should intervene and grant relief since it was unconscionable for the non-mistaken party to insist that the contract be performed.[128] The case could not be brought within existing principles governing unilateral mistake at common law.[129] The lack of legal principle did not entail that the governing framework for the trades was the express contract terms between the users of the platform and the platform itself. Rather, Lord Mance regarded it as the task of the law to develop the necessary rules to address the problems generated by algorithmic contracting.

The judgments in the case manifest two different views on algorithmic contracting. Lord Mance regards the problem as one that contract law (or equity) must fix. The extant contract law rules are inadequate to deal with the problem at hand, necessitating that new rules be fashioned that can effectively regulate the difficulties thrown up by the innovation. For the majority, party autonomy applies with full force, irrespective of any absurdity in result. One suspects that which of these turns out to be the road legally travelled by depends on pragmatic factors, notably which approach better facilitates automated contract dealing and generates investor confidence. Theoretical matters of doctrinal purity, principled consistency, coherence, or even justice and fairness may not carry determinative weight. Though the Singapore Court of Appeal pointed out the isolated context within which the algorithms operated, others have sounded a note of caution. Lord Sales, writing extra-judicially, has noted that

> coding algorithms are closed systems. As written, they may not capture everything of potential significance for the resolution of a human problem. With the human application of law, the open-textured nature of ideas like justice and fairness creates the possibility for

[127] Above n. 122 at [98]. [128] Above n. 122, per Lord Mance [173].
[129] Above n. 122, per Lord Mance [182].

> immanent critique of the rules being applied and leaves room for wider values, not explicitly encapsulated in law's algorithm, to enter the equation leading to a final outcome.[130]

Lord Sales recognises the problems that result from capitulation to decision by computers: 'access to public services is being depersonalised. The individual seems powerless in the face of machine systems and loses all dignity in being subjected to their control. The movement here threatens to be from citizen to consumer and then on to serf.'[131] In the automated world, criteria of consent and the intention of the parties are substantively emptied of any significance. To the extent that our law of contract claims to uphold and safeguard these values, it too may simply become redundant.

6.4 Conclusion

Three factors likely to impinge on common law development in the future were examined in this chapter. First, the idea that contract law is a commodity that should primarily serve the interests of commercial contractors (usually by upholding the terms of the contract). Second, the declining use of adjudication and litigation to resolve disputes, rooted in an anti-litigation culture across society and an emphasis on ADR within courts themselves. Third, the impact of automation in contracting, in particular the possibility of 'smart contracts' usurping contract law functions. All of these pose a significant threat to the future of the common law rules. Developments in information and communication technologies potentially remove the role of state institutions in facilitating certain transactions, reducing further the significance of the law of contract and ushering in private forms of contract enforcement subject to minimal legal control (and that may seek actively to bypass such control). The lack of contract cases being litigated to trial and judgment is likely to compound the commercialisation of the common law of contract and further entrench the formalistic model of contract law rules. These factors contribute to general contract law degeneration, continuing and accentuating the program to empty contract law of normative significance and damage its capacity to communicate a normative message about contracting. They indicate a broader project of the privatisation and automation of justice. In the next chapter we will consider if there are any possibilities for common law revival.

[130] Lord Sales, 'Algorithms, Artificial Intelligence and the Law' Sir Henry Brooke Lecture for BAILII, Freshfields Bruckhaus Deringer (12 November 2019), p. 6.

[131] Lord Sales, 'Algorithms, Artificial Intelligence and the Law', p. 9.

7

The Possibility of Common Law Revival

This chapter explores the potential for the revival of the common law of contract. It must be recognised that there are many barriers to contract doctrinal development, and not all of these have been erected by courts. Courts are not responsible for government policy concerning how justice may best be served, nor for the cuts to litigation funding. The rise of regulation, the growth in private ordering through contracts and technological innovations are products of societal, not legal, change. Nevertheless the emphasis here is on the possibility of judicial action to reverse some of the movements we have explored in this work. No doubt this can be castigated as more ideal than practically realisable. But these two are not mutually exclusive. Contract scholars with a more pragmatic or practical approach to the subject have long maintained that contract law must do more to distinguish different contracting contexts and to develop appropriate rule sets accordingly.[1] Judicial decision-making in recent years seems to have moved contract law in a commercial direction, prioritising commercial interests and concerns in the elucidation of contract rules. That said, there are areas of contract law where courts have not unquestioningly applied the classical model of contract law but have appealed to broader considerations than the traditional contract model might admit. We saw some instances of this in Chapter 2 during

1 David Campbell, 'The Relational Constitution of the Discrete Contract' in David Campbell and Peter Vincent-Jones (eds.) *Contract and Economic Organisation* (Dartmouth, 1996), pp. 40, 43–45; Hugh Collins, *Regulating Contracts* (Oxford University Press, 1999); David Campbell and Hugh Collins, 'Discovering the Implicit Dimensions of Contracts' in David Campbell, Hugh Collins and John Wightman (eds.) *Implicit Dimensions of Contract* (Hart Publishing, 2003), pp. 25–27. Stewart Macaulay, 'The Real and the Paper Deal: Empirical Pictures of Relationships, Complexity and the Urge for Transparent Simple Rules' in David Campbell, Hugh Collins and John Wightman (eds.) *Implicit Dimensions of Contract* (Hart Publishing, 2003), p. 51; Roger Brownsword, *Contract Law: Themes for the Twenty-First Century*, 2nd ed. (Oxford University Press, 2006); Catherine Mitchell *Contract Law and Contract Practice* (Hart Publishing, 2013).

contract's welfarist and contextualist period. The recent engagement with the concept of relational contracting demonstrates a judicial ambition (admittedly not shared by all) to create a more responsive, contextual and flexible contract law. Courts could go further however. The public policy dimensions of a contractualised society, and the regulatory framework within which a contract exists, could be drawn upon to gain a deeper understanding of the contracting environment in which an agreement is created and performed.

Courts should also re-engage with the task of developing contract law principle. Cultivating and articulating the general principles that underpin contract law is entirely in keeping with common law method, yet judges appear increasingly disengaged from this crucial aspect of the judicial role. The ambivalence displayed in some quarters towards the concept of relational contract demonstrates this. Nevertheless, judicial reluctance to develop contract law principle is not universal. Developments in England (for example, in the law of illegality as developed in *Patel* v. *Mirza*[2]) and innovations in other common law jurisdictions (such as the organising principle of good faith and approach to unconscionability in Canada[3]) are indicative of an alternative direction for common law that could supply the necessary inspiration. There is a further consideration here. During the nineteenth century, legal rules were regarded as having an educational effect.[4] Judges of the time appreciated that their decisions would have future implications and that they could affect the behaviour of people subject to the rules. This educative effect was regarded as more important than doing justice in the individual case. However, the belief in this educative capacity of the rules declined after the 1850s. The more complex the rules became, the less valuable they were for communicating values and expectations about behaviour.[5] This educative function of the common law should be revived. Even if judges harbour doubts that rules can influence behaviour, they will appreciate that the rules announced and applied by them indicate the normative commitments of contract law. In formulating responses, judges are a conduit for communicating contract values and have a role in moulding a society's contract culture. At present, too many contract abuses are perpetrated through the operation of freedom of contract. The judicial reluctance to interfere with the operation of contract terms, and

2 [2017] AC 467.

3 *Bhasin* v. *Hyrnew* [2014] SCC 71; [2014] 3 SCR 494; *Uber Technologies Inc* v. *Heller* [2020] SCC 16.

4 Patrick S. Atiyah, *The Rise and Fall of Freedom of Contract* (Oxford University Press, 1979), p. 357.

5 Atiyah, *Rise and Fall*, p. 394.

unwillingness to consider the broader policy implications of contracting on one-sided terms and conditions contributes to this. We saw in earlier chapters that values in contract have changed throughout the law's past. But this capacity for change is easily extinguished. Presently the signs are not positive for the possibility of common law renewal or revival. To establish this, we turn first to consider the concept of relational contracting and the allied implied term of good faith. Developments here exemplify the common law's potential for innovation while also exposing the influential forces that resist it.

7.1 Relational Contracting outside Contract Law

First gaining prominence in the 1960s and 1970s, thanks to the pioneering work of Ian Macneil,[6] relational contracts hitherto have largely been a matter of academic as opposed to judicial interest.[7] Since 2013, however, the concept of the relational contract has been making an impression on English contract law, albeit mainly in the lower courts. Generally speaking, relational contracts are characterised by co-operative, often long-term, relationships between parties, usually occurring within productive settings that generate a degree of interdependence and a need for collaboration. It has long been conceded that such relationships are poorly regulated by classical contract law and that standards-based and contextual forms of reasoning are necessary to identify the expectations generated by the parties' relationship and draw them into the determination of the case.[8] It is perhaps no coincidence that the re-emergence of formalism in contract legal reasoning has prompted judges to consider whether some contractual relationships require a different response to that meted out by the classical law. The difficulty is that while the formalist turn in contract law provides an immediate stimulus for the production of an alternative model of contract, it is also an unlikely, even hostile, environment in

6 See generally, Ian Macneil, *The Relational Theory of Contract: Selected Works of Ian Macneil*, David Campbell (ed.) (Sweet and & Maxwell, 2001).

7 Although earlier judicial engagement appeared in *Total Gas Marketing Ltd* v. *Arco British Ltd* [1998] 2 Lloyd's Law Rep 209. Lord Steyn identified an anticipated fourteen-year relationship as a relational contract but he went on to say that no special rules applied to such agreements (218). See also *Dymocks Franchise Systems (NSW) Pty* v. *Todd and others* [2002] UKPC 50; [2002] 2 All ER (Comm) 849. Lord Browne-Wilkinson recognised that franchise agreements 'were not ordinary commercial contracts but contracts giving rise to long-term mutual obligations in pursuance of what amounted, in substance, to a joint venture and therefore dependent upon co-ordinated action and co-operation' at [63].

8 Ian R. Macneil, 'Relational Contract Theory: Challenges and Queries' (2000) 94 *Northwestern University Law Review* 877, 881.

which to nurture relational contract principles into existence. Most of the lower court judgments in support of relational contracts are heavily fact-dependent and have limited precedential value. Beyond recognising that a category of relational contracts may exist, appeal courts have shown little inclination to develop a set of coherent rules to apply to them. Authoritative principles are lacking on the defining features of a relational contract and the legal consequences that should follow a finding of 'relationality'.[9] As a result, it appears that the relational contract idea will be incorporated into the law on implied terms: the implied obligation of good faith, which follows the finding that the parties are in a relational contract in the case law, will only operate if the traditional 'business efficacy' test is satisfied.[10] The possibility of an obligation of good faith being implied into all relational contracts as a matter of law and policy appears to be receding, due to fears about creating uncertainty. Lurking here may be a judicial reluctance to disturb the long-standing conviction that it is precisely the lack of a general good faith duty that makes England a favoured jurisdiction for contract enforcement.[11]

One reason why English contract law may resist importing relational values of co-operation, contextualism and standards-based reasoning into contract is that relational contracting can be found almost everywhere beyond the courtroom. This may make it easier for the law to exclude relational values on the basis that these values reflect contract life, not contract law. That is too limited a view, however, since relational principles frequently play a role in contract regulation. Regulatory regimes promulgate guidance and codes of practice replete with obligations of good faith and co-operation in regulated relationships. As we have noted previously, the Grocery Code of Practice must be incorporated into contracts between retailers and suppliers. The code imposes non-excludable duties of fair dealing and good faith on the parties.[12] Similarly,

[9] It is becoming clear that there is no room for implied term of good faith, even in relational contracts (however defined) where comprehensive express terms exist and are interpreted as providing an answer to whatever contract problem has arisen on the facts: *Marks and Spencer plc* v. *BNP Paribas Securities Services Trust Co Ltd* [2016] AC 742; *Teesside Gas Transportation Ltd* v. *CATS North Sea Ltd* [2019] EWHC 1220 (Comm).

[10] See recent decisions such as *Russell* v. *Cartwright and others* [2020] EWHC 41 (Ch); *TAQA Bratani Ltd & Ors* v. *RockRose UKCS8 LLC* [2020] EWHC 58 (Comm); *UTB LLC* v. *Sheffield Utd* [2019] EWHC 2322 (Ch).

[11] See Paul S. Davies, 'Excluding Good Faith and Restricting Discretion' in Paul S. Davies and Magda Raczynska (eds.) *Contents of Commercial Contracts: Terms Affecting Freedoms* (Hart Publishing, 2020), p. 89 for a recent example of this sort of critique, at 98–99. See also Magda Raczynska, 'Good Faiths and Contract Terms' in same volume 65, p. 82 ff.

[12] *Groceries Supply Code of Practice* (4 August 2009) Part 2, Principle of Fair Dealing.

noting a need for a shift in culture and behaviour in retail financial markets, the Financial Conduct Authority (FCA) has proposed a new consumer duty owed by financial firms to consumers, a classification that would include small and medium enterprises. The proposed consumer duty would require regulated firms to prioritise the interests of the consumer over the firm's interests, deliver good outcomes for consumers and act in good faith.[13] It is hoped that this will instigate change in the banking sector to restore public trust and accountability in the financial services industry. The FCA has not yet decided if breach of this duty should give rise to a private right of action on the part of the consumer. The FCA's Principles for Business already state that 'a firm must pay due regard to the interests of its customers and treat them fairly'[14] and that 'a firm must pay due regard to the information needs of its clients, and communicate information to them in a way which is clear, fair and not misleading'.[15] This FCA starting point is in complete contrast with the common law assumption of adversarial and self-interested contractors meeting in a market to hammer out a deal in a climate of competition. We have already seen that the common law has not drawn upon these wider regulatory expectations and purposes in determining the extent of analogous private law rights.

Legislation has also transparently incorporated relational values into some contractual arrangements. The Corporate Insolvency and Governance Act 2020 curtails a supplier's contractual right to terminate a supply agreement or make other contract changes if the customer enters an insolvency procedure.[16] Where the statute applies, it reverses the common law tendency to uphold termination clauses, provided carefully drafted and the termination is in accordance with the terms. Common law has shown little inclination to place any limit on contractual rights to terminate, such as by requiring these rights to be exercised in good faith or for genuine reasons.[17] The extraordinary interventions into contracts during the Covid-19 public health emergency

[13] Financial Conduct Authority, *A New Consumer Duty* CP21/13 (May 2021), paras 1.11 and 2.21. Reference to good faith is in para 2.25. Good faith is defined in the consultation as 'a standard of conduct characterised by honesty, fair and open dealing and consistency with the reasonable expectations of consumers': 3.25.

[14] Financial Conduct Authority, *Handbook: Principles for Business*, 2.1, Principle 6.

[15] Financial Conduct Authority, *Handbook: Principles for Business*, 2.1, Principle 7.

[16] Section 14 Corporate Insolvency and Governance Act 2020, inserting a new s 233B in the Insolvency Act 1986.

[17] See, for example, *Compass Group UK and Ireland Ltd (t/a Medirest)* v. *Mid Essex Hospital Services NHS Trust* [2013] EWCA Civ 200 [64].

further indicate the divergence of current contract law from the relational values underpinning exchange and economic activity. The impact of the pandemic has been severe, touching on every area of society and economy, including contract performance. In the same way the pandemic made glaringly obvious who were the essential workers upon whom we all rely, it also exposed the inadequacy of formal contract law to respond to the contractual fallout from the crisis. An unprecedented range of measures were introduced encouraging firms to treat contracting partners fairly and reasonably.[18] In some cases, the right to enforce contract terms was suspended. The Coronavirus Act 2020 placed a moratorium on landlords seeking to evict residential tenants[19] and prevented forfeiture of business tenancies for non-payment of rent during the pandemic.[20] Other measures included a voluntary code of practice to inform negotiations between commercial landlords and tenants concerning rent payments and arrears during the outbreak.[21] The code urges the parties to 'act reasonably, swiftly, transparently and in good faith' to identify 'mutual solutions'.[22] The proliferation of informal codes of practice, concept and guidance notes exhorting collaboration, co-operation, good faith and dialogue during the pandemic served to accentuate the transactional and individualistic disposition of English contract law.[23] The proposed solutions for dealing with the consequences of the crisis demonstrated relational theory in action, notably drawing upon the relational contract norms identified by Macneil: preservation of the relationship, maintaining values of mutuality, flexibility, contractual solidarity and propriety of means.[24]

The plea for a broadly anti-contract and relational response to the emergency threw into relief the dysfunction of classical contract law. This arises from English contract law's discreteness, that is, its preference for complete (or almost complete) presentiation (bringing the future into the present through planning), a highly objective and attenuated notion of consent and the

[18] Cabinet Office, *Guidance on Responsible Contractual Behaviour in the Performance and Enforcement of Contracts Impacted by the Covid-19 Emergency* (7 May 2020).

[19] Section 81 and Schedule 29 Coronavirus Act 2020.

[20] Section 82(1) Coronavirus Act 2020.

[21] Ministry for Housing, Communities and Local Government, *Code of Practice for Commercial Property Relationships During the Covid-19 Pandemic* (6 April 2021).

[22] *Code of Practice for Commercial Property*, [14] and [17].

[23] See, for example, the British Institute of International and Comparative Law, *Breathing Space: Concept n. 1 on the Effect of the Pandemic on Commercial Contracts* (April 2020); Cabinet Office, *Guidance on Responsible Contractual Behaviour* (above n. 18); Construction Leadership Council, *Covid-19 Contractual Best Practice Guidance* (7 May 2020), para 2.4.

[24] Ian R. Macneil, 'Values in Contract: Internal and External' (1983) 78 *Northwestern University Law Review* 340, 349.

separation of the contract from wider aspects of the productive relationship.[25] The discrete model equates contracting with an impersonal transaction motivated by self-interest over joint interest and created between adversarial contracting parties. The automation of consent by the 'I agree' click embraces and takes to an extreme the discrete version of contract: detailed and bureaucratic advance planning, presentiation via complex terms, single 'moment in time' creation of the contract and relative stability of that contract thereafter, minimising the relational aspects of the deal (such as those expectations created by branding, reputation, previous experience or the negotiating process). Similarly the use of 'no reliance' terms to impose a 'non-advisory' standard on a contractual relationship is precisely motivated by the desire to eliminate from the contract the relational aspects of the association between bank staff and customer, particularly in what might turn out to be a very long relationship involving high dependence and reliance. The point of the discrete agreement is precisely to distil the relationship down to its core elements, which are represented by the written terms. Although there might be some halting and imperfect recognition of relational values in contract, in many ways the relational features of a contract will be rendered irrelevant in a discrete law. A formalistic law may drive the endeavour to develop alternative principles for relational contracts, but it makes it almost impossible to deliver them. This becomes apparent when we consider the attempt in English law to create a relational contract jurisprudence.

7.2 Developing Relational Contract Law

Though the concept of relational contracts is known in the law, especially in the employment context,[26] the idea gained more sustained attention following Mr Justice Leggatt's judgment in *Yam Seng Pte Ltd* v. *International Trade Corporation Ltd.* The judge implied a term of good faith in a distributorship agreement between two sole traders on the basis that it was a relational contract, that is, the agreement involved 'a longer term relationship

[25] David Campbell, 'Ian Macneil and the Relational Theory of Contract' in Ian Macneil, *The Relational Theory of Contract: Selected Works of Ian Macneil*, David Campbell (ed.) (Sweet and & Maxwell, 2001), pp. 3, 21.

[26] *Johnson* v. *Unisys Ltd* [2003] 1 AC 518, per Lord Steyn at [20]; *Braganza* v. *BP Shipping Ltd* [2015] 1 WLR 1661, per Lord Hodge at paras [54] and [61]; Lizzie Barmes, 'Common Law Implied Terms and Behavioural Standards at Work' (2007) 36 *Industrial Law Journal* 35, 42.

between the parties which they make a substantial commitment'.[27] The judge remarked:

> Such "relational" contracts . . . may require a high degree of communication, co-operation and predictable performance based on mutual trust and confidence and involve expectations of loyalty which are not legislated for in the express terms of the contract but are implicit in the parties' understanding and necessary to give business efficacy to the arrangements. Examples of such relational contracts might include some joint venture agreements, franchise agreements and long term distributorship agreements.[28]

The judge noted that many contractual contexts are informed by implicit but shared norms of behaviour, including trust and honesty.[29] In this analysis, Mr Justice Leggatt showed some appreciation of the core of relational theory – social context is essential to understanding the exchange, and the express terms do not necessarily incorporate the expectations of trust, co-operation and information-sharing that are generated by the context. The context will usually involve uncertainty in the contracting environment that militates against detailed advanced planning of specific and measurable outcomes. Instead, the parties may commit only to open-ended obligations dealing with processes and behaviours.

The case law following Mr Justice Leggatt's statement illustrates some of the difficulties of carving out principles of relational contract within a broadly discrete contract law. Judges have attempted to rein in the concept of relational contracts, and make the application of the label more predictable, by identifying the precise circumstances when a contract will be determined to be relational and the exact consequences of that finding. The problem is that the relational contract concept resists being structured in such a way, since, as Macneil tells us, ultimately all contracts are relational.[30] Consider Mr Justice Fraser's pathbreaking decision in *Bates* v. *The Post Office*. In his judgment, Mr Justice Fraser proposed nine non-exhaustive criteria relevant to the identification of a relational contract.[31] The first of these was the negative requirement that 'there must be no specific express terms in the contract that prevents a duty of good faith being implied into the contract'.[32] For a classical-style contract law, this is determinative. For relational contract theory, however,

[27] *Yam Seng Pte Ltd* v. *International Trade Corporation Ltd* [2013] 1 Lloyd's Rep 526, [2013] EWHC 111 [142].

[28] *Yam Seng* [142].

[29] *Yam Seng* [134]–[135] and [138].

[30] Macneil, 'Values in Contract: Internal and External', 341–42.

[31] *Bates* v. *Post Office Ltd No 3* [2019] EWHC 606 (QB), [2019] All ER (D) 100 [725]–[726].

[32] *Bates* [725].

this analysis proceeds from the wrong starting point: the social context of the agreement determines how much weight is to be attached to the contract text. Although Mr Justice Fraser thought that detailed terms did not prevent a contract being a relational one,[33] from a practical point of view detailed express terms are almost always likely to be afforded pre-eminence, crowding out the possibility that the contract will be relational in the sense recognised by law. Where express terms exist, there is simply no room for the operation of any implied terms.[34] In contract documents containing mixed commitments, as where textual formalism (clearly expressed termination rights, entire agreement or no oral modification clauses) appears alongside softer obligations (good faith, co-operation, loyalty to the contract purpose, partnering attitude), courts allow unequivocally expressed legal rights to eclipse the aspirational statements manifesting the agreement's relational qualities. In *Kabab-Ji SAL* v. *Kout Food Group*, where the contract contained a no oral modification clause as well as an express stipulation that the contract was to be performed and interpreted in good faith, Lord Justice Flaux in the Court of Appeal remarked that 'the fact that the provisions are to be interpreted in good faith cannot justify an interpretation which goes beyond what has been agreed or which seeks to rewrite the Agreement'.[35] This treats the good faith obligation as an outlier, an approach perfectly in keeping with the classical law priority to enforce context-reducing over context-expanding terms.

A contract may well fall into the class of relational agreements that Mr Justice Leggatt identifies (distributorships, joint ventures, franchises) but this does not entail that good faith duties will be owed and will be implied into the contract.[36] Even in long-term or co-operative relationships (which might otherwise be described as 'relational contracts') the implied term of good faith has been held to have no application when a party is exercising termination or other rights in accordance with the contract's express terms.[37] This allows judges to give notional recognition to the concept of 'relational contract' while

[33] *Bates* [732]; see also *Amey Birmingham Highways Ltd* v. *Birmingham City Council* [2018] EWCA Civ 264 at [92].

[34] *Essex County Council* v. *UBB Waste (Essex) Ltd* [2020] EWHC 1581 (TCC) [106], [113], [148].

[35] *Kabab-Ji SAL (Lebanon)* v. *Kout Food Group (Kuwait)* [2020] EWCA Civ 6 [65].

[36] In *Carewatch Care Services Ltd* v. *Focus Caring Services Ltd* [2014] EWHC 2313 (Ch), a good faith term was not implied in a franchise agreement with detailed terms [109]–[111]; in *Hamsard 3147 Ltd* v. *Boots UK Ltd* [2013] EWHC 3251, [2013] All ER (D) 12, a joint venture agreement was held not to include the good faith duty.

[37] See *Cathay Pacific Airlines Ltd* v. *Lufthansa Technik AG* [2019] EWHC 1789 (Ch), [202]; *Ilkerler Otomotiv Sanayai ve Ticaret Anonim Sirketi* v. *Perkins Engines Co Ltd* (CA) [2017] 4 WLR 144; *MSC Mediterranean Shipping Co SA* v. *Cottonex Anstalt* [2016] EWCA Civ 789 at

emptying it of any significance as a source of additional or alternative obligations not reflected in the express terms. This is illustrated by *TAQA Bratani Ltd* v. *RockRose*. The judge described a joint operating agreement (JOA) concerning the Brae Fields in the North Sea as a relational contract but nevertheless held that no good faith provision could be implied in contradiction of the express terms.[38] The contract of one of the operators could therefore be cancelled on notice, without giving any substantive reason. This was in the face of expert evidence on the importance of co-operation between parties involved in UK Continental Shelf activities and an industry norm that reasons would be given for terminating a JOA. The claimants relied on written reports from the regulator of the North Sea oil and gas industry to corroborate the existence of the norm of co-operation between participants in the business,[39] but the judge regarded this as irrelevant to the operation of contractual rights that were unqualified and absolute.[40]

The judicial approach here illustrates the tendency to regard the contract as creating a separate and isolated legal world that does not draw any normative controlling standards from the context. In addition, it reinforces that a contract is underpinned by a norm of self-interest,[41] even where party expectations draw heavily on relational values. Mr Justice Pelling's analysis of the contract in *TAQA* demonstrates all the characteristics of *discreteness and not relationality*. Macneil anticipates that there are circumstances when the parties will impose discreteness on their contractual dealings for good reasons,[42] but this is not how the judge's reasoning proceeds. The conclusion about discreteness merely follows from the form of the contract – long detailed terms dealing exactly with the contingency that has arisen. Whether the agreement should be analysed using alternative tools and expectations – such as those informed by the regulatory framework stressing the need for co-operation – is not considered.

[45]; *TSG Building Services* v. *South Anglia Housing Ltd* [2013] BLR 484; *Compass Group UK and Ireland Ltd (t/a Medirest)* v. *Mid Essex Hospital Services NHS Trust* [2013] EWCA Civ 200.

38 *TAQA Bratani Ltd* v. *RockRose UKCS8 LLC* [2020] EWHC 58 (Comm).

39 *TAQA* [39]. Compare ogauthority.co.uk/regulatory-framework/commercial-good-practice/ and Oil and Gas Authority, *The OGA Strategy* (16 December 2020); see also Sir Ian Wood, *UKCS Maximising Recovery Review: Final Report* (24 February 2014), p. 6; *The Maximising Economic Recovery Strategy for the UK*, p. 12, para 28, referenced in *TAQA* at [58].

40 *TAQA* [39] and [53].

41 Thus in *TAQA* Mr Justice Pelling notes from the evidence that joint venturers are 'hard nosed commercial parties' whose interests 'will not be wholly aligned' at [61].

42 Ian R. Macneil, 'Relational Contract Theory: Challenges and Queries', 877, 895–96.

Courts often recognise that a long-term agreement involving repeat obligations may give rise to different expectations on the part of contractors than a discrete transaction.[43] Similarly, implied duties to co-operate have a long pedigree in the common law.[44] Nevertheless, the classical law preference is for parties to stipulate terms dealing with variation, discretionary powers, circumstances where renegotiation might be expected and good faith in the documented agreement.[45] Contract law is predicated on the view that whatever behaviour is required to be displayed by a contractor can be expressed with greater certainty in terms of verifiable actions with observable outcomes: to share profit, engage in certain dispute resolution procedures (such as mediation rather than adversarial arbitration or litigation), comply with information exchange regimes and so on. The judicial expectation may be that these obligations are expressed in fairly clear, unambiguous language that expresses hard outcomes and the effects of non-compliance, rather than vaguer standards describing the expected behaviour. Thus, while a stipulated contractual duty to act with 'loyalty' to a project is not likely to be legally enforceable, a liquidated damages clause stipulating a payment in excess of the claimant's likely pecuniary losses on breach may be enforceable if it protects a claimant's legitimate interest in performance. In this way, the defendant's loyalty may be maintained and incentivised by sanctions designed to deter breach.

English courts may be unreceptive to the relational contract idea because of its association with the implied term of good faith. The antipathy of English contract law towards general duties of good faith is well known. The suggestion that relational contracts should have an obligation of good faith implied as a matter of legal policy is particularly controversial. In *Bates* v. *Post Office Ltd* Mr Justice Fraser distinguished between terms implied as a consequence of the finding that the contract is a relational one and terms implied on the basis of business efficacy.[46] This suggests that where there is a finding that a contract is relational, the implied term of good faith operates as a matter of law, although the parties would be able to exclude its operation.[47] In *Al Nehayan*

[43] See, for example, *Globe Motors Inc* v. *TRW Lucas Varity Electric Steering Ltd* [2014] EWHC 3718 (Comm), [75].

[44] *Mackay* v. *Dick* (1881) 6 App Cas 251 at 263; *Mona Oil Equipment & Supply Co Ltd* v. *Rhodesia Railways Ltd* (1949) 83 Lloyds Law Rep 173; *Swallowfalls Ltd* v. *Monaco Yachting & Technologies SAM* [2014] EWCA Civ 186.

[45] The Court of Appeal in *Globe Motors* reiterated that it is up to the parties to put express good faith clauses into their contracts: [2016] EWCA Civ 396 [63]–[64].

[46] See *Bates*, above n. 31, at [770].

[47] *Bates* [725].

v. *Kent*, Lord Justice Leggatt also suggested the good faith term could be implied in law in circumstances where the contract was relational.[48] Davies has commented that this demonstrates the 'hardening' of the implied term into one that will be implied in law into all 'relational contracts' unless contrary to the express terms. He regards *Bates* as the apogee of this development.[49]

Recent judicial engagement with the implied term of good faith suggests otherwise however. Judges have sought to limit the impact of the implied term by subsuming it within the traditional law so that the good faith obligation will only arise when the traditional doctrinal tests for implied terms in fact are satisfied.[50] The concept of the relational contract as a distinct category recognised in law, mandating a specific response, is likely to disappear from the analysis, with only the implied term of good faith remaining. Mr Justice Fancourt in *UTB LLC* v. *Sheffield Utd Ltd* thought the decision in *Bates* displayed 'the tendency to substitute for the question whether a reasonable reader of the contract would consider a term to be necessary or obvious the question of whether a contract is a "relational" contract'.[51] Similarly, in *Russell* v. *Cartwright* the starting point for the judge was not whether the contract was relational but whether the traditional tests for implied terms were met.[52] On these analyses, the development of a separate category of relational contracts serves no purpose. Evidently, a term of good faith may need to be implied on business efficacy grounds in order to make a contract work as a *relational contract*. The Canadian case of *Bhasin* v. *Hyrnew* suggests that good faith is necessary to give business efficacy to some agreements.[53] In English law this possibility is usually precluded where detailed terms exist.[54] Far from having significance as an alternative form of analysis or as providing a different explanatory framework to the classical law, the idea of relational contract appears likely to be drawn into the classical contract model.

[48] *Sheikh Tahnoon Bin Saeed Bin Shakhboot Al Nehayan* v. *Kent* [2018] EWHC 333 [167].

[49] Davies, 'Excluding Good Faith and Restricting Discretion', 96.

[50] See *Globe Motors, Inc & Ors* v. *TRW Lucas Varity Electric Steering Ltd* [2016] EWCA Civ 396; [2017] 1 All ER (Comm) 601: 'an implication of a duty of good faith will only be possible where the language of the contract, viewed against its context, permits it. It is thus not a reflection of a special rule of interpretation for this category of contract' per Lord Justice Beatson [68].

[51] *UTB LLC* v. *Sheffield Utd Ltd* [2019] EWHC 2322 [201]. The judge notes at [198] 'while certain types of joint venture agreements may require the implication of such a term, in order to give them business efficacy, other types of joint venture agreements may not do so'.

[52] *Russell* v. *Cartwright* [2020] EWHC 41 (Ch) [87].

[53] *Bhasin* v. *Hyrnew*, above n. 3 [24]. Approach confirmed in *C M Callow Inc* v. *Zollinger* [2020] SCC 45.

[54] *Marks and Spencer plc* v. *BNP Paribas Securities Services Trust Co Ltd* [2016] AC 742.

The admirable judicial effort to develop legal rules to respond to the particular features of relational contracts demonstrates that common law has considerable potential for innovation. But we also see here the difficulties of embedding real change within judicial reasoning about contracts. A stumbling block for the law is the uncertainty surrounding relational contracts themselves. Thus, while the long-term nature of the business relationship may be a factor, in isolation contract length is neither sufficient nor necessary to identify a relational contract.[55] Goetz and Scott observe that a contract is 'said to be relational to the extent that the parties are incapable of reducing important terms ... to well defined obligations'.[56] This is probably the crux of the relational contract – the expectations generated are difficult to capture in express terms at the point of agreement but are fleshed out by the course of performance and day-to-day co-operation between the parties.[57] Mr Justice Fraser in *Bates* acknowledged this as one of the criteria for identifying a relational contract.[58] Contract actions are more important than contract texts. The key factor in identifying the relational contract is uncertainty in the contracting environment that precisely precludes presentiation in the manner presumed achievable by the classical law.[59] That is to say, the agreement arising cannot be reduced to a 'transaction' motivated wholly by the pursuit of self-interest.

The impulse amongst some members of the judiciary to recognise a category of relational contracts reflects the realisation that the present law is resolutely *not* relational. But it seems unlikely that the recent judicial engagement with relational contracts evidences any kind of permanent paradigm shift in contract legal reasoning. This failure to fully engage with the relational contract idea is disappointing. Courts are hampered within the classical law by the need to map out the contours of relational contracts with some certainty.

55 *Monde Petroleum SA* v. *Westernzagros Ltd* [2016] EWHC 1472 (Comm), [2016] 2 Lloyd's Rep 229 at [250]; *General Nutrition Investment Company* v. *Holland and Barrett International Ltd* [2017] EWHC 746 (Ch). See also *Cathay* v. *Lufthansa* (above n. 37) where the agreement was a long-term contract but no good faith term was implied.

56 Charles J. Goetz and Robert E. Scott, 'Principles of Relational Contracts' (1981) 67 *Virginia Law Review* 1089 at 1091. See also *Dunkin' Brands Canada Ltd* v. *Bertico Inc* [2015] QCCA 624, [62] describing a relational contract as a long-term arrangement that does not spell out all of its terms.

57 David Campbell, 'Good Faith and the Ubiquity of Relational Contract' (2014) 77 *Modern Law Review* 475, 479.

58 *Bates* v. *Post Office Ltd* at [725].

59 See *Cathay* v. *Lufthansa*, above n. 37, [218]; *Al Nehayan* v. *Kent*, above n. 48, [167] and [174]; *UTB* v. *Sheffield Utd Ltd* above n. 10 [200].

This facilitates the containment of the concept. Yet, at its foundation, the idea of a relational contract is not disruptive to contracting reality, only to the assumed and imposed *classical contract law* reality. As Lord Justice Leggatt has pointed out, 'the enforcement of basic norms of commerce and of fair and honest dealing is an essential function of a system of commercial law.'[60] Nevertheless, resistance emanates from those judges who perhaps fear the principle of good faith in relational contract may prove impossible to silo. It is particularly telling that cases where the good faith duty has been recognised usually involve contractual relationships between individuals where the obligations are performed personally.[61] Courts may be reluctant to apply the same standards in agreements between complex organisations, acting through agents and employees, where detailed paperwork discharges multiple functions. Courts are also doubtful about the wisdom of imposing 'other-regarding' norms on self-interested and adversarial contracting parties.[62] The fear that standards-based reasoning will interfere with the exercise of contractual rights is advanced as one of the reasons for the appearance of context-limiting contract terms, such as entire agreement clauses, acknowledgements of non-reliance and 'no oral modification' provisions.[63]

Most of the judgments examining relational contracts have been delivered in lower courts. First instance decisions do not create precedents and are readily distinguishable on their facts, making it harder for the concept to implant itself securely within contract law. The piecemeal approach to legal development does not necessarily lend itself to producing authoritative rules to identify and govern relational contracts. It is also clear that some judges are less than enthusiastic about the idea of a separate category of contracts. The recent case law has been preoccupied with specifying the limitations on the concept and ensuring that it does not interfere with the operation of contractual rights appearing in the documents. Similarly, the implied term of good faith will be utilised only when the facts demand it. Good faith is not treated as an external standard according to which contractor behaviour can be reviewed and censured. This would entail acknowledging that contract rights may be subject to the operation of a broad principle, inviting uncertainty into the law.

60 *Al Nehayan* v. *Kent* [187]. See also first instance judgment in *Astor Management AG* v. *Atalaya Mining Plc & Ors* [2017] EWHC 425 at [98].

61 *Yam Seng* v. *ITC*, above n. 27; *Al Nehayan* v. *Kent*; *Bristol Ground School Ltd v Intelligent Data Capture Ltd* [2014] EWHC 2145; *Bates* v. *Post Office Ltd*, above n. 31.

62 *Carewatch*, above n. 36, [109]–[111].

63 Jonathan Morgan, 'Contracting for Self-Denial: On Enforcing "No Oral Modification" Clauses' (2017) 76 *Cambridge Law Journal* 589, 600–01.

The reticence in English law towards developing general principles is not necessarily seen in other jurisdictions.

7.3 Principled Development of the Common Law Elsewhere

Common law courts elsewhere have been bolder in cultivating innovative principles of contract law. In *Bhasin* v. *Hyrnew* the Canadian Supreme Court noted that the good faith duty in contract had a fluctuating justification. Good faith was sometimes imposed as a 'legal incident' of a contract, sometimes as the result of the operation of the 'presumed intention of the parties' or else derived from a process of contract interpretation.[64] The court in the case preferred the view that good faith was an organising principle of contract law. The principle of good faith was not an incident of a particular type of *contract* but an incident of the *law*. As for what good faith required, the court maintained that 'parties generally must perform their contractual duties honestly and reasonably and not capriciously or arbitrarily'.[65] The court in *Bhasin* viewed the principle as providing support for other more specific rules and also as the foundation upon which other new rules could be developed and justified.[66] Importantly, the good faith duty was not discharged merely by acting in accordance with the contract terms. Good faith was an independent standard according to which performance could be appraised and the exercise of express contractual rights moderated. For the court, express terms did not set out an unassailable framework that could override the duty of honest performance.[67] The duty 'operates irrespective of the intentions of the parties, and is to this extent analogous to equitable doctrines which impose limits on the freedom of contract, such as the doctrine of unconscionability'.[68] The organising principle has justified more specific actions taken to protect parties. It has been used to ascribe responsibility to a franchisor for failing to monitor franchisees and halt brand decline,[69] to invalidate the exercise of contract termination rights when one party has misled the other[70] and to control the

64 *Bhasin* v. *Hyrnew,* above n. 3, [48] and [52].

65 *Bhasin* v. *Hyrnew* [63].

66 *Bhasin* v. *Hyrnew* [66].

67 Stephen Waddams, *Sanctity of Contracts in a Secular Age* (Cambridge University Press, 2019), p. 108.

68 *Bhasin* v. *Hyrnew* above n. 3 at [74]. This was confirmed in *C M Callow Inc* v. *Zollinger,* above n. 53 – the duty of honesty in contractual performance is a part of the 'organising principle' of good faith and is a doctrine of contract law [3].

69 *Dunkin' Brands Canada Ltd* v. *Bertico Inc,* above n. 56.

70 *C M Callow Inc* v. *Zollinger,* above n. 53.

use of discretionary powers by ensuring the discretion is exercised in line with the purposes of the contract.[71] Good faith formed the organising or umbrella principle under which these more specific interventions drew meaning and justification.[72]

The contrast with English contract law is stark. The idea of good faith as an organising principle was rejected by the Court of Appeal in *MSC Mediterranean Shipping Co SA* v. *Cottonex Anstalt.*[73] English courts might regard the impugned behaviour in the Canadian cases as harsh instances of the exercise of contractual rights but ultimately justifiable according to the contract framework. The motive of a contracting party in exercising express and absolute contractual rights is irrelevant, and while the actions may be unsavoury, they are generally not unlawful if in accordance with the terms (the operation of any mandatory rules aside). In English law, the parties are entitled to pursue their self-interest within the dictates of the contract's terms. Interestingly, the Canadian Supreme Court in *Bhasin* did not believe their approach interfered with the pursuit of self-interest. A contracting party can prioritise their own interests, provided they do not offend the basic duty of honesty.[74] For the Supreme Court, contract law includes the organising principle of good faith as an irreducible minimum of *contracting*. The court thereby acknowledged that the law stipulates the standards within which all contracting takes place in order to be identified as 'contracting' at all. The court in *Bhasin* did warn against using the principle of good faith as an excuse to engage in judicial moralism or a form of discretionary justice.[75] As for the content of the duty, the court stressed it involved having regard to the legitimate interests of the other party, although it did not require acting to serve those interests in all cases.[76] The overriding factor is that the contract remains *a contract* where there is an exchange. As Macneil has argued, *reciprocity* ('the principle of getting something back for something given'[77]) is a common contract norm, so there is no question that contract can require

[71] *Wastech Services Ltd* v. *Greater Vancouver Sewerage and Drainage District* [2021] SCC 7.

[72] *Bhasin* v. *Hyrnew,* above n. 3 [64].

[73] Per Lord Justice Moore-Bick [2016] EWCA Civ 789 at [45].

[74] *Bhasin* v. *Hyrnew,* above n. 3, per Cromwell J at [65], [70] and [86].

[75] *Bhasin* v. *Hyrnew,* above n. 3, [70].

[76] *Overlook* v. *Foxtel* [2002] NSWSC 17 [67]. In *CPC Group Ltd* v. *Qatari Diar Real Estate Investment Company* [2010] EWHC 1535 (Ch) at [246] Mr Justice Vos interpreted an explicit good faith obligation as requiring the parties 'to adhere to the spirit of the contract ... and to observe reasonable commercial standards of fair dealing, and to be faithful to the agreed common purpose, and to act consistently with the justified expectations of the parties'.

[77] Macneil, 'Values in Contract: Internal and External', 347.

complete subordination of one's interest to another. Nevertheless, this does not entail that the pursuit of self-interest is the sole value contract protects.

The articulation of good faith as an organising principle is not an isolated incident of a common law jurisdiction travelling in a different direction to English courts. Canadian judges have demonstrated willingness to invoke unconscionability more readily than their English counterparts and to reform it in the light of contemporary challenges. In *Uber Technologies Inc* v. *Heller*[78] the Supreme Court of Canada used unconscionability to invalidate a dispute resolution clause in a standard form service contract between a Canada-based food delivery driver and the Uber platform. Standard form contracts are a ubiquitous feature of the digital platform and sharing economy. The clause mandated arbitration in the Netherlands and for the defendant driver to pay significant upfront costs. The term was located in a software licencing and services agreement some fourteen pages in length. The court noted the significant disparity in bargaining power between the parties and the lack of negotiation in the terms that had resulted in the improvident bargain. The case outcome suggests that the vulnerability of the weaker party, which is necessary for a finding of unconscionability, can be relative to the strength and sophistication of the other party. Vulnerability is not limited to situations where the weaker party is labouring under some disability, manifest disadvantage or specific weakness that the stronger party has knowingly sought to exploit. The court thought such a restriction was at odds with the equitable roots of the unconscionability doctrine.[79] Australian courts have adopted a similar line in relation to the statutory unconscionability rules operating in Australia.[80]

Apparent in these decisions is an aspiration to develop common law doctrine and *to communicate* the values inherent in the practice of contracting. The view of the Canadian Supreme Court is that the good faith duty of honest performance is a doctrine of the law of contract, not justified on the basis of interpretation or implied terms.[81] This contrasts with English law's reluctance to develop good faith except by way of the traditional implied terms route.

78 *Uber Technologies Inc* v. *Heller* (Supreme Court of Canada) [2020] SCC 16.

79 *Uber Technologies Inc.* v. *Heller* [82].

80 *Australian Competition and Consumer Commission* v. *Quantum Housing Group Pty Ltd* [2021] FCAFC 40, [91], dealing with statutory unconscionability under s 21 of the Australian Consumer Law code.

81 See, for example, *Wastech,* above n. 71: 'it is appropriate to recognize the duty to exercise discretion in good faith as a general doctrine of contract law. Like the duty of honest performance, it need not find its source in an implied term in the contract, but rather it operates in every contract irrespective of the intentions of the parties' [91].

This technique is individualistic and fact-dependent. It prevents the courts articulating clear statements of the standards of contract behaviour that are not hedged about with qualifiers, limitations and exceptions. The Canadian approach also reflects a different understanding of common law reasoning. It accepts that what may start out as an amorphous principle will gain structure, boundaries and a degree of certainty through being applied to the different facts and contexts presented in actual cases. English common law, however, concerned with maintaining certainty, seeks to position the new development within the existing rules. As we have seen, some of the recent decisions on relational contracts have sought to assimilate the concept into the existing doctrinal framework of implied terms. This move immediately neutralises the development, negating what is innovative and distinctive about relational contracting. In the process, we lose the possibility of differentiating more transparently and systematically between different types of contracts or contracting parties and to develop alternative rules that correlate to these differences. The reluctance in English law to recognise the relational contract as requiring an extraordinary or distinctive legal approach springs from the legal assumptions on which commercial contract law turns – chief of which is that it is predicated upon discrete transactions conducted at arm's length between stoical, self-interested and rational utility-maximisers. There is little to suggest this acontextual model of contract has been seriously challenged by the concept of relational contracting.

7.4 English Common Law Innovations

There are mandatory rules of English contract law that have been subject to recent review and restatement by senior courts. Developments in the law of illegality and the legal control of discretionary powers in contracts demonstrate that courts cannot avoid dealing with difficult questions of policy and the public interest in the operation of contract rights. Despite engagement being unavoidable, the judicial response to these matters has generated controversy. In *Patel* v. *Mirza*,[82] Lord Toulson in the Supreme Court rejected a rule-based method of determining when illegality bars a claim in favour of a flexible 'range of factors' approach. In *Patel*, maintaining the integrity of the legal system was identified as the relevant overriding policy in determining the consequences of illegality. Lord Toulson remarked:

[82] [2017] AC 467.

> The essential rationale of the illegality doctrine is that it would be contrary to the public interest to enforce a claim if to do so would be harmful to the integrity of the legal system. . . . In assessing whether the public interest would be harmed in that way, it is necessary a) to consider the underlying purpose of the prohibition which has been transgressed and whether that purpose will be enhanced by denial of the claim b) to consider any other relevant public policy on which the denial of the claim may have an impact and c) to consider whether denial of the claim would be a proportionate response to the illegality, bearing in mind that punishment is a matter for the criminal courts.[83]

Lord Toulson's policy-based method for determining the effects of illegality, in particular the judicial responsibility to weigh the various factors of each specific case in reaching a decision, did not win universal support amongst other members of the Supreme Court. Perhaps predictably, a minority argued for a rule-based method for the operation of the illegality defence, notwithstanding the profound difficulty of reducing the illegality doctrine to a few succinct precepts.[84] Expansion of judicial discretion, with negative consequences for certainty in the law, was a particular fear in the minority judgments.[85] Given the wide application of the illegality defence, and the varying severity of circumstances that may trigger illegality, the rule-based approach appears entirely misconceived. It is, however, in keeping with the formalist aversion to conferring any relatively open-ended power on judges in private law matters.

While *Patel* demonstrates the continuing importance and influence of policy-based reasoning in contract, the courts' approach to discretionary powers shows they are mindful of the limits on party autonomy. Contract terms may confer a discretion on one of the parties in relation to any future decision-making under the contract, such as granting permissions and approvals, determining the contractual entitlement of the other, assessing whether a standard has been reached or a performance criterion satisfied, and so on.[86] Those academic commentators that support a robust interpretation of freedom of contract are naturally critical of any general legal power to

83 *Patel* v. *Mirza* [120].

84 See critique of Lord Toulson's approach in *Patel* v. *Mirza* by Lord Sumption, Lord Mance and Lord Clarke. See also Andrew Burrows, 'Illegality after *Patel v Mirza*' (2017) 70 *Current Legal Problems* 55, endorsing the 'range of factors' method.

85 *Patel* v. *Mirza*, per Lord Sumption at [226], [239], [261].

86 See generally Richard Hooley, 'Controlling Contractual Discretion' (2013) 72 *Cambridge Law Journal* 65, 68ff; Michael Bridge, 'The Exercise of Contractual Discretion' (2019) 135 *Law Quarterly Review* 227, 235ff.

review the exercise of a discretion conferred by contract.[87] Yet it could be argued that the power of review only demonstrates that courts are mindful that the use of discretion without constraint by one party may render aspects of the bargain completely illusory for the other.[88] Controls on discretionary powers are a clear indication of courts' willingness to oversee the exercise of freedoms conferred on one party to the agreement to ensure they are not abused. This maintains the value of reciprocity by preventing one party using non-negotiated terms to transform the contract into a one-sided instrument. There is evidence that legal control on discretionary powers is necessary and important.[89] Controls on discretionary powers are therefore entirely in keeping with contract law rationale that a contract is an exchange. Controls are also a manifestation of the judicial concern with procedural fairness.

The fear that the legal power to constrain contract discretion will lead to judicial overreaching appears exaggerated. Judicial authority to review the exercise of contract discretions is relatively modest. Discretionary powers are usually controlled through the mechanisms of interpretation and implied terms. The interpretative questions include whether the power conferred by the contract terms is a discretion at all and whether the discretion has been exercised in accordance with its terms and in relation to a matter falling within its scope. What is interpreted as an absolute contractual right, such as the right to terminate, will generally not be subject to any controls on the basis of good faith, reasonableness or rationality.[90] Many purported 'discretions' up for review may fall at this initial hurdle. In distinguishing the absolute right from the discretionary power, it has been said that a discretion involves a choice amongst alternatives, whereas an absolute contract right, which involves a

[87] See, for example, Jonathan Morgan, 'Resisting Judicial Review of Discretionary Contractual Powers' [2015] *Lloyd's Maritime and Commercial Law Quarterly* 483.

[88] *Equitable Life Assurance Society* v. *Hyman* [2002] 1 AC 408, 459 per Lord Steyn, articulating the presumption of the parties that directors would not exercise a discretion in a way that conflicted with contractual rights.

[89] See Competition and Markets Authority, *Care Homes Market Study: Final Report* (30 November 2017). The Competition and Markets Authority noted widespread use of terms conferring broad discretions on care homes to increase residents' fees (para 11.30) and a wide discretion to terminate the contract at short notice (11.39). Terms also allowed the homes to continue to charge fees even after the death of a resident (11.45).

[90] See discussion in *Mid Essex Hospital Services NHS Trust* v. *Compass Group UK and Ireland Ltd (t/a Medirest)* [2013] EWCA Civ 200, [83] and [91]. In the Canadian case of *Callow* v. *Zollinger* (above n. 53) the Supreme Court of Canada held that a contractual duty to act honestly attached to a contractual right to terminate and was not discharged simply by a contractor acting in accordance with their termination rights, [37] and [84].

binary yes-no decision, does not.[91] This distinction between absolute rights and discretionary powers is a fine one, and not easily drawn in the abstract.[92] Admittedly, while the determination of whether one party has exercised a contractual right or a discretionary power may turn on interpretation of the clause (does it involve a binary choice or a range of options from which to choose?), an element of ex post facto rationalisation may be involved: a determination that a party has exercised a contractual *right* if the courts are not minded to interfere (as with termination rights) and a contractual *discretionary power* if they are.[93]

Nevertheless, even if the discretion is reviewable, the implied terms controlling its exercise are not stringent. The power must be exercised subject to requirements of honesty, good faith and genuineness and in the absence of perversity and irrationality.[94] In a mortgage agreement, the contractual discretion to vary interest rates payable under the mortgage was held subject to an implied term that 'the discretion ... should not be exercised dishonestly, for an improper purpose, capriciously or arbitrarily'.[95] Other formulations have stressed the need for the discretion to be exercised 'honestly and in good faith for the purposes for which it was conferred'.[96] A contractor can exercise the discretion with attention to their own interests, but the manner of its exercise must be justifiable. The law is doing little more here than articulating what is a reasonable expectation. It is hard to perceive of any contractor agreeing with the proposition that the counterparty's decision-making process can be irrational, capricious, arbitrary or conducted in bad faith. These tests do not necessarily mandate an outcome from the discretion. In *Paragon Finance plc* v. *Nash*, for example, while the implied term required the lender to act reasonably, in the sense of not exercising the discretion in a way that no reasonable lender, acting reasonably, would do (so-called *Wednesbury*

91 *Monde Petroleum SA* v. *Westernzagros Ltd*, above n. 55, [266], drawing on *Mid Essex Hospital Services NHS Trust* v. *Compass Group UK and Ireland* at [83].

92 Bridge, 'The Exercise of Contractual Discretion', 237–38.

93 Bridge, 'The Exercise of Contractual Discretion', 237.

94 *Socimer International Bank Ltd* v. *Standard Bank London Ltd* [2008] EWCA Civ 116; [2008] 1 Lloyd's Rep 558, per Lord Justice Rix at [66] and [106].

95 *Paragon Finance plc* v. *Nash (and others)* [2002] 1 WLR 685 [32]. Reliance was placed on dicta in *Abu Dhabi National Tanker Co* v. *Product Star Shipping Ltd (The Product Star) (No 2)* [1993] 1 Lloyd's Rep 397: '[w]here A and B contract with each other to confer a discretion on A, that does not render B subject to A's uninhibited whim' per Lord Justice Leggatt at 404.

96 *Ludgate Insurance Co Ltd* v. *Citibank NA* [1998] Lloyd's Rep IR 221 per Lord Justice Brooke at [35].

unreasonableness, latterly in the contractual context termed 'irrationality'[97]), this did not impose a duty on the contractor to charge a reasonable interest rate or a rate not significantly out of line with other lenders, only to act for a genuine reason (in this case the lender's own straitened financial circumstances) in raising rates.[98] Thus the controls attempt to chart a path between the extremes of an unfettered power to do whatever the decision-maker likes at one end and a requirement for the decision-maker to demonstrate an objectively reasonable outcome from the discretion at the other. The qualification on the discretion is procedural rather than substantive, and it requires a degree of means-end rationality. Thus in *Nash* the lender could have charged very high interest rates, provided they showed they had a reason – a legitimate business interest to advance – in doing so. Without this reason, the exercise of discretion is likely to breach the implied term.[99] In addition, the decision-maker must act *honestly*, that is, hold an honest belief that the exercise of discretion is necessary to secure the legitimate interest.[100] The line of authority on discretionary powers demonstrates that courts can impose principled limits on the exercise of freedom of contract, although in truth the reference to 'legitimate interests' of a contractor, as we have seen in other contexts, stresses the individualistic nature of the assessment.

The precise implementation of the controls on discretionary powers may vary widely with the context. In a commercial context, for example, there is no requirement to balance the legitimate interest pursued in exercising the contractual discretion (assuming a legitimate interest is made out) with the interests of the other party.[101] In a relational contract context, the standard to be expected in the exercise of the discretionary power may be higher. While it may be argued that this demonstrates the uncertainty inherent in any judicial power to review, it could be maintained that this only shows that courts rightly differentiate between types of contract and contractor. This is a welcome departure from the tendency to apply the same commercial contract standard indiscriminately across a diverse range of contracting circumstances. *Braganza* v. *BP Shipping Ltd* concerned a decision taken by an employer that 'in their opinion' an employee had committed suicide, rendering his widow ineligible for death-in-service benefits. The Supreme Court, in reviewing the

[97] *Socimer International Bank Ltd* v. *Standard Bank London Ltd*, above n. 94, [66].

[98] *Paragon Finance* v. *Nash* [41].

[99] *BHL* v. *Leumi ABL Limited* [2017] EWHC 1871.

[100] See Hooley, 'Controlling Contractual Discretion', 72.

[101] *Property Alliance Group Ltd* v. *Royal Bank of Scotland* [2018] EWCA Civ 355 [169].

decision, stated that the requirement was that 'the decision is made rationally (as well as in good faith) and consistently with its contractual purpose'.[102] Drawing on public law, the Supreme Court stated that this involved, first, a question of process-rationality (were the right matters taken into account in reaching the decision?) and, second, a question of outcome-rationality (did the decision-maker nevertheless reach a conclusion so unreasonable that no reasonable decision-maker could have reached it?). This formulation suggests a court may more readily interfere in the decision if they feel relevant matters have not been considered (process) and, in the light of that, the outcome was clearly unreasonable (substance). Lady Hale intimated that the employment context of the decision in *Braganza* meant it would not necessarily apply in the same way in a commercial setting.[103] In a business context it would be expected that greater emphasis is placed on process rationality (the decision is justifiable in the pursuit of a legitimate interest) and honesty, rather than substantive and objective reasonableness, or whether the decision-maker has paid sufficient attention to the effect that the decision may have on the other party.

The controls on discretionary powers are not an interference with freedom of contract but a proper exercise of legal authority to determine how far freedom of contract extends. The parties are not prevented from stipulating the standards that the decision-maker must reach in exercising a discretion, or placing a limit on the power, within the contract terms. In that case, the discretion is not unqualified, and there will be no implied term concerning how it is exercised.[104] In a consumer contract the exercise of discretionary powers or unilateral rights to vary contract terms will be subject to the controls in the unfair terms legislation.[105] Ultimately, the question is an interpretative one raising the same issue that appears in relation to a number of different contractual powers: is the exercise of the discretion in the service of a legitimate interest of the decision-maker? Is the manner in which the discretion is exercised proportionate to advancing or protecting that legitimate interest, bearing in mind the value of reciprocity in contractual relationships? These controls are justified to ensure we have a law of contract at all.

[102] *Braganza* v. *BP Shipping Ltd*, above n. 26, [30].

[103] *Braganza* [32]; per Lord Hodge at [54], [55]. Although see *BHL* v. *Leumi ABL Limited* for a different approach.

[104] *Federal Mogul Asbestos Personal Injury Trust* v. *Federal Mogul Ltd and others* [2014] EWHC 2002 [120].

[105] Section 62(4) Consumer Rights Act 2015.

7.5 The Limitations on Litigation

One of the main arguments of this book is that the law of contract has for too long reflected the interests and concerns of commercial contractors. As a result, the general principles of contract law are diminishing in importance as a significant regulatory force in contracting. One evident problem is the difficulty of bringing non-commercial contract disputes before courts. The situation of declining funding for litigation is not likely to improve, and it is beyond the means of many individuals to bring cases to court. In addition there are clear signs that the litigation of 'ordinary' disputes is to be discouraged. If an identifiable group is affected by a widespread and legally questionable contracting practice, then regulatory action may be appropriate. As we have seen, however, regulatory action often proceeds independently of legal proceedings, with the result that regulatory enforcement does not necessarily impinge on common law development. To the extent that individuals are deterred from taking action due to lack of resources, the level of risk involved and the likelihood of small recompense, group proceedings may provide a partial answer. Recent case law has demonstrated the significance of Group Litigation Orders in getting contract law issues affecting non-commercial actors before courts. Thus the important decision on relational contracts in *Bates* v. *The Post Office Ltd* was the result of proceedings commenced under a Group Litigation Order. Group litigation can be pursued under the civil procedure rules, but each claimant must consent.[106] A similar possibility for collective litigation to challenge poor market practices arises under Collective Proceedings Orders (CPOs). Unlike Group Litigation Orders, CPOs enable a representative claimant to pursue a legal action for anti-competitive behaviour on behalf of a potentially vast and indeterminate class of claimants, provided the claims raise the same or similar issues of fact or law.

The efficacy of these orders was recently given a boost by the Supreme Court decision in *Mastercard Incorporated* v. *Merricks*.[107] The case concerned the refusal by the Competition Appeal Tribunal to certify a CPO in relation to a claim against Mastercard for breaching competition rules by charging unlawfully high interchange fees over a sixteen-year period from 1992 to 2008. The breach was thought to affect some forty-six million UK adults. In its judgment, the Supreme Court removed some of the barriers to certification of the representative claimant (chiefly centred around the difficulty of proving loss) and ordered the decision on the CPO to be remitted to the Competition

[106] CPR Part 19 III. [107] *Mastercard Incorporated* v. *Merricks* [2021] 3 All ER 285.

Appeal Tribunal. Though CPOs are limited to the operation of the Competition Act 1998 (the Consumer Rights Act 2015 established the procedure in an amendment to the Act), they mark an attempt to deal with anticompetitive practices. These practices are often established and pursued through the use of contract terms. The returns by way of damages for each claimant in the class for these mass actions for breach of competition law are likely to be nominal, but the public interest in such action, and the possibility for legal development that it raises, is potentially highly significant. At the very least, it provides an important channel for challenging commercial contracting cultures and behaviours that contribute to the pursuit of predatory and exploitative practices by big business in the market.

While providing routes and remedies for weaker contracting parties to seek redress, the impact of these developments on general contract law is likely to be limited. As we have seen with regard to relational contracts, legal developments that are confined to lower courts are likely to remain in flux for a considerable time or may fail to become embedded in the law at all. The processes for mounting appeals are designed to tease out whether there is serious issue to be tried involving an important issue of legal principle or practice or an issue of public importance, as well as a substantial prospect of success. Thus section 69(3)(c) and (d) of the Arbitration Act 1996 provides that leave to appeal from an arbitration award will be granted only if 'the question is one of general public importance and the decision of the tribunal is at least open to serious doubt, and that, despite the agreement of the parties to resolve the matter by arbitration, it is just and proper in all the circumstances for the court to determine the question'. Under the Civil Procedure Rules, permission to appeal to the Court of Appeal is granted only if that court considers that 'the appeal would have a real prospect of success; and raises an important point of principle or practice or there is some other compelling reason for the Court of Appeal to hear it'.[108] In refusing or allowing permission to appeal, a judge is asked to indicate whether 'there appear to be conflicting authorities; there is a point of practice and procedure of significant importance; there is a point of general principle and importance in the development of the substantive law; a number of appeals on similar points suggest that a theme, or trend, is developing which the Court of Appeal needs to consider'.[109] Appeals to the Supreme Court will be allowed for an 'arguable

[108] Part 52 CPR.

[109] HM Courts and Tribunals Service, Form N460: *Reasons for Allowing or Refusing Permission to Appeal.*

point of law of general public importance'.[110] This might suggest that, ultimately, the reason why contract cases show a distinct lack of diversity is because many of the issues raised by contracts (non-commercial contracts in particular) are not thought worthy of trial or appeal. The project to contractualise society is so ingrained and established that it no longer raises any issue of general contract principle or requires a revisiting of principle: the principles upon which it is based are beyond any meaningful revision.[111]

Similarly, it is clear that it is becoming more and more difficult to justify adjudication as a method for resolving contract disputes. As yet, a court's jurisdiction cannot be completely ousted by contract terms. Any attempt to do so would be void as contrary to public policy.[112] But alternative dispute resolution is increasingly encouraged within courts themselves. While there are directions as to when a case should be directed to mediation, there is no equivalent provision under the Civil Procedure Rules for identifying the relevant features of cases that should be directed towards trial. At present, it appears the legal importance of a case is not regarded as a ground for reasonable refusal to mediate. Potential for an authoritative ruling to contribute to the body of common law rules, or to provide clarity on a long-contentious issue, may be one relevant criterion for earmarking a case for trial. This is not just a matter of identifying those cases that, for whatever reason, are regarded as unsuitable for mediation. Rather it would involve track allocation according to factors beyond the money value of the claim, including the implications of the case for the continued renewal of common law principle. Change is unlikely, however, given the influential tide of opinion against litigation. The public interest argument for trials is often derided as 'idealistic' or a 'principled objection' that is substantially outweighed by practical factors concerning speed of resolution, cost and dispute disposal.[113] Courts struggling with caseloads are also used as evidence that there is little

[110] Supreme Court Practice Direction 3.3.3.

[111] Francis Reynolds, 'Commercial Law' in Louis Blom-Cooper, Brice Dickson and Gavin Drewry (eds.), *The Judicial House of Lords 1876–2009* (Oxford University Press, 2009), pp. 700, 710, noting the relative decline in commercial cases reaching the House of Lords.

[112] *Lee* v. *The Showmen's Guild of Great Britain* [1952] 2 QB 329; *R (on the application of UNISON)* v. *The Lord Chancellor* [2020] AC 869, fees for taking a case to the Employment Tribunal were unlawful as against the 'constitutional right of access to the courts . . . inherent in the rule of law', per Lord Reed [66].

[113] Civil Justice Council, *Compulsory ADR* (June 2021), at para 81; Civil Mediation Council, *Response to the Civil Justice Council's Report "Compulsory ADR"* (13 July 2021) noting that the anti-compulsory ADR argument is 'based on a more idealistic, rather than realistic, view of the function of justice and the court system today' (para 10).

danger to the rule of law by cases being directed towards settlement.[114] There is scant consideration of whether courts are exposed to a sufficient diversity of cases to maintain the general legal principles surrounding one of the most basic and important tools of social organisation: the contract.

7.6 Conclusion

The practical limitations on continued common law development in contract are considerable. This is not to deny that there have been areas of progress in common law where judges have taken the opportunity to refresh or restate important principles. The law on the effect of illegality on contracts is one recent example. However, illegality represents a relatively exceptional instance of direct judicial engagement with broader policy issues affecting general contract law. The outcome – endorsement of a flexible 'range of factors' approach to the operation of illegality – has not won universal support. Relational contracting is another area of common law innovation that has attempted to change contract law along principled lines in response to the realisation that not all contracts will fit within the classical law framework. At present, however, the relational contract development is at risk of being absorbed within existing rules on implied terms. The chance presented by relational contracts to weaken the hold of the classical law paradigm by developing alternative forms of analysis in contract is in danger of being squandered. Through the decisions examined in this chapter, courts have demonstrated that originality in contract common law is still possible. But these developments are vulnerable and liable to fail when located within a formal law that does not admit innovation easily and where significant impediments to change are presented by the legal system. The attempted advances considered here have been subject to criticism for introducing uncertainty into the law to the detriment of commercial contractors. In view of this, we can expect that the influence that the complex commercial contract exerts over contract law is not likely to be surrendered at any time soon. Innovations that strengthen the formal classical law model are likely to be received more readily into current judicial decision-making. But new techniques that challenge the classical law are necessary if contract law is to still maintain some meaningful general powers of review over the range of contracting activity.

[114] Civil Justice Council, *Compulsory ADR*, at para 84.

8

Conclusion

The judicially created rules of contract law provide an invisible framework that underpins and facilitates much contracting activity. Yet the role of contract law in policing many contracts approaches vanishing point. Current law is largely content to enforce express terms in the documented contract, with stark consequences for ensuring justice and fairness in contractual relationships. The role of private ordering through contracts has expanded the reach of contract but made little impression on contract law. The methods by which contracts come into existence, and notionally create binding obligations, have become more insidious. Consumers enter into contracts through remote and automated processes (via the Internet) over which they have little control and on standard terms whose legal validly is frequently untested. The dwindling significance of contract law is also evident in the commercial sphere. Commercial exchange is managed through complex and multi-faceted contractual mechanisms, but the enforcement of these contracts relies on social systems and norms (trust, reputation networks, informal codes and internal procedures) rather than domestic contract law. Similarly, international trade is governed by model rules, standard form contracts and bespoke regulation promulgated by specialist industry organisations, not legal institutions. Developments in information and communication technology, such as the advent of 'smart contracts', potentially remove the role of state institutions in facilitating certain transactions, reducing further the significance of the law of contract and ushering in private forms of contract enforcement subject to minimal legal scrutiny.

The English common law response to these pressures has been to retreat back to a formal, insular and minimalistic model, justified by 'freedom of contract'. This model is tailored to the interests and concerns of commercial contractors. The commercial turn in contract reflects a judicial perception that domestic contract law must remain competitive (cost-sensitive) against other jurisdictions in the international market for commercial law and legal services.

The judicial focus on presenting contract law as an attractive product for sole use by commercial contractors reduces further the generality, scope and regulatory effectiveness of contract law in society and erodes its capacity to reflect normative values, such as upholding the protection of reasonable expectations and preventing abuse and exploitation of weaker parties through the operation of contract forms. One effect of this impoverishment of the general principles of contract law is that much contracting activity is conducted beyond the scope of legal control, despite the questionable terms contained in many of these contracts (the Student Loan Agreement; the non-disclosure agreement). There is no realistic prospect of determinative rulings on many important issues concerning the role of contract in society. The vagaries of litigation and the inadequacy of common law rules fashioned to appeal predominantly to commercial contractors preclude it. The substantive weakening of the institution of contract law in a society heavily dependent on contracts has implications that have not seriously been addressed by courts.

Legal scrutiny of our contracts matters. Contract law, and the common law in particular, provides the support that enables the use of contracts not only to protect and enhance our freedom of action but also to curtail it, often in ways that are less than transparent. This is particularly evident when the party autonomy, upon which the general law of contract so heavily relies for its justification, is supposedly established through proxies for genuine agreement, such as clicking boxes on computer screens that incorporate standard terms and conditions into an agreement. That these scenarios are accepted as giving rise to obligations is largely because of the precepts of general contract law and its founding principle of freedom of contract. But contract law engagement with the deeper policy questions raised by the use of contracts in these contexts has been minimal. The growth of consumer contracting in the second half of the twentieth century, the resurgence of free market economic ideology over the past forty years, a simultaneously less paternalistic yet more regulatory state, changes in the economic organisation and production methods of firms, and technological advances affecting the way citizens procure goods and services have been significant social drivers behind the expansion of contracting in liberal societies, particularly contracting on standard terms. Nevertheless, the law has also played its part in elevating contracts to the dominant position in our society that they now occupy. Most of the contract general principles upon which modern contracts rely, to a greater or lesser extent, are derived from the common law: the authoritative statements of legal principle produced by judges in the course of resolving contract disputes in courts and the interpretation and re-interpretation of these principles by other judges in accordance with a doctrine of precedent.

Current contract principles are also associated with the classical law of contract, that is, the contract rules developed by courts during the course of the nineteenth century. These rules had manifest significance in shaping some important elements of our understanding of contracts: what contracts look like, how we become bound to them, what rights they confer and the legitimate avenues of escape. The classical law of contract is committed to a heavily formalistic model of what it means 'to contract'. This formality is in many ways a virtue. It prioritises certainty and predictability in the rules, which is prized in commerce. But contract law's focus on freedom of contract, party autonomy and objectivity also facilitates commitment by stealth and inertia, rendering the process of assuming contractual obligation liable to exploitation and abuse. Despite its dubious legacy in legitimising the bureaucratic model of contract (bureaucratic in the sense of 'a particular form of governance of human affairs dominated by reasoned and detailed planning'[1]) that confronts us on a daily basis, the general and common law rules of contract exercise little direct oversight over many aspects of the modern contracting process and the agreements that result from it.

Courts do recognise that contracts might have unwelcome or negative social effects. But currently it is not reckoned to be any part of the common law to act as a corrective to this. The judicial role is presented as a relatively neutral one of simply enforcing the agreed terms. As McBride has observed, there is a risk that contract law will '"eat itself" through the courts' too slavishly giving effect to the formalist ideal of "party autonomy"'.[2] The overarching commitment to autonomy compounds the problem of inequality of bargaining power and accords excessive significance to contractual documents. The commercial paradigm that informs contract law exerts a damaging effect on contract legal reasoning, and a significantly imbalanced contract law has resulted – rules developed in the context of negotiated agreements have been applied indiscriminately and inappropriately. Common law has sacrificed the development of its general principles on altars of certainty and party autonomy.

The common law is a flexible system, well-equipped to respond to transformations in contracting practice. This feature should ensure its continued renewal and relevance. Indeed, the manifest shift back to classical law values

[1] Ian R. Macneil, 'Bureaucracy and Contracts of Adhesion' (1984) 22 *Osgoode Hall Law Journal* 5, 8.

[2] Nicholas J. McBride, *Key Ideas in Contract Law* (Hart Publishing, 2017), p. 18.

appears to reverse the move towards a more contextual style of contract law that judges embraced towards the end of the last century. In contrast to this more reflexive and expectations-led approach, current common law, in England at least, increasingly excludes itself from a role as ultimate general authority on contract matters. The common law rules of contract, while still claiming relevance to the basics, are increasingly dispensable in the details. While an expendable contract law may suit commercial contractors, it has stark consequences for law's capacity to ensure justice and fairness across the range of contractual relationships.

This work sought to examine the implications of a disappearing contract law in a society heavily dependent on private ordering through contracts. Contract law diminishment is evident in the substantive weakening of the institution of contract law, particularly the common law, both internally in the law (the revival of classical norms in contract legal reasoning) and externally (the appropriation of many of contract law's functions by private processes). This diminishment has potentially considerable negative consequences. Shadowy though the legal role may be, a contract is, ultimately, a relationship defined by legal rules. Contract law remains the ultimate arbiter of what is and is not permissible in making, performing and enforcing voluntary agreements. Courts perform an important function in announcing publicly the legal rules and standards that govern contracting – even when only filling in the gaps left by the absence of other forms of regulation. This extends to communicating the values that contract should embody. Since it is impossible for courts to adjudicate every contract dispute, or develop a distinct legal position on every contract-based problem, the relevance of these values stretches beyond the immediate audience for contract's detailed rules. In showing excessive deference to the interests of one particular audience in their legal reasoning, to the exclusion of others, courts may distort these values in damaging ways. In short, courts bear a substantial responsibility for a society's contract culture. The downsides of the privatisation of contract regulation are also readily apparent. The attempt to conduct the entirety of contracting activity largely outside the confines of a national legal system, or beyond effective legal control, raises issues about access to justice, legitimacy and accountability in decision-making and the rule of law.[3] Given the accelerated rate at which the functions of contracts and contract law are assumed by artificial intelligence, these problems seem likely to become more acute, creating a new kind of

[3] Margaret Jane Radin, *Boilerplate: The Fine Print, Vanishing Rights and the Rule of Law* (Princeton University Press, 2013).

contract-based servitude.[4] Contract may be the paradigm concept of private law, and the sphere of protection for private arrangements, but as custodians of the common law judges have a duty to maintain it in order to serve the public interest. Yet never has it seemed more likely that the common law will be reduced to 'an ossuary'.[5]

An immediate response to these points is to say that the availability of alternatives to law means that common law does not need to adapt. Or that the overshadowing of the common law rules is not a matter of concern: we simply do not require traditional law to occupy the same role or perform the same functions that it once did. The complex, modern, administrative state delivers public goods, its democratic mandate and its laws in ways that do not need to appeal to the normative values inherent in a coherent system of principle but relies instead on criteria of regulatory or functional effectiveness.[6] This development wholly militates against the possibility of a unified system based on an ideal of coherence. Understandably then, the common law rules have become marginal to all but a minor subset of transactions – those discrete agreements whose parties are embroiled in an adversarial dispute in a dysfunctional relationship. Other forms of contract can have different considerations applied by alternative methods of enforcement and dispute resolution.

It is true that there are many normative frameworks, apart from the law, that support contracting. But one result of these overlapping systems is an increasingly fragmented and piecemeal landscape of contract regulation that does not pursue any obvious value. Traditional contract law attempts to retain its commitment to the principles of freedom of contract and party autonomy but only by excluding most contracts – and contracting environments – from its consideration. Atiyah observed that legislative interventions that substantially interfered with freedom of contract were regarded by lawyers as not 'affecting the principles of contract itself: there, free choice remains, in theory, the ultimate basis of the law'.[7] Brownsword noted in his examination of the

4 Lord Sales, 'Algorithms, Artificial Intelligence and the Law' The Sir Henry Brooke Lecture for BAILII (12 November 2019), p. 9.

5 Lord Toulson, *Kennedy* v. *The Charity Commission* [2014] 2 WLR 808 at [133]; quoted by Lord Thomas, 'Developing Commercial Law through the Courts: Rebalancing the Relationship between the Courts and Arbitration', BAILII Lecture (9 March 2016), at para 22.

6 Edward L. Rubin, 'From Coherence to Effectiveness: A Legal Methodology for the Modern World' in Rob van Gestel, Hans-W. Micklitz, and Edward L. Rubin (eds.) *Rethinking Legal Scholarship: A Transatlantic Dialogue* (Cambridge University Press, 2017), pp. 310, 350.

7 Patrick S. Atiyah, *An Introduction to the Law of Contract*, 5th ed. (Oxford University Press, 1999), p. 23.

decision in *Suisse Atlantique* that senior courts always held fast to the faith that the common law of contract did not need to distinguish between different types of contract. The same rule set was applicable, notwithstanding appreciable differences in contract context.[8] A clear statement of this, and its implications, comes from Lord Wilberforce in the case: '[t]he principle that the contractual intention is to be ascertained – not just grammatically from words used, but by consideration of those words in relation to commercial purpose (or other purpose according to the type of contract) – is surely flexible enough, and though it may be the case that adhesion contracts give rise to particular difficulties in ascertaining or attributing a contractual intent, which may require a special solution, those difficulties need not be imported into the general law of contract nor be permitted to deform it.'[9] The creation of too many distinctive categories or exceptions to the operation of a rule or principle may raise an excess of policy issues that are best regarded as a matter for parliament, not judges.[10] The common law of contract therefore regards itself as the last refuge for the values of freedom and autonomy in the regulatory and administrative state. This foundation upon which the common law is based is increasingly unstable and unfit for most modern contracting circumstances. The inability of the model to assimilate and reflect the changes in contract practice is the biggest weakness in the law, and some of its implications have been explored in the course of this work.

Contract law has not always been committed to a single vision or value. Alternative models or explanations of contract have emerged over time, prompted by encroachment from other areas of law into contract's territory. Amongst others we have seen reliance principles developed to account for the recourse to tort in order to remedy classical law's perceived shortcomings; the effects of EU harmonisation, globalisation and transnationalism; the articulation of principles of reasonable expectation and welfarism to account for consumer protection; and relational contract to explain the findings of empirical studies of business relationships. Yet none of these have endured nor made any permanent inroads into some basic common law understandings. Instead, aspects of the classical law have been forcefully reasserted, and these dalliances with alternative explanations or models explained away as deviant departures

[8] Roger Brownsword, 'Suisse Atlantique Société d'Armement Maritime SA v. NV Rotterdamsche Kolen Centrale' in Charles Mitchell and Paul Mitchell (eds.) *Landmark Cases in the Law of Contract* (Hart Publishing, 2008), pp. 299–314.

[9] *Suisse Atlantique Société d'Armement Maritime SA* v. *NV Rotterdamsche Kolen Centrale* [1967] 1 AC 361, per Lord Wilberforce, 434.

[10] Brownsword, 'Suisse Atlantique', p. 313.

from the basic foundations of the law. The price of this purity is substantial obsolescence. Contract law may have clung to a semblance of coherence around the ideas of freedom, autonomy and consent, but only by distancing itself from the societal effects of major changes in contract practice and regulation over the past decades and abjuring doctrinal development in favour of expanding the scope of contract interpretation and commitment to upholding express terms. The concepts that supposedly form the core of contract – voluntariness and consent – have been emptied of much of their meaning and importance.

We might be quite content with this state of affairs. After all, there are plenty of private fora to deal with contract disputes. But private dispute resolution and regulation are not always adequate substitutes for law. Private processes do not contribute to the corpus of public legal rules governing the operation of contracts in society. Regulation does not produce general rules that can be applied by analogy across other contracting contexts. While it is both unrealistic and unjustified to expect common law rules to develop responses to the entire range of challenges generated by contracts, the failure of common law to engage with some pressing problems surrounding modern contracting raises the risk of legal stagnation and, ultimately, contract law irrelevance.

Given that commercial contractors can create their own rules, and expect to have them upheld, it is right to ask whether contract law should limit its role to providing defaults for commercial contractors or whether it should develop principles to encompass a broader regulatory role over contract matters in society. Contract law can no doubt sustain its position as an island where autonomy is the prime value, amidst a growing number of alternative forms of contract governance that have whittled away at its foundational principles. There will be enough commercial contractors generating disputes about terms to keep the law in business for a while yet. But such a law will have little to contribute to the important task of controlling the abuse and exploitation of contract norms and have nothing to say about the role of contract in society.

Select Bibliography

Ackermann, Thomas, 'Private Production of Transnational Regulation through Standard Form Contracts' in Horst Eidenmüller (ed.) *Regulatory Competition in Contract Law and Dispute Resolution* (Verlag C. H. Beck/Hart Publishing/Nomos, 2013), 142

Adams, John N. and Brownsword, Roger, 'The Ideologies of Contact' (1987) 7 *Legal Studies* 205

Adams, John N. and Brownsword, Roger, 'More in Expectation than Hope: The Blackpool Airport Case' (1991) 54 *Modern Law Review* 281

Adams, John N. and Brownsword, Roger, 'The Unfair Contract Terms Act: A Decade of Discretion' (1988) 104 *Law Quarterly Review* 94

Aldohni, Abdul Karim, 'The UK New Regulatory Framework of High-Cost Short-Term Credit: Is There a Shift Towards a More "Law and Society" Based Approach?' (2017) 40 *Journal of Consumer Policy* 321

Allen, Jason G., 'Wrapped and Stacked: "Smart Contracts" and the Interaction of Natural and Formal Language' (2018) 14 *European Review of Contract Law* 307

Andrews, Neil, *Contract Law*, 2nd ed. (Cambridge University Press, 2015)

Arestis, Philip and Sawyer, Malcolm, 'The Neoliberal Experience of the United Kingdom' in Alfredo Saad-Filho and Deborah Johnston (eds.) *Neoliberalism: A Critical Reader* (Pluto Press, 2005), 199

Armour, John, 'Brexit and Financial Services' (2017) 33 *Oxford Review of Economic Policy* S54

Arvind, T. T., 'Contract Transactions and Equity' in Larry A. DiMatteo, Qi Zhou, Séverine Saintier and Keith Rowley (eds.) *Commercial Contract Law: Transatlantic Perspectives* (Cambridge University Press, 2013), 146

Atiyah, Patrick S., 'Contracts, Promises and the Law of Obligations' in Patrick S. Atiyah, *Essays on Contract* (Oxford University Press, 1990), 10

Atiyah, Patrick S., 'Freedom of Contract and the New Right' in Patrick S. Atiyah, *Essays on Contract* (Oxford University Press, 1990), 355

Atiyah, Patrick S., *An Introduction to the Law of Contract*, 5th ed. (Oxford University Press, 1995)

Atiyah, Patrick S., *The Rise and Fall of Freedom of Contract* (Oxford University Press, 1979)

Auckland, Cressida and Goold, Imogen, 'Claiming in Contract for Wrongful Conception' (2020) 136 *Law Quarterly Review* 45

Ayres, Ian, 'Targeting Repeat Offender NDAs' (2018) 71 *Stanford Law Review Online* 76

Ayres, Ian and Gertner, Robert, 'Filling Gaps in Incomplete Contracts: An Economic Theory of Default Rules' (1989) 99 *Yale Law Journal* 87

Ayres, Ian and Gertner, Robert, 'Majoritarian vs Minoritarian Defaults' (1999) 51 *Stanford Law Review* 1591

Baker, John H., 'The Rise and Fall of Freedom of Contract by P.S. Atiyah' (1980) 43 *Modern Law Review* 467

Baker, John H., 'From Sanctity of Contract to Reasonable Expectation?' (1979) 32 *Current Legal Problems* 17

Bakos, Yannis, Marotta-Wurgler, Florencia, and Trossen, David R., 'Does Anyone Read the Fine Print? Consumer Attention to Standard-Form Contracts' (2014) 43 *Journal of Legal Studies* 1

Bantekas, Ilias, 'The Globalisation of English Contract Law: Three Salient Illustrations' (2021) 137 *Law Quarterly Review* 330

Barmes, Lizzie, 'Common Law Implied Terms and Behavioural Standards at Work' (2007) 36 *Industrial Law Journal* 35

Barnett, Randy E., 'Consenting to Form Contracts' (2002) 71 *Fordham Law Review* 627

Beale, Hugh, (ed.) *Chitty on Contracts*, 33rd ed. (Sweet & Maxwell, 2020)

Beale, Hugh and Dugdale, Tony, 'Contracts between Businessmen: Planning and the Use of Contractual Remedies' (1975) 2 *British Journal of Law and Society* 45

Beale, Ned, 'Access to Financial Justice: Three Financial Services Conduct Scandals, and a Proposal for Reform' (2018) 33 *Journal of International Banking Law and Regulation* 153

Beatson, Jack, 'Public Law Influences in Contract Law' in Jack Beatson and Daniel Friedmann (eds.) *Good Faith and Fault in Contract Law* (Oxford University Press, 1995), 263

Becher, Shmeul I. and Benoliel, Uri, 'Sneak in Contracts: An Empirical and Legal Analysis of Unilateral Modification Clauses in Consumer Contracts' (2020) 55 *Georgia Law Review* 657

Beever, Allan, *Rediscovering the Law of Negligence* (Hart Publishing, 2007)

Ben-Shahar, Omri, 'The Tentative Case against Flexibility in Commercial Law' (1999) 66 *University of Chicago Law Review* 781

Ben-Shahar, Omri and Pottow, John A. E., 'On the Stickiness of Default Rules' (2006) 33 *Florida State University Law Review* 651

Benoliel, Uri, 'The Interpretation of Commercial Contracts: An Empirical Study' (2017) 69 *Alabama Law Journal* 469

Bernstein, Lisa, 'Merchant Law in a Merchant Court: Rethinking the Code's Search for Immanent Business Norms' (1996) 144 *University of Pennsylvania Law Review* 1765

Bernstein, Lisa, 'Opting Out of the Legal System: Extralegal Contractual Relations in the Diamond Industry' (1992) 21 *Journal of Legal Studies* 115

Bernstein, Lisa, 'Private Commercial Law in the Cotton Industry: Creating Co-operation through Rules, Norms and Institutions' (2001) 99 *Michigan Law Review* 1724

Bernstein, Lisa, 'The Questionable Empirical Basis of Article 2's Incorporation Strategy: A Preliminary Study' (1999) 66 *University of Chicago Law Review* 710

Bernstein, Lisa and Volvovsky, Hagay, 'Not What You Wanted to Know: The Real Deal and the Paper Deal in Consumer Contracts: Comment on the Work of Florencia Marotta-Wurgler' (2015) 12 *Jerusalem Review of Legal Studies* 128

Biggins, John and Scott, Colin, 'Public-Private Relations in a Transnational Private Regulatory Regime: ISDA, the State and OTC Derivatives Market Reform' (2012) 13 *European Business Organization Law Review* 309

Birks, Peter, *An Introduction to the Law of Restitution*, rev. ed. (Oxford University Press, 1989)

Bix, Brian H., 'Contract Law and the Common Good' (2018) 9 *William & Mary Business Law Review* 373

Black, Julia, 'Decentring Regulation: Understanding the Role of Regulation and Self-Regulation in a "Post-Regulatory" World' (2001) 54 *Current Legal Problems* 103

Borowicz, Maciej, 'Private Power and International Law: The International Swaps and Derivatives Association' (2015) 8 *European Journal of Legal Studies* 46

Braithwaite, Jo, 'Law After Lehmans' LSE Law, Society and Economy Working Papers 11/2014

Braithwaite, Jo, 'The Origins and Implications of Contractual Estoppel' (2016) 132 *Law Quarterly Review* 120

Braithwaite, Jo, '*Springwell*-watch: New Insights into the Nature of Contractual Estoppel' LSE Law Society and Economy Working Paper No 12/2017

Braithwaite, Joanne P., 'Standard Form Contracts as Transnational Law: Evidence from the Derivatives Markets' (2012) 75 *Modern Law Review* 779

Braithwaite, John, 'The Regulatory State?' in Robert E. Goodin (ed.) *The Oxford Handbook of Political Science* (Oxford University Press, 2011), 217

Bridge, Michael, 'Exceptions Clauses and Contractual Frustration Clauses' (2020) 136 *Law Quarterly Review* 1

Bridge, Michael, 'The Exercise of Contractual Discretion' (2019) 135 *Law Quarterly Review* 227

Bridge, Michael, 'Good Faith, the Common Law and the CISG' (2017) 22 *Uniform Law Review* 98

Bridge, Michael and Braithwaite, Jo, 'Private Law and Financial Crises' (2013) 13 *Journal of Corporate Law Studies* 361

Brown, Henry H., 'Equity' (1914) 26 *Juridical Review* 338

Brownsword, Roger, 'After Investors: Interpretation, Expectation and the Implicit Dimension of the "New Contextualism"' in David Campbell, Hugh Collins, and John Wightman (eds.) *Implicit Dimensions of Contract* (Hart Publishing, 2003), 103

Brownsword, Roger, 'Contract Law, Co-operation, and Good Faith: The Movement from Static to Dynamic Market-Individualism' in Simon Deakin and Jonathan Michie (eds.) *Contracts, Cooperation, and Competition: Studies in Economics, Management, and Law* (Oxford University Press, 1998)

Brownsword, Roger, *Contract Law: Themes for the Twenty-First Century*, 2nd ed. (Oxford University Press, 2006)

Brownsword, Roger, 'The Law of Contract: Doctrinal Impulses, External Pressures, Future Directions' (2014) 31 *Journal of Contract Law* 73

Brownsword, Roger, 'The Philosophy of Welfarism and its Emergence in the Modern English Law of Contract' in Roger Brownsword, Geraint G. Howells, and Thomas Wilhelmsson (eds.) *Welfarism in Contract Law* (Dartmouth, 1994), 21

Brownsword, Roger, 'Smart Contracts: Coding the Transaction, Decoding the Legal Debates' in Philipp Hacker, Ioannis Lianos, Georgios Dimitropoulos, and Stefan Eich (eds.) *Regulating Blockchain: Techno-Social and Legal Challenges* (Oxford University Press, 2019), 311

Brownsword, Roger, 'Suisse Atlantique Société d'Armement Maritime SA v. NV Rotterdamsche Kolen Centrale' in Charles Mitchell and Paul Mitchell (eds.) *Landmark Cases in the Law of Contract* (Hart Publishing, 2008), 299

Brownsword, Roger, van Gestel, Rob A. J., and Micklitz, Hans-W., (eds.) *Contract and Regulation: A Handbook on New Methods of Law Making in Private Law* (Edward Elgar Publishing, 2017)

Brownsword, Roger, Howells, Geraint, and Wilhelmsson, Thomas, (eds.) *Welfarism in Contract Law* (Dartmouth, 1994)

Burrows, Andrew, 'Illegality after *Patel v Mirza*' (2017) 70 *Current Legal Problems* 55

Burrows, Andrew, *A Restatement of the English Law of Contract* (Oxford University Press, 2016)

Burrows, Andrew, *Thinking About Statutes: Interpretation, Interaction, Improvement* (Cambridge University Press, 2017)

Burrows, Andrew, 'We Do This at Common Law but That in Equity' (2002) 22 *Oxford Journal of Legal Studies* 1

Calabresi, Guido, *A Common Law for the Age of Statutes* (Harvard University Press, 1982)

Campbell, David, 'Good Faith and the Ubiquity of Relational Contract' (2014) 77 *Modern Law Review* 475

Campbell, David, 'Ian Macneil and the Relational Theory of Contract' in David Campbell (ed.) *The Relational Theory of Contract: Selected Works of Ian Macneil* (Sweet and Maxwell, 2001), 3

Campbell, David, 'The "Market" in the Theory of Regulation' (2018) 27 *Social and Legal Studies* 545

Campbell, David, 'Reflexivity and Welfarism in the Modern Law of Contract' (2000) 20 *Oxford Journal of Legal Studies* 477

Campbell, David, 'The Relational Constitution of the Discrete Contract' in David Campbell and Peter Vincent-Jones (eds.) *Contract and Economic Organisation* (Dartmouth, 1996), 40

Campbell, David 'Relational Contract and the Nature of Private Ordering: A Comment on Vincent-Jones' (2007) 14 *Indiana Journal of Global Legal Studies* 279

Campbell, David, 'The Undeath of Contract: A Study in the Degeneration of a Research Programme' (1992) 22 *Hong Kong Law Journal* 20.

Campbell, David and Allan, James, 'Procedural Innovation and the Surreptitious Creation of Judicial Supremacy in the United Kingdom' (2019) 46 *Journal of Law and Society* 347

Campbell, David and Collins, Hugh, 'Discovering the Implicit Dimensions of Contracts' in David Campbell, Hugh Collins, and John Wightman (eds.) *Implicit Dimensions of Contract* (Hart Publishing, 2003), 25

Campbell, David and Halson, Roger, 'By Their Fruits Shall Ye Know Them' (2020) 79 *Cambridge Law Journal* 405

Carr, Chris A. and Jencks, Michael R., 'The Privatization of Business and Commercial Dispute Resolution: A Misguided Policy Decision' (1999) 88 *Kentucky Law Journal* 183

Cartwright, Peter 'Publicity, Punishment and Protection: The Role(s) of Adverse Publicity in Consumer Policy' (2012) 32 *Legal Studies* 179

Casey, Donal and Scott, Colin, 'The Crystallization of Regulatory Norms' (2011) 38 *Journal of Law and Society* 76

Charny, David, 'The New Formalism in Contract' (1999) 66 *University of Chicago Law Review* 842

Chiu, Iris H.-Y. and Brener, Alan H., 'Articulating the Gaps in Financial Consumer Protection and Policy Choices for the Financial Conduct Authority – Moving Beyond the Question of Imposing a Duty of Care' (2019) 14 *Capital Markets Law Journal* 217

Choi, Stephen J. and Gulati, G. Mitu, 'Contract as Statute' (2006) 104 *Michigan Law Review* 1129

Cohen, Morris R., 'The Basis of Contract' (1933) *Harvard Law Review* 553

Collins, Hugh, 'Flipping Wreck: Lex Mercatoria on the Shoals of Ius Cogens' in Stefan Grundmann, Florian Möslein, and Karl Riesenhuber (eds.) *Contract Governance: Dimensions in Law and Interdisciplinary Research* (Oxford University Press, 2015), 383

Collins, Hugh, *The Law of Contract*, 4th ed. (Butterworths, 2003)

Collins, Hugh, *Regulating Contracts* (Oxford University Press, 1999)

Collins, Hugh, 'Regulatory Competition in International Trade: Transnational Regulation through Standard Form Contracts' in Horst Eidenmüller (ed.) *Regulatory Competition in Contract Law and Dispute Resolution* (Verlag C H Beck, Hart Publishing, Nomos, 2013), 121

Cooper, Betsy, 'Judges in Jeopardy! Could IBM's Watson Beat Courts at Their Own Game?' (2011) 121 *Yale Law Journal Online* 87

Coote, Brian, 'The Function of Exception Clauses' in Rick Bigwood (ed.) *Contract as Assumption: Essays on a Theme* (Hart Publishing, 2010)

Coote, Brian, 'The Second Rise and Fall of Fundamental Breach' (1981) 55 *Australian Law Journal* 788

Cooter, Robert D., 'Decentralized Law for a Complex Economy' (1994) 23 *Southwestern University Law Review* 443

Cooter, Robert D., 'Decentralized Law for a Complex Economy: The Structural Approach to Adjudicating the New Law Merchant' (1996) 144 *University of Pennsylvania Law Review* 1643

Cotterell, Roger, 'Transnational Communities and the Concept of Law' (2008) 21 *Ratio Juris* 1

Cranston, Ross, 'Theorizing Transnational Commercial Law' (2007) 42 *Texas International Law Journal* 597

Cuccuru, Pierluigi, 'Beyond Bitcoin: An Early Overview on Smart Contracts' (2017) 25 *International Journal of Law and Information Technology* 179

Dagan, Hanoch, Dorfman, Avihay, Kreitner, Roy, and Markovits, Daniel, 'The Law of the Market' (2020) 83 *Law and Contemporary Problems* i

Dagan, Hanoch and Heller, Michael, *The Choice Theory of Contracts* (Cambridge University Press, 2017)

Daintith, Terence, 'Government Companies as Regulators' (2019) 82 *Modern Law Review* 397

Davies, Paul S., 'Bad Bargains' (2019) 72 *Current Legal Problems* 253

Davies, Paul S., 'Excluding Good Faith and Restricting Discretion' in Paul S. Davies and Magda Raczynska (eds.) *Contents of Commercial Contracts: Terms Affecting Freedoms* (Hart Publishing, 2020), 89

Devlin, Lord, 'The Relation between Commercial Law and Commercial Practice' (1951) 14 *Modern Law Review* 250

Diamond, A., 'Codification of the Law of Contract' (1968) 31 *Modern Law Review* 36

Dietz, Thomas, *Global Order Beyond Law* (Hart Publishing, 2014)

Dingwall, Robert and Cloatre, Emilie, 'Vanishing Trials?: An English Perspective' (2006) 7 *Journal of Dispute Resolution* 51

Diplock, Lord, 'The Law of Contract in the Eighties' (1981) 15 *University of British Columbia Law Review* 371

Dworkin, Ronald, *Law's Empire* (Fontana, 1986)

Eidenmüller, Horst, 'Regulatory Competition in Contract Law and Dispute Resolution' in Horst Eidenmüller (ed.) *Regulatory Competition in Contract Law and Dispute Resolution* (Verlag C H Beck, Hart Publishing, Nomos, 2013), 1

Eigen, Zev J., 'When and Why Individuals Obey Contracts: Experimental Evidence of Consent, Compliance, Promise and Performance' (2012) 41 *Journal of Legal Studies* 67

Eldridge, John, 'Contract Codification: Cautionary Lessons from Australia' (2019) 23 *Edinburgh Law Review* 204

Ellickson, Robert C., *Order Without Law* (Harvard University Press 1994)

Enonchong, Nelson, 'The Modern English Doctrine of Unconscionability' (2018) 34 *Journal of Contract Law* 211

Epstein, Richard A., 'Confusion about Custom: Disentangling Informal Customs from Standard Contractual Provisions' (1999) 66 *University of Chicago Law Review* 821

Etherton, Sir Terence, 'Equity and Conscience', Eldon Professor's Lecture, Northumbria University (24 October 2017)

Fairweather, Karen, 'Redressing Inequality in Personal Credit Transactions: 1700–1974' in Kit Barker, Simone Degeling, Karen Fairweather, and Ross Grantham (eds.) *Private Law and Power* (Hart Publishing, 2016), 53

Farrow, Trevor C. W., *Civil Justice, Privatization and Democracy* (University of Toronto Press, 2014)

Feinman, Jay M., 'Relational Contract Theory in Context' (2000) 94 *Northwestern University Law Review* 737

Feinman, Jay M., 'Un-Making Law: The Classical Revival in the Common Law' (2004) 28 *Seattle University Law Review* 1

Finck, Michèle, 'Blockchains: Regulating the Unknown' (2018) 19 *German Law Journal* 665

Fiss, Owen M., 'Against Settlement' (1984) 93 *Yale Law Journal* 1073

Fiss, Owen M., 'The Bureaucratization of the Judiciary' (1983) 92 *Yale Law Journal* 1442

Fiss, Owen M., 'The History of an Idea' (2009) 78 *Fordham Law Review* 1273

Freeland, Mark R., 'Government by Contract and Public Law' [1994] *Public Law* 86

Freeman, Jody, 'The Contracting State' (2000) 28 *Florida State University Law Review* 155

Furth-Matzkin, Meirav and Sommers, Roseanna, 'Consumer Psychology and the Problem of Fine Print Fraud' (2020) 72 *Stanford Law Review* 503

Gardner, John, 'The Contractualisation of Labour Law' in Hugh Collins, Gillian Lester, and Virginia Mantouvalou (eds.) *Philosophical Foundations of Labour Law* (Oxford University Press, 2018), 33

Gava, John, 'Dixonian Strict Legalism: Wilson v. Darling Island Stevedoring and Contracting in the Real World' (2010) 30 *Oxford Journal of Legal Studies* 519

Gava, John, 'False Lessons from the Real Deal: Campbell, Collins and Wightman on Implicit Dimensions of Contract – Discrete, Relational, and Network Contracts?' (2005) 21 *Journal of Contract Law* 182

Gava, John, 'How Should Judges Decide Commercial Contract Cases?' (2013) 30 *Journal of Contract Law* 133

Gava, John and Greene, Janey, 'Do We Need a Hybrid Law of Contract? Why Hugh Collins is Wrong and Why It Matters' (2004) 63 *Cambridge Law Journal* 605

Genn, Hazel, *Judging Civil Justice* (Cambridge University Press, 2010)

Genn, Hazel, 'Why the Privatisation of Civil Justice is a Rule of Law Issue' 36th F A Mann Lecture (19 November 2012)

Gharagozlou, Alireza M., 'Unregulable: Why Derivatives May Never Be Regulated' (2010) 4 *Brooklyn Journal of Corporate Financial and Commercial Law* 269

Giancaspro, Mark, 'Is a 'Smart Contract' Really a Smart Idea? Insights From a Legal Perspective' (2017) 33 *Computer Law & Security Review* 825

Gill, Chris, Mullen, Tom, and Vivian, Nial, 'The Managerial Ombudsman' (2020) 83 *Modern Law Review* 797

Gilmore, Grant, *The Death of Contract* (Ohio University Press, 1974)

Gilson, Ronald J., Sabel, Charles F., and Scott, Robert E., 'Contract and Innovation: The Limited Role of Generalist Courts in the Evolution of Novel Contract Forms' (2013) 88 *New York University Law Review* 170

Goetz, Charles J. and Scott, Robert E.,'Principles of Relational Contracts' (1981) 67 *Virginia Law Review* 1089

Goff, Lord, 'Commercial Contracts and the Commercial Court' [1984] *Lloyd's Maritime and Commercial Law Quarterly* 382

Golden, Jeffrey B., 'Setting Standards in the Evolution of Swap Documentation' (1994) 13 *International Financial Law Review* 18

Goode, Roy, 'Perpetual Trustee and Flip Clauses in Swap Transactions' (2011) 127 *Law Quarterly Review* 1

Goodhart, William and Jones, Gareth, 'The Infiltration of Equitable Doctrine into English Commercial Law' (1980) 43 *Modern Law Review* 489

Gordley, James, *Foundations of Private Law* (Oxford University Press, 2006)

Gordon, Jeffrey Steven, 'Silence for Sale' (2020) 71 *Alabama Law Review* 1109

Green, Sarah and Sanitt, Adam, 'Smart Contracts' in Paul S. Davies and Magda Raczynska (eds.) *Commercial Contracts: Terms Affecting Freedoms* (Hart Publishing, 2020), 191

Grey, Thomas C., *The New Formalism,* Stanford Public Law and Legal Theory Working Paper Series, 5 (6 September 1999) www.papers.ssrn.com/paper.taf?abstract-id=200732

Gulati, Mitu and Scott, Robert E., *The 3½ Minute Transaction* (University of Chicago Press, 2013)

Hadfield, Gillian K., 'Where Have All the Trials Gone? Settlements, Nontrial Adjudications, and Statistical Artifacts in the Changing Disposition of Federal Civil Cases' (2004) 1 *Journal of Empirical Legal Studies* 705

Hale, Lady, 'Legislation or Judicial Law Reform: Where Should Judges Fear to Tread?' Society of Legal Scholars Conference, 7 September 2016

Hanbury, H. G., 'The Field of Modern Equity' (1929) 45 *Law Quarterly Review* 196

Harden, Ian, *The Contracting State* (Open University Press, 1992)

Hart, H. L. A., *The Concept of Law*, 1st ed. (Oxford University Press, 1961)

Hartkamp, Arthur S., Hesselink, Martijn W., Hondius, Ewoud, Mak, C., and Du Perron, Edgar, (eds.) *Towards a European Civil Code*, 4th ed. (Wolters Kluwer, 2010)

Harvey, David, *A Brief History of Neoliberalism* (Oxford University Press, 2007)

Hedley, Steve, 'Looking Outward or Looking Inward? Obligations Scholarship in the Early 21st Century' in Andrew Robertson and Tang Hang Wu (eds.) *The Goals of Private Law* (Hart Publishing, 2009), 193

Hedley, Steve, 'The Rise and Fall of Private Law Theory' (2018) 134 *Law Quarterly Review* 214

Hedley, Steve, 'Tort: The Long Goodbye' (8 April 2020) www.ssrn.com/abstract=3571950

Hedley, Steve, 'Two Laws of Contract, or One?' in T. T. Arvind and Jenny Steele (eds.) *Contract Law and the Legislature* (Hart Publishing, 2020), 147

Hillman, Robert A. and Rachlinski, Jeffrey J., 'Standard-Form Contracting in the Electronic Age' (2002) 77 *New York University Law Review* 429

Hodge, Lord, 'Judicial Development of the Law of Contract in the United Kingdom' (2017) 85 *George Washington Law Review* 1587

Hodge, Lord, 'Technology and the Law' Dover House Lecture (10 March 2020)

Hoffman, David A. and Lampmann, Eric., 'Hushing Contracts' (2019) 97 *Washington University Law Review* 165

Hooley, Richard, 'Controlling Contractual Discretion' (2013) 72 *Cambridge Law Journal* 65

Horwitz, Morton J., 'The Historical Foundations of Modern Contract Law (1974) 87 *Harvard Law Review* 917

Howells, Geraint G. and Bently, Lionel, 'Judicial Treatment of Extortionate Credit Bargains: Part 1' [1989] *Conveyancer and Property Lawyer* 164

Howells, Geraint G. and Bently, Lionel, 'Loansharks and Extortionate Credit Bargains: Part 2' [1989] *Conveyancer and Property Lawyer* 234

Ibbetson, David, *An Historical Introduction to the Law of Obligations* (Oxford University Press, 2001)

Ibbetson, David, 'Revolutions in Private Law?' in Sarah Worthington, Andrew Robertson, and Graham Virgo (eds.) *Revolution and Evolution in Private Law* (Hart Publishing, 2018), 20

Kar, Robin Bradley and Radin, Margaret J., 'Pseudo-contract and Shared Meaning Analysis' (2019) 132 *Harvard Law Review* 1135

Katz, Avery W., 'Taking Private Ordering Seriously' (1996) 144 *University of Pennsylvania Law Review* 1745

Kennedy, Duncan, *A Critique of Adjudication* (Harvard University Press, 1998)

Kennedy, Duncan, 'Form and Substance in Private Law Adjudication' (1976) 89 *Harvard Law Review* 1685

Kennedy, Duncan, 'A Transnational Genealogy of Proportionality in Private Law' in Roger Brownsword, Hans-W. Micklitz, Leone Niglia, and Stephen Weatherill (eds.) *The Foundations of European Private Law* (Hart Publishing, 2011)

Kim, Nancy S., *Wrap Contracts* (Oxford University Press, 2013)

Kimel, Dori, 'The Choice of Paradigm for Theory of Contract: Reflections on the Relational Model' (2007) 27 *Oxford Journal of Legal Studies* 232

Konradi, Wioletta, 'The Role of Lex Mercatoria in Supporting Globalized Transactions: An Empirical Insight into the Governance Structure of the Timber Industry' in Volkmar Gessner (ed.) *Contractual Certainty in International Trade* (Hart Publishing, 2009), 49

Kraus, Jody P. and Scott, Robert E., 'The Case against Equity in American Contract Law' (2020) 93 *Southern California Law Review* 1323

Lacey, Nicola, 'The Metaphor of Proportionality' (2016) 43 *Journal of Law and Society* 27

Landes, William M. and Posner, Richard A., 'Adjudication as a Private Good' (1979) 8 *Journal of Legal Studies* 235

Lando, Ole and Beale, Hugh, (eds.) *The Principles of European Contract Law, Parts I and II* (Kluwer, 2000)

Larrain, Maria and Prufer, Jens, 'Trade Associations, Lobbying, and Endogenous Institutions' (2015) 7 *Journal of Legal Analysis* 467

Lau, Kwan Ho and Tan, Ben Mathias, 'Basis Clauses and the Unfair Contract Terms Act 1977' (2014) 130 *Law Quarterly Review* 377

Law Commission, *Digital Assets: Electronic Trade Documents – A Consultation Paper* CP 254 (30 April 2021).

Law Commission, *Electronic Commerce – Formal Requirements in Commercial Transactions: Advice from the Law Commission* (December 2001)

Law Commission, *Electronic Execution of Documents* Law Com No 386 (2019)

Law Commission, *Law of Contract: The Parol Evidence Rule* No 154 (1986)

Law Commission, *Smart Contracts: Call for Evidence* (December 2020)

Law Commissions (England and Scotland), *Building Families through Surrogacy: A New Law,* Joint Consultation Paper 244/167, (June 2019)

Leff, Arthur A., 'Contract as Thing' (1970) 19 *American University Law Review* 131

Legrand, Pierre, 'Against a European Civil Code' (1997) 60 *Modern Law Review* 44

Lemley, Mark A., 'Terms of Use' (2006) 91 *Minnesota Law Review* 459

Levi, Edward H., '*An Introduction to Legal Reasoning*' (1948) 15 *University of Chicago Law Review* 501

Linarelli, John, 'Global Legal Pluralism and Commercial Law' in Paul Schiff Berman (ed.) *Oxford Handbook on Global Legal Pluralism* (Oxford University Press, 2020), 689

Luban, David, 'Settlements and the Erosion of the Public Realm' (1995) 83 *Georgetown Law Journal* 2619

Macaulay, Stewart, 'Non-Contractual Relations in Business: A Preliminary Study' (1963) 28 *American Sociological Review* 55

Macaulay, Stewart, 'The Real and the Paper Deal: Empirical Pictures of Relationships, Complexity and the Urge for Transparent Simple Rules' in David Campbell, Hugh Collins, and John Wightman (eds.) *Implicit Dimensions of Contract* (Hart Publishing, 2003), 51

Macdonald, Elizabeth, 'When is a Contract Formed by the Browse-wrap Process?' (2011) 19 *International Journal of Law and Information Technology* 285

MacMillan, Catharine, 'The Impact of Brexit upon English Contract Law' (2016) 27 *King's Law Journal* 420

MacMillan, Catharine, 'Private Law and Public Concerns: Non-Disclosure Agreements in English Contract Law' in Paul S. Davies and Magda Raczynska (eds.) *Contents of Commercial Contracts: Terms Affecting Freedoms* (Hart Publishing, 2020), 315

Macneil, Ian, *The Relational Theory of Contract: Selected Works of Ian Macneil*, David Campbell (ed.) (Sweet & Maxwell, 2001).

Macneil, Ian R., 'Bureaucracy and Contracts of Adhesion' (1984) 22 *Osgoode Hall Law Journal* 5

Macneil, Ian R., 'Contracts: Adjustment of Long-Term Economic Relations under Classical, Neoclassical and Relational Contract Law' (1978) 72 *Northwestern University Law Review* 854

Macneil, Ian R., 'The Many Futures of Contract' (1974) 47 *Southern California Law Review* 691

Macneil, Ian R., 'Relational Contract Theory: Challenges and Queries' (2000) 94 *Northwestern University Law Review* 877

Macneil, Ian R., 'Values in Contract: Internal and External' (1983) 78 *Northwestern University Law Review* 340

Macneil, Ian R., 'Whither Contracts?' (1969) 21 *Journal of Legal Education* 403

Maine, Henry Sumner, *Ancient Law* (John Murray, 1861 Cambridge University Press, 2012)

Markesinis, Basil S., 'An Expanding Tort Law – The Price of a Rigid Contract Law' (1987) 103 *Law Quarterly Review* 354

Marks, Colin P., 'Online Terms as *In Terrorem* Devices' (2019) 78 *Maryland Law Review* 247

Marotta-Wurgler, Florencia, 'What's in a Standard Form Contract – An Empirical Analysis of Software License Agreements' (2007) 4 *Journal of Empirical Legal Studies* 677

Mattli, Walter, 'Private Justice in a Global Economy: From Litigation to Arbitration' (2001) 55 *International Organization* 919

MacCormick, Neil, *Legal Reasoning and Legal Theory*, revised ed. (Oxford University Press, 1994)

McKinney, Scott A., Landy, Rachel, and Wilka, Rachel, 'Smart Contracts, Blockchain, and the Next Frontier of Transactional Law' (2018) 13 *Washington Journal of Law, Technology and Arts* 313

McMeel, Gerard, 'Documentary Fundamentalism in the Senior Courts: The Myth of Contractual Estoppel' [2011] *Lloyd's Maritime and Commercial Law Quarterly* 185

Mensch, Betty, 'Freedom of Contract as Ideology' (1981) 33 *Stanford Law Review* 753

Merry, Sally Engle, 'Legal Pluralism' (1988) 22 *Law and Society Review* 869

Mik, Eliza, 'From Automation to Autonomy: Some Non-existent Problems in Contract Law' (2020) 36 *Journal of Contract Law* 205

Mik, Eliza, 'The Resilience of Contract Law in Light of Technological Change' in Michael Furmston (ed.) *The Future of the Law of Contract* (Routledge, 2020), 112

Mik, Eliza, 'Smart Contracts: A Requiem' (2019) 36 *Journal of Contract Law* 70

Mik, Eliza, 'Smart Contracts: Terminology, Technical Limitations and Real World Complexity' (2017) 9 *Law, Innovation and Technology* 269

Mik, Eliza, 'The Unimportance of Being Electronic or – Popular Misconceptions about Internet Contracting' (2011) 19 *International Journal of Law and Information Technology* 324

Millett, Peter J., (Lord Justice) 'Equity's Place in the Law of Commerce' (1998) 114 *Law Quarterly Review* 214

Mitchell, Catherine, *Contract Law and Contract Practice* (Hart Publishing, 2013)

Mitchell, Catherine, 'Contracts and Contract Law: Challenging the Distinction between the Real and Paper Deal' (2009) 29 *Oxford Journal of Legal Studies* 675

Mitchell, Catherine, *Interpretation of Contracts*, 2nd ed. (Routledge, 2018)

Mitchell, Catherine, 'Leading a Life of its Own? The Roles of Reasonable Expectation in Contract Law' (2003) 23 *Oxford Journal of Legal Studies* 639

Moorhead, Richard, 'Professional Ethics and NDAs: Contracts as Lies and Abuse' in Paul S. Davies and Magda Raczynska (eds.) *Contents of Commercial Contracts: Terms Affecting Freedoms* (Hart Publishing, 2020), 339

Moorhead, Richard and Hinchly, Victoria, 'Professional Minimalism: The Ethical Consciousness of Commercial Lawyers' (2015) 42 *Journal of Law and Society* 387

Morgan, Bronwen and Yeung, Karen, *An Introduction to Law and Regulation* (Cambridge University Press, 2007)

Morgan, Jonathan, *Contract Law Minimalism: A Formalist Restatement of Commercial Contract Law* (Cambridge University Press, 2013).

Morgan, Jonathan, 'Contracting for Self-Denial: On Enforcing "No Oral Modification" Clauses' (2017) 76 *Cambridge Law Journal* 589

Morgan, Jonathan, 'Opting for "Documentary Fundamentalism": Respecting Party Choice for Entire Agreement and Non-Reliance Clauses' in Paul S. Davies and Magda Raczynska (eds.) *Contents of Commercial Contracts: Terms Affecting Freedoms* (Hart Publishing, 2020), 239

Morgan, Jonathan, 'Resisting Judicial Review of Discretionary Contractual Powers' [2015] *Lloyd's Maritime and Commercial Law Quarterly* 483

Morrison, Alan D. and Wilhelm, William J. Jr, 'Trust, Reputation and Law: The Evolution of Commitment in Investment Banking' (2015) 7 *Journal of Legal Analysis* 363

Möser, Katharina, 'Making Sense of the Numbers: The Shift from Nonconsensual to Consensual Debt Relief and the Construction of the Consumer Debtor' (2019) 46 *Journal of Law and Society* 240

Möslein, Florian, 'Legal Boundaries of Blockchain Technologies: Smart Contracts as Self-Help?' in Alberto De Franceschi and Reiner Schulze (eds.) *Digital Revolution – New Challenges for Law* (C H Beck Nomos, 2019), 313

Mulcahy, Linda, 'The Collective Interest in Private Dispute Resolution' (2013) 33 *Oxford Journal of Legal Studies* 59

Mulcahy, Linda, *Legal Architecture: Justice, Due Process and the Place of Law* (Routledge, 2011)

Mulcahy, Linda and Teeder, Wendy, 'Are Litigants, Trials and Precedents Vanishing After All?' *Modern Law Review* (forthcoming) www.ssrn.com/abstract=3880274

Mummery, Sir J., 'Commercial Notions and Equitable Potions' in Sarah Worthington (ed.) *Commercial Law and Commercial Practice* (Hart Publishing, 2003)

Murray, Edward, 'Lomas v Firth Rixson: "As you were!"' (2013) 8 *Capital Markets Law Journal* 395

Murray, John E. Jr, 'Contract Theories and the Rise of Neoformalism' (2002) 71 *Fordham Law Review* 869

Neuberger, Lord, 'Equity, ADR, Arbitration and the Law: Different Dimensions of Justice' Fourth Keating Lecture (19 May 2010)

Neuberger, Lord, 'Has Mediation Has Its Day?' Gordon Slynn Memorial Lecture (10 November 2010)

Nolan, Donal, 'The Classical Legacy and Modern English Contract Law' (1996) 59 *Modern Law Review* 603

Ogus, Anthony, *Regulation: Legal Form and Economic Theory* (Hart Publishing, 2004)

Oldham, James, *English Common Law in the Time of Mansfield* (University of North Carolina Press, 2004)

Oman, Nathan B., *The Dignity of Commerce* (University of Chicago Press, 2016)

Paech, Phillip, 'The Governance of Blockchain Financial Networks' (2017) 80 *Modern Law Review* 1073

Partnoy, Frank and Skeel, David A. Jr, 'The Promise and Perils of Credit Derivatives' (2007) 75 *University of Cincinnati Law Review* 1019

Phipps, Charles, Harman, William, and Teasdale, Simon, *Toulson and Phipps on Confidentiality*, 4th ed. (Sweet & Maxwell, 2020)

Posner, Eric A., 'Law, Economics and Inefficient Norms' (1996) 144 *University of Pennsylvania Law Review* 1697

Posner, Richard A., 'The Path Away from the Law' (1997) 110 *Harvard Law Review* 1039

Powell, John Joseph, *Essay Upon the Law of Contract and Agreements*, Vol 1 (J. Johnson, 1790)

Raczynska, Magda, 'Good Faiths and Contract Terms' in Paul S. Davies and Magda Raczynska (eds.) *Contents of Commercial Contracts: Terms Affecting Freedoms* (Hart Publishing, 2020), 65

Raczynska, Magda and Davies, Paul S. 'Freedom of Contract and Terms Affecting Freedoms' in Paul S. Davies and Magda Raczynska (eds.) *Contents of Commercial Contracts: Terms Affecting Freedoms* (Hart Publishing, 2020), 1

Radin, Margaret Jane, *Boilerplate: The Fine Print, Vanishing Rights and the Rule of Law* (Princeton University Press, 2013)

Radin, Margaret Jane, 'The Deformation of Contract in the Information Society' (2017) 37 *Oxford Journal of Legal Studies* 505

Rajah, Vijaya Kumar, 'W(h)ither Adversarial Commercial Dispute Resolution?' (2017) 33 *Arbitration International* 17

Ramseyer, J. Mark, 'Contracting for Sex in the Pacific War' (2021) 65 *International Review of Law and Economics* (article 105971)

Ramseyer, J. Mark, 'Indentured Prostitution in Imperial Japan: Credible Commitments in the Commercial Sex Industry' (1991) 7 *Journal of Law, Economics and Organization* 89

Rauterberg, Gabriel V. and Verstein, Andrew, 'Assessing Transnational Private Regulation of the OTC Derivatives Market: ISDA, the BBA, and the Future of Financial Reform' (2013) 54 *Virginia Journal of International Law* 9

Resnik, Judith, 'Diffusing Disputes: The Public in the Private of Arbitration, the Private in Courts, and the Erasure of Rights' (2015) 124 *Yale Law Journal* 2804

Resnik, Judith, 'Managerial Judges' (1982) 96 *Harvard Law Review* 376

Reynolds, Francis, 'Commercial Law' in Louis Blom-Cooper, Brice Dickson, and Gavin Drewry (eds.) *The Judicial House of Lords 1876–2009* (Oxford University Press, 2009), 700

Reynolds, Piers and Collins, Anthony, 'Non-advised sales of Financial Products: An End to Caveat Emptor' (2018) 33 *Journal of International Banking Law and Regulation* 148

Richman, Barak D., 'Firms, Courts, and Reputation Mechanisms: Towards a Positive Theory of Private Ordering' (2004) 104 *Columbia Law Review* 2328

Riles, Annelise, 'The Anti-Network: Private Global Governance, Legal Knowledge, and the Legitimacy of the State' (2008) 56 *American Journal of Comparative Law* 605

Rowlingson, Karen, Appleyard, Lindsey, and Gardner, Jodi, 'Payday Lending in the UK: The Regul(aris)ation of a Necessary Evil?' (2016) 45 *Journal of Social Policy* 527

Rubin, Edward L., 'From Coherence to Effectiveness: A Legal Methodology for the Modern World' in Rob van Gestel, Hans-W. Micklitz, and Edward L. Rubin (eds.)

Rethinking Legal Scholarship: A Transatlantic Dialogue (Cambridge University Press, 2017)

Sales, Lord, 'Algorithms, Artificial Intelligence and the Law' Sir Henry Brooke Lecture for BAILII, Freshfields Bruckhaus Deringer (12 November 2019)

Sales, Lord, 'Being a Supreme Court Justice in 2030' Law and the Digital World Cour de Cassation Seminar, (16 April 2021)

Sales, Lord, 'The Interface Between Contract and Equity' Lehane Memorial Lecture, Sydney (29 August 2019)

Samet, Irit, *Equity: Conscience Goes to Market* (Oxford University Press, 2018)

Samuel, Geoffrey, *A Short Introduction to Judging and to Legal Reasoning* (Edward Elgar Publishing, 2016)

Samuel, Richard, 'Tools for Changing Banking Culture: FCA Are You Listening?' (2016) 11 *Capital Markets Law Journal* 129

Savelyev, Alexander, 'Contract Law 2.0: 'Smart' Contracts as the Beginning of the End of Classic Contract Law' (2017) 26 *Information & Communications Technology Law* 116

Schwarcz, Steven L., 'Private Ordering' 97 (2002) *Northwestern University Law Review* 319

Schwenzer, Ingeborg, 'Global Unification of Contract Law' (2016) 21 *Uniform Law Review* 60

Scott, Robert E., 'The Case for Formalism in Relational Contract' (2000) 94 *Northwestern University Law Review* 847

Scott, Robert E., 'The Death of Contract Law' (2004) 54 *University of Toronto Law Journal* 369

Scott, Robert E., 'The Paradox of Contracting in Markets' (2020) 83 *Law and Contemporary Problems* 71

Selden, John, *The Table-Talk of John Selden* (Cambridge University Press, 2015)

Shaffer, Gregory C., 'How Business Shapes Law: A Socio-Legal Framework' (2009) 42 *Connecticut Law Review* 147

Shiffrin, Seana V., 'Remedial Clauses: The Overprivatization of Private Law' (2016) 67 *Hastings Law Journal* 407

Shleifer, Andrei, *The Failure of Judges and the Rise of Regulators* (MIT Press, 2012)

Simpson, A. W. B., 'Contract: The Twitching Corpse' (1981) 1 *Oxford Journal of Legal Studies* 265

Simpson, A.W.B., 'The Horwitz Thesis and the History of Contracts' (1979) 46 *University Chicago Law Review* 533

Sklaroff, Jeremy M., 'Smart Contracts and the Cost of Inflexibility (2017) 166 *University of Pennsylvania Law Review* 263

Slawson, W. David, 'Standard Form Contracts and Democratic Control of Lawmaking Power' (1971) 84 *Harvard Law Review* 529

Smith, Stephen A., *Atiyah's Introduction to the Law of Contract*, 6th ed. (Oxford University Press, 2005)

Snyder, David V., 'Private Law Making' (2003) 64 *Ohio State Law Journal* 371

Steiner, Eva, 'Challenging (Again) the Undemocratic Form of the Common Law: Codification as a Method of Making the Law Accessible to Citizens' (2020) 32 *Kings Law Journal* 27

Stevens, Robert, *Torts and Rights* (Oxford University Press, 2007)

Steyn, Lord, 'Contract Law: Fulfilling the Reasonable Expectations of Honest Men' (1997) 113 *Law Quarterly Review* 433

Strauss, Emily, 'Crisis Construction in Contract Boilerplate' (2019) 82 *Law and Contemporary Problems* 163

Study Group on a European Civil Code/Research Group on the Existing EC Private Law (Acquis Group), (eds.) *Principles, Definitions and Model Rules on European Private Law – Draft Common Frame of Reference* (Sellier, 2009).

Sumption, Lord, 'Law and the Decline of Politics' Reith Lecture, Lecture 1 (21 May 2019)

Sumption, Lord, 'A Question of Taste: The Supreme Court and the Interpretation of Contracts' (2017) 17 *Oxford University Commonwealth Law Journal* 301

Susskind, Richard, *Online Courts and the Future of Justice* (Oxford University Press, 2019)

Swain, Warren, *The Law of Contract 1670–1870* (Cambridge University Press, 2015)

Tan, Zhong Xing, 'Disrupting Doctrine: Revisiting the Doctrinal Impact of Relational Contract Theory' (2019) 39 *Legal Studies* 98

Tan, Zhong Xing, 'The Proportionality Puzzle in Contract Law: A Challenge for Private Law Theory' (2020) 33 *Canadian Journal of Law and Jurisprudence* 215

Teubner, Gunther, 'Legal Irritants: Good Faith in British Law or How Unifying Law Ends Up in New Divergences' (1998) 61 *Modern Law Review* 11

Thomas, Lord, 'Developing Commercial Law through the Courts: Rebalancing the Relationship between the Courts and Arbitration' BAILII Lecture (9 March 2016)

Thomas, Lord, 'Keeping Commercial Law Up to Date' Jill Poole Memorial Lecture, Aston University (8 March 2017)

Trakman, Leon E., 'Public Responsibilities Beyond Consent: Rethinking Contract Theory' (2016) 45 *Hofstra Law Review* 217

Twigg-Flesner, Christian, *The Europeanisation of Contract Law*, 2nd ed. (Routledge, 2013)

Van Loo, Rory, 'The New Gatekeepers: Private Firms as Public Enforcers' (2020) 106 *Virginia Law Review* 467

Varuhas, Jason N.E., 'The Socialisation of Private Law: Balancing Private Right and Public Good' (2021) 137 *Law Quarterly Review* 141

Vincent-Jones, Peter, 'Contractual Governance: Institutional and Organizational Analysis' (2000) 20 *Oxford Journal of Legal Studies* 317

Vincent-Jones, Peter, *The New Public Contracting* (Oxford University Press, 2006)

Vincent-Jones, Peter, 'The New Public Contracting: Public versus Private Ordering?' (2007) 14 *Indiana Journal of Global Legal Studies* 259

Vos, Sir Geoffrey, 'Cryptoassets as Property: How can English Law Boost the Confidence of Would-be Parties to Smart Legal Contracts?' Joint Northern Chancery Bar Association and University of Liverpool Lecture (2 May 2019)

Vos, Sir Geoffrey, 'The Relationship between Formal and Informal Justice' Hull University (26 March 2021)

Vos, Sir Geoffrey, 'Technological Challenges for English Law and Jurisdiction' ISDA Virtual Annual Legal Forum (10 March 2021)

Waddams, Stephen, *Sanctity of Contracts in a Secular Age* (Cambridge University Press, 2019)

Walters, Adrian, 'Individual Voluntary Arrangements: A 'Fresh Start' for Salaried Consumer Debtors in England and Wales?' (2009) 18 *International Insolvency Review* 5

Weinrib, Ernest, *The Idea of Private Law* (Harvard University Press, 1995)

Werbach, Kevin, *Blockchain and the New Architecture of Trust* (MIT Press, 2018)

Werbach, Kevin, 'Trust, But Verify: Why the Blockchain Needs the Law' (2018) 33 *Berkeley Technology Law Journal* 487

Werbach, Kevin and Cornell, Nicolas, 'Contracts *Ex Machina*' (2017) 67 *Duke Law Journal* 313

Wheeler, Sally, 'Modelling the Contracts of the Future' (2017) 26 *Griffith Law Review* 593

Whitford, William C., 'Relational Contracts and the New Formalism' (2004) *Wisconsin Law Review* 631

Whittaker, Simon., 'Unfair Terms in Commercial Contracts and the Two Laws of Competition: French Law and English Law Contrasted' in (2019) 39 *Oxford Journal of Legal Studies* 404

Wielsch, Dan, 'Global Law's Toolbox: Private Regulation by Standards' (2012) 60 *American Journal of Comparative Law* 1075

Wightman, John, *Contract: A Critical Commentary* (Pluto Press, 1996)

Wilkinson-Ryan, Tess, 'Do Liquidated Damages Encourage Breach? A Psychological Experiment' (2010) 108 *Michigan Law Review* 633

Wilkinson-Ryan, Tess, 'Justifying Bad Deals' (2020) 169 *University of Pennsylvania Law Review* 193

Wilkinson-Ryan, Tess, 'Legal Promise and Psychological Contract' (2012) 47 *Wake Forest Law Review* 843

Wilkinson-Ryan, Tess and Baron, Jonathan, 'Moral Judgment and Moral Heuristics in Breach of Contract' (2009) 6 *Journal of Empirical Legal Studies* 405

Williamson, Oliver E., *The Economic Institutions of Capitalism* (Free Press, 1985)

Woodward, William J., 'Neoformalism in a Real World of Forms' (2001) *Wisconsin Law Review* 971

Wright, Aaron and De Filippi, Primavera, 'Decentralized Blockchain Technology and the Rise of Lex Cryptographia' (2015) www.ssrn.com/abstract=2580664,

Yates, David, *Exclusion Clauses in Contracts*, 2nd ed. (Sweet & Maxwell, 1982)

Yeung, Karen, 'Regulation by Blockchain: The Emerging Battle for Supremacy between the Code of Law and Code as Law' (2019) 82 *Modern Law Review* 207

Yip, Man and Lee, James, 'The Commercialisation of Equity' (2017) 37 *Legal Studies* 647

Zuckerman, Adrian, 'Artificial Intelligence – Implications for the Legal Profession, Adversarial Process and Rule of Law' (2020) 136 *Law Quarterly Review* 427

Index

www.ingramcontent.com/pod-product-compliance
Lightning Source LLC
LaVergne TN
LVHW052307200926
848481LV00002B/491
* 9 7 8 1 0 0 9 0 7 7 3 9 2 *